WHERE'S MY GUITAR?

BERNIE MARSDEN

WHERE'S MY GUITAR?

An Inside Story of British Rock and Roll

4th ESTATE • London

4th Estate
An imprint of HarperCollins*Publishers*
1 London Bridge Street
London SE1 9GF

www.4thEstate.co.uk

First published in Great Britain in 2019 by 4th Estate

1

A catalogue record for this book is
available from the British Library

ISBN 978-0-00-835655-2

Set in Sabon
Printed and bound in Great Britain by
CPI Group (UK) Ltd, Croydon

To Fran,
who always knows where my guitar is.
B x

CONTENTS

Praise for Bernie Marsden   ix
Introduction   1
Preface   3

1. New York, New York, 1980   5
2. Going to my Home Town   7
3. Look Through Any Window   13
4. Welcome to the Real World   29
5. To the City   43
6. Dance on the Water   59
7. PALs with Deep Pockets   81
8. Whitesnake   95
9. Free Flight   121
10. Come an' Get It   137
11. Look At Me Now   159
12. Baked Alaska   175
13. Shooting the Breeze   191
14. In the Company of Snakes   223
15. Going Again on my Own   241

Afterword: Guitars and the Sickness They Induce   253
Seminal Moments in my Musical Education   263

Acknowledgements   273

PRAISE FOR
BERNIE MARSDEN

Pat Cash, tennis champion

'There wouldn't be many guitar fans who haven't heard a Bernie Marsden riff somewhere along the road. That goes for anyone alive in the '80s and early '90s, guitar fan or not. My first awareness of Bernie was during the glory years of Whitesnake while I was travelling the world making a career in tennis. Great album after great album, catchy riffs with melodic yet rocking solos. It was post-Whitesnake that I discovered the Marsden voice in its full extent, his most recent blues albums showing those talents. As a Rory Gallagher fan his *Bernie Plays Rory* album was more than a worthy tribute – a pure joy. No wonder he is applauded throughout the blues and rock world as one of the iconic musicians of his generation.'

Dónal Gallagher, brother of Rory

'Rory's admiration for Bernie as both a musician and as a person was huge and I share my late brother's sentiments. Actions speak louder than words – Bernie was the first guitarist allowed to perform with Rory's Stratocaster after his passing. In addition to his own great abilities, Bernie carries the torch!'

Steve Lukather, Toto

'Bernie is part of the legendary wave of British blues-rock players I heard that had it all. His soul, chops and sound resonated with me. He is also a first-class gentleman and when he came to meet me and see me the first time Toto played in London in the very early '80s he brought Jeff Beck and Gary Moore. Like I wasn't intimidated enough by *him* … ha, ha! This started a lifelong friendship. Bernie is one of the best in every way and I am honoured to call him my friend – and he is one badass guitar player!'

Ian Paice, Deep Purple

'Bernie is one of those rare musicians who can play whatever is required of him. Rock, blues, pop, you name it and he will do it, and do it very well! A talent in itself. But the other string to his bow is his writing. Back in the Whitesnake days it was obvious that without those songs, the band would have found it much harder to break through and enjoy the success it achieved. Those songs started out from Bernie's imagination. No Bernie – no songs.'

Paul Jones, musician and broadcaster

'I think the first time I played with Bernie was when he sat in with the Blues Band at a gig in Swindon, and I thought, Wow – this heavy metal guy can really play the blues! As time went on, I discovered that the blues (and soul) have informed all his work. The other thing I admire about Bernie is his humility. I've seen it on many occasions – not least the times when he's contributed to my charity gigs at Cranleigh Arts Centre.'

Warren Haynes, the Allman Brothers Band

'I first met Bernie in 1991 when the Allman Brothers came to Europe. There was a benefit at the Hard Rock in London and a bunch of us went and wound up jamming. I heard Bernie play and not only did he play great but he had the best sounding rig of anyone on stage. When it came time for us to play I asked him if I could play through his gear, saying something like, "You've got the only good-sounding rig on stage." He laughed and obliged. We became instant friends and have played together numerous times since. I really love his economy of notes and the fact that the most important thing to him is to get a good sound first (which he seems to be able to do with any setup) and then take it from there.'

Zak Starkey, The Who

'If I had never met Bernie Marsden I would never have spent three years sitting on his garden furniture in the back of a transit crying with laughter and playing the real blues all over the UK, Europe, Northampton and JBs Dudley.

There is Whitesnake, yes, but let's not forget Bernie's great pop sensibility in his work with Mickie Most in the '70s. Bernie is a dear friend for life who never actually paid me but taught me so much about playing with empathy, sincerity, emotion, and fucking huge balls that I owe him at least forty quid.

We bonded over Freddie King, who I was lucky enough to see play once. Bernie has Freddie King's shoes and he's getting ready to dust his broom in the palace of the king. A perfect hideaway to stumble into while steppin' out, walkin' by himself and … sorry I digress as usual – here I go again.'

Elkie Brooks, singer

'Having always been a huge fan of blues music and its various transitions throughout the years, there is nothing better than to hear it played with style and integrity. Bernie Marsden has both in abundance.

We did not work together until 2002 when I was appearing at the Maryport Blues Festival, Cumbria. Bernie was on the bill with his own band that night and I asked him if he would like to get up and do a few numbers with my band later. It was a special night and the atmosphere in the marquee was electric. Bernie added his own dynamic to our sound and it was a great gig. A few years later I called up Bernie and asked if he would possibly come on the road with us for a few months … so off we went! He was such a marvellous addition and a real pleasure to play with.

Among the stunning array of songs Bernie has written, I really fell in love with "A Place in my Heart". A real testament to a true talent.'

Bob Harris, broadcaster

'We first met in 1970, just before I joined Radio 1. I was a DJ at the Country Club, a very cool north London rock venue where Bernie appeared with Skinny Cat. Even now I can remember Bernie's playing – "just like a ringing a bell", as Chuck Berry would say. He was a fabulously expressive, economical guitarist. At a time when speed seemed to be of the essence, Bernie's style was relatively understated but beautifully constructed, already demonstrating his intuitive knowledge of what spaces to fill and how much space to leave. It's a rare gift.

Since then, as we know, he has enjoyed massive success as a player, writer, Hollywood film score composer and a member of one of the biggest bands in the world but despite all the head-turning fame, he has always kept his feet on the ground.

Recently, Bernie joined me in my home studio to play an acoustic session for my TeamRock show, *Bob Harris Rocks*, a full-circle moment. He has deep respect for and amazing knowledge of the players who helped influence his style and who laid the foundations of so much of the music we've loved and supported these past forty-six years.

It feels good to have known Bernie all this time and to have shared many great moments. They all really mean a lot. I have massive respect for him as a superb musician but even more than that, I cherish him as a friend.'

Jack Bruce, Cream

'When I saw Bernie leaving Abbey Road Studios as I arrived, I said to him, "Turn around, man, you're playing on my new album!" This was the best move I ever made. Bernie's delicacy of touch hides the great power of his playing. He has that amazing quality of making every note sound like the only possible note that could be played – and that's before you consider the depth of his sound. He is simply fantastic.'

BB King

Email from Juergen Hoelzle of FRS Radio Stuttgart: 'In 1996 I had the pleasure of interviewing BB King for my radio show. We talked of many things, I don't need to give you a break-down. Well, except one thing, which it has occurred to me that you might not be even aware of. Near the end I asked, "Can white men feel and sing the blues?"

His answer surprised more than a few people and the room was buzzing when he said, "Most of them don't 'cos they do not have the soul for it, sure they can play the blues, but that's not the point. You have to feel the blues, you must go deep into the blues, open your mind and soul. In my opinion there are only a handful of white musicians in the world who can play the Blues like they should be played: Eric Clapton, Jeff Beck, Peter Green, Jonny Lang, John Mayall, and don't forget that Whitesnake guy, Bernie Marsden, he got it too. It is not because of their technique, it's also not their bluesy voices, it's just simple, they have the blues and that's it.'

INTRODUCTION

I first met Bernie Marsden in Musicland Studios in Munich when Paice Ashton Lord (PAL) had come to town to make their debut album, *Malice in Wonderland*. I'd popped in to say hello. Bernie was the singer and guitarist with PAL. I found him welcoming, charming and personable. Who could have known that within a few years we'd be making Whitesnake a band to be reckoned with worldwide?

The second time I saw him was in London. PAL had folded and Bernie quite boldly suggested himself for the band I was putting together after Deep Purple. He immediately established himself by playing and singing great, and bringing his excellent sense of derisive humour to the mix, which was a *huge* part of early Whitesnake.

Bernie, Micky and I wrote the songs that created Whitesnake's sonic identity and helped to make the band a household name. The vocal blend of the three of us worked refreshingly well and our choruses inspired the creation of the Almighty Whitesnake Choir – ah, sweet memories.

Bernie was truly an invaluable band-mate, friend, musician and co-composer of many of my favourite Whitesnake songs, particularly 'Walking in the Shadow of the Blues' and 'Here I Go Again', probably our most recognised and successful song. It has served us and continues to serve us very well, hasn't it, ol' son?

'Tis a biggie, for sure ...

I am so happy we are back in each other's good books and get to jam together whenever I have the pleasure of performing in our home country.

Happy trails, ol' chap.

David Coverdale, Lake Tahoe, 2019

PREFACE

Over nearly fifty years on the road as a professional musician in different cities, countries and continents, I have often thought about Brian Davies.

Brian was a couple of years above me at secondary school in the Sixties in Buckingham, my home town just north-west of London. He was always friendly to me and was an all-round good guy. I remember him being a particularly good athlete: good at running, long jump and javelin. His girlfriend at the time was Diane Jones, someone who I secretly worshipped from my lowly position in the younger classes. I played football with him at school and later for Buckingham Town Juniors. I was a decent enough player but I always thought that he was a very good footballer.

As far as I could see, Brian Davies had it all. We got along well without being close friends. He left school two years before I did, but we still saw each other at football games and sometimes at the pub when I might have been playing the guitar. My playing had always fascinated Brian.

The last time I saw Brian was in 1970 at the corner of Buckingham's West Street and School Lane, where we had a short chat. He said he was no longer with Diane Jones and that he hadn't been able to play football much of late. I told him that I still wanted to be a professional musician; Brian and I had often talked about our dreams. I thought he looked a little grey. Under his arm he carried an old-fashioned glass medicine bottle full of a lurid green liquid. I told him not to drink too much of it: whatever was inside looked as though it might kill him. I could not have been more wrong about that – he had actually been prescribed it to treat a cancer, Hodgkin's lymphoma. Brian passed away later that same year. I was deeply shocked. He was so young, just 21, and I was only 19. Brian had always encouraged me to be a professional musician. He championed my ability and said that I shouldn't ever give up. I still think about Brian Davies a lot.

At every milestone I have reached, a little piece of Brian has been there with me. Whether it was stepping off the plane for the first time in Japan, getting the phone call to say 'Here I Go Again' had reached US No. 1, or receiving my honorary degree from the University of Buckingham, I've always thought of him.

1.

NEW YORK, NEW YORK, 1980

On 9 October 1980, the Whitesnake tour bus driver drove over the Brooklyn Bridge and into Manhattan. My mind was racing and I was full of excitement although I tried to appear cool. At last I was in New York City.

David Coverdale walked up the bus, smiling, and shook my hand. He knew what it meant to me. He had been the one to shake my hand the first time I landed in the USA, in San Francisco. He had felt the same the first time he came here, with Deep Purple. I stared at the skyscrapers. It seemed as though there were so many. I couldn't wait to see Times Square, the Brill Building, Radio City, and Carnegie Hall.

My thoughts drifted to the shows I had done at school concerts, carnivals, wedding receptions, pubs and birthday parties, and in village halls. I felt a huge sense of nostalgia. I looked around the bus, taking in the musicians I was playing with: Jon Lord, Ian Paice, Neil Murray, Micky Moody, and David Coverdale, all now in the same band as me.

Madison Square Garden – here I come.

This had been a huge goal for me since my teenage years, when I listened to live boxing on my portable radio from MSG. I explored the venue by myself when we arrived. I felt like a kid. I wanted to find those boxing dressing rooms and be able to stand in the very spots Joe Louis, Rocky Marciano, Joe Frazier, Muhammad Ali and the Raging Bull himself, Jake La

Motta, prepared for the biggest fights of their lives. Marilyn Monroe sang 'Happy Birthday' to JFK here, and the likes of the Jackson 5, Stevie Wonder and Alice Cooper had performed there.

Whitesnake would open for Jethro Tull that night in front of some 15,000 people as part of our US tour. I had been frustrated many times in previous years by tours in the US being cancelled for various reasons but now all of that was unimportant. It had taken less than eight years to go from my local town hall to Madison Square Garden. No time at all really.

We stayed at the famous Navarro Hotel, a magnificent gothic building overlooking Central Park. Its residents included film stars, poets, musicians, singers and artists and Jacqueline Susann wrote *Valley of the Dolls* there in the 1940s. Musical guests included Jimi Hendrix, the Kinks, the Rolling Stones, the Grateful Dead and Jim Morrison. I shared an elevator with actor James Caan when I arrived. Sonny Corleone and me in a lift! I tried to be the cool Englishman as Mr Caan smiled, 'Nice socks.' I had completely forgotten that I was holding a spare pair lent by Mick Moody. 'Take care with those socks,' said James Caan as he got out.

Whitesnake had no creative management whatsoever but had managed to get to America. That was testament to how together we were at the time. We were ready and it was our time to go global. I was back on the bus and heading for Madison Square Garden in no time. The gig was over far too fast. Jethro Tull's audience liked us a lot, although we were practically unknown in America. Jon Lord and Ian Paice received the biggest recognition as Deep Purple still meant something to the fans.

Time to break America – that was the plan. But plans don't always work out, do they? Let's go back to the start.

2.

GOING TO MY HOME TOWN

I was born on 7 May 1951 in Westfields estate in Buckingham, an extremely quiet town of between 2,000–3,000 souls. My mum and dad were working-class parents and, boy, did they work hard. When I was four we moved to a brand-new council house in Overn Avenue. This was a triumph – my parents had earned their new house, and they loved it. It was my castle.

Buckingham had old-fashioned shops, rather than supermarkets – butchers, greengrocers, a wool shop, a saddler, two gentlemen's outfitters and a very good toyshop. Walter Tyrell, the fruit-and-vegetable man, delivered to our estate twice a week, his overloaded cart drawn by one of his small ponies. Brook's Dairies delivered milk and orange juice daily, also by horsepower.

My Victorian-built primary school was in Well Street. I got on well with the teachers, except deputy head W. T. Benson. I don't know why he took such a dislike to me. When I was seven he ridiculed me in front of the class for a spelling mistake. All he did was make me realise that I rather enjoyed being the centre of attention – a sign of things to come!

I failed my eleven-plus and went to the secondary modern. I never did go to university, but in 2015 the University of Buckingham honoured me with a master's degree for services to music and Buckingham! I accepted with a great deal of pride. My dad was there with my wife, Fran, and daughters Charlotte and Olivia. I wish that my mum could have seen it, but she passed away the previous year. I did find it ironic to be mingling with brilliant academics who had years of hard study under their belts when I had received only a very average education myself. Some of my teachers had also taught my mother some thirty years earlier. Imagine that! How could they possibly relate to my generation?

I was twelve when President Kennedy was shot in November 1963. I remember being scared by my mum's reaction. 'There will definitely be a war if the Russians did it.' I went to the pictures that night, but I couldn't take my mind off JFK and impending doom. I had butterflies in my stomach the whole time. Young people in that cold war period lived in constant fear of the Russians and another world war. But the USSR was innocent, this time, and therefore not going to bomb us off the planet.

Beatles records had started hitting the charts that year – they cheered America up, and they cheered the world up. In my head, it was the Beatles who beat the Russians – I was convinced of that fact. They also ended the reign of the artists I had grown up with in my household – middle-of-the-road stars like Joe Loss, Jess Conrad, David Whitfield, Pearl Carr and Teddy Johnson and Perry Como. Meanwhile, Lonnie Donegan, Joe Brown, Cliff Richard and the Shadows survived and managed to stay with the new army. I had become a fan of a few of them: Joe Brown, Cliff Richard and Marty Wilde. They seemed splendid. Their shiny guitars fascinated me. I watched them on *Ready Steady Go!*, *Juke Box Jury*, and *Thank Your Lucky Stars*.

My cousin Sylvia Chalmers was a huge fan of Elvis, but she was older than me. Merseybeat was the happening thing and all I could think about was guitars. But now came the hard bit for an almost-teen. Just how do I learn to play the guitar?

There were no musicians in either side of my family. The first person I ever saw playing the guitar in the flesh was Roger Williamson from Northampton. He played 'Apache' by the Shadows at my cousin Jean's wedding reception in 1961 and I think he had a gleaming red Fender Stratocaster. I didn't really know how to judge but I thought he played really well. He played 'Shakin' All Over' by Johnny Kidd and the Pirates, a seminal song with the guitar riff of the period. Guitarists today still rate it. London session guitarist Joe Moretti plays those brilliant parts on a white Fender Telecaster.

I was fortunate at a ridiculously young age to have seen acts at Buckingham Town Hall and in the surrounding towns. There was always the potential for danger, with fights breaking out during sets, but I used to sneak in the back of the town hall and climb into an old lighting box to watch the bands on Friday nights, usually fibbing to my folks that I was visiting my grandparents. I saw Screaming Lord Sutch and the Savages – at a time when there was with the real possibility that Ritchie Blackmore was playing guitar – Joe Brown and the Bruvvers, maybe Neil Christian and the Crusaders with Jimmy Page on guitar, Freddy 'Fingers' Lee, Mike Sarne and Bert Weedon. I was bitten by the excitement, alone up there, with the hall full to bursting.

I was in Steeple Claydon hall one Saturday night in 1964 to see the Primitives, and I thought they were fabulous. I got as close to the stage as I could. I had never seen men with such long hair – I was more than impressed. They made two singles for Pye Records and Jimmy Page played on both of them, I'm told. They came from Oxford but their home could have been Jupiter as far as I was concerned. I had seen them on the TV, and now I was a few feet away from them. I was captivated.

I used to see a guitarist from nearby Winslow when I was 14. Nipper – his real name was Gerald Rogers – had quite a reputation and often played weddings. His group was the Originals – Les Castle, Snowy Jeffs, Nipper and either Keith Fenables or Maurice Cracknell singing. Nipper played guitar. One night at the Verney Arms I heard them do Muddy Waters's 'Hoochie Coochie Man'. It was a revelation to hear local guys play this, and play it well.

My cousin Keith Aston had somehow got a guitar but I was under strict instructions not to touch it. I did, of course. I found it a hugely pleasurable experience, just holding it and touching the neck. I didn't really understand the feeling, it just felt right. I had to have my very own guitar and I bugged my folks until they caved in. Finally I had a very old and very used acoustic Spanish guitar. It wasn't particularly good, I knew that even then, cheap and hard to play, especially for a beginner. It was almost impossible to hold one or two notes down, let alone a chord. I persevered until my fingers bled, skin coming off the tips. My hand ached beyond description and became such a painful claw that Mum asked me why my fingers were such a mess. She was genuinely concerned. I practised every single day for months on end and, gradually, the pain subsided, although the worn-out instrument remained extremely difficult to play. This was how I learnt my craft, and what a miracle that I, and countless others all over the country, were prepared to go through this pain barrier.

I astonished my folks one evening when I was able to play along with the theme tunes from *Coronation Street* and *Dixon of Dock Green*. They were both very enthusiastic but I told them that, even though I had improved, the guitar was holding me back. I thought my heavy hint was a bit of a long shot but to my delight they agreed. Thank you, TV theme writers!

I saved every penny from my paper round, and had been saving all my birthday and Christmas money for a couple of years. I had enough money for a deposit! Dad said he would help me out as much as he could. 'How do we get an electric guitar?' he said. I knew exactly where. I had been there before.

3.

LOOK THROUGH ANY WINDOW

When I was 13 I spent a few days in at my aunt Doreen's house in Hampstead, London. I was allowed to make a bus trip on my own after promising I would see the town but not get off the bus.

I boarded the no. 24 from Hampstead to Pimlico, a round trip of about three hours. It remains a great way to see central London. I sat in the prime seat – front, upstairs – and went to Camden Town, Marylebone Road, Gower Street, Trafalgar Square into Whitehall. Sitting there all alone I saw Nelson's Column, the Houses of Parliament, Big Ben, Westminster Abbey and more, all sights I had only seen in pictures or TV. It was very exciting.

On the return leg I glanced up at 114 Charing Cross Road, the Selmer Music Store – the UK's sole importer of American guitars. It was a life-changing moment. I had promised not to leave the bus, but what could I do? I had seen Selmer's window, full of Fender, Gibson, and Epiphone guitars. It was fate. If I had been sitting on the left-hand side of that bus, I would never have noticed. I was down those bus stairs and off the footplate without thinking.

There were bass guitars, amplifiers, and custom-coloured Strats that I'd only ever seen in catalogues. The archtop Gibsons in the store were almost two hundred pounds, an unreal amount of money. One side of the store stocked brass instruments with the famous Selmer badge on them, all very well but of no interest to me, really, the guitars had me totally spellbound. Selmer's was a magic kingdom. The Beatles had been in this very store, as had the Hollies and the Applejacks.

I spent over two hours in the shop but it took me an hour before I actually plucked up the courage to touch one. The assistants were very nice and I took a Fender Stratocaster down from the wall and dared to ask how much it was. The answer was 140 guineas, the equivalent of around £165. This was an incredible amount of money. That very same model today would be worth £30,000 or more.

It eventually dawned that my aunt and uncle would be wondering where the hell I was as I'd been gone for three hours longer than expected – oops. I apologised, told them where I had been and promised not to do it again.

The next day I was on the twenty-four again, this time getting off at Cambridge Circus. I walked up Charing Cross Road and to my delight I discovered many more guitar shops – Macari's, Pan Music. I returned to Selmer's where I heard a famous band were also browsing – could it be John, Paul, or George, or maybe Tony Hicks or Graham Nash? No, it was just the Bachelors, brothers Con and Dec Cluskey buying new Gibson acoustics. The Bachelors were one of my mum's favourites.

It wasn't until later visits that I met the Merseybeats, also Chris Curtis, the drummer with the Searchers. I had taken a guitar from the wall, totally out of my price range, of course, and was playing it quietly. Curtis said I was a very good player and invited me to his flat in Chelsea. I accepted his invitation – he was a pop star, after all, and had a chauffeur-driven car. I still don't believe it, but I got in the car with a man I had just met. With hindsight, that could have been a terrible scenario.

He said that he would cook at the flat. Jon Lord later told me that he was probably elsewhere in the flat at the time – Jon was ten years older than me and was just then starting the project with Chris that would later become Deep Purple. As it turned out, there were only Cornflakes in Chelsea and so that was the meal. I did feel a little strange, eating cereal with Mr Curtis, and wondering why I was there. I should also say that Chris was very nice to me, and nothing whatsoever questionable happened. Maybe he had in mind that I could have been the guitarist for Roundabout, but I was only a young teenager. Jon would later pull my leg about that day, especially at breakfast in a hotel on the road where there were Cornflakes around.

I got to know Denmark Street's shops well and when my dad asked me where we could get an electric guitar, I was ready. Dad was the guarantor for the hire purchase agreement. Selmer had a special offer on the Colorama 2 by the German company Hofner, whose guitars were very popular, reasonably priced and good quality. It was the one for me. The monthly repayments were quite high, but I really didn't care: and I had my first electric guitar!

I held the green plastic case tightly as we went home. I thought the guitar was beautiful. It was finished in a cream colour, had twin pickups and a tremolo arm. I took it everywhere – my mum often said that I was chained to it. I couldn't believe how much easier it was to play than my Spanish acoustic. There was just one more thing …

'You never said anything about a bloody amplifier!' said my dad.

I pleaded with him and we acquired a five-watt Dallas amp from Butler's furniture shop in Buckingham. I practised daily and our next-door neighbour, Tom Tranter, who worked nights, soon had his own name for my setup. He called it 'That bloody electric thing.'

I quickly improved at the guitar while my grades at school plummeted (although I did get a B-plus for music). The art teacher said in his year report, 'I have never known such an idle and yet so charming boy.' I rather liked that.

The first real group I was in was the Jokers: I must have been about 14. They were already an established act with Eric Jeffs on bass, Stan Church on drums, Dave Brock (not the future Hawkwind leader!) as the vocalist and second guitarist, and Steve Rooney the lead guitarist. Eric played bass guitar left-handed, à la McCartney – but strung normally and played upside down.

In the practice room at the youth club I immediately realised the underpowered Dallas was useless in this company. I knew I needed a bigger amp but I didn't have any money, and asking Dad was out of the question. Guitarist Steve owned a six-input amplifier with a massive thirty watts of power which I used via Dave. Steve found me – a young upstart – playing all the guitar licks he knew plus quite a few that he didn't and, worse still, playing them through his massive amp. Having both of us in the band was never going to work. The upstart 14-year-old was already shining brighter than Steve and he left the band – and took the big amp with him. Dave Brock had a lovely, blue Watkins Dominator amp which he lent me. I wish I still had it, a very collectable amplifier.

Steve later told me he left the band because he wanted to spend more time with his girlfriend. I was amazed. Even at 14, I couldn't understand why anybody would want to spend time with a girl instead of being the guitarist in the Jokers.

I was very keen, practising all the time, learning Chuck Berry riffs and Bo Diddley songs, and I settled in very quickly. We had a major upset when drummer Stan Church left after a member of his family was jailed for the manslaughter of a local girl. The case even made national TV. I was very young and quite frankly confused. I didn't understand why this had to have such an impact on my band – was having the name Church the reason?

Roger Hollis replaced Stan as our drummer. He lived near me in Overn Avenue, and was an early heavy metal drummer: he really did hit them hard. We practised every Tuesday and Thursday evening, when the sound of the judo lessons in the upper room was louder than the band. Amps were soon to become a lot louder – thank you, Jim Marshall.

We had another setback when there was a robbery and all of the Jokers' equipment was stolen. The story made front page of the *Buckingham Advertiser* and they sent a photographer who asked us to look appropriately sad. I felt a bit of a fraud as the only equipment I owned was safely back at home: I would never, ever leave my guitar behind.

The Jokers ran out of steam and I came across the Originals, whose guitarist Nipper Rogers had been such an inspiration to me. On one Sunday afternoon I was playing acoustic guitar in the garden of the King's Head. Originals' singer Keith 'Diver' Fenables heard me playing, asked who I was, and then disappeared. He had gone to tell drummer Les Castle about this new kid playing the guitar. He casually asked me if I could play any of their songs and I said yes, I could.

'Good,' he smiled back at me. 'Be here at seven tonight.'

It dawned on me that I had just signed myself up to a gig. Nipper Rogers' job took him away from the area and the Originals couldn't do any gigs – until this particular Sunday! I was petrified: not only had I only played their songs in my bedroom, but Nipper was streets ahead of me as a guitar player My mouth had said that I could do it and so now I would play in a pub packed with punters.

I arrived at the King's Head at about six, very nervous, and a little panicked because I didn't have an amplifier. Les Castle was setting up his drum kit and had a big smile.

'Well, you are young, my boy,' he said, pointing to Nipper's Burns Orbit 3 amplifier. 'Use that.' Les, Keith and I played in a corner of the main bar without a bass player. I kept my head down to avoid making any eye contact with the audience. I was pleased not to hear any booing after the first few songs. Les Castle gave me another smile.

'Fabulous, my boy, carry on like that!'

We played 'I Can Tell', 'Shakin' All Over', 'Green Green Grass of Home', 'Twist and Shout', 'Kansas City', 'Look Through Any Window' and 'Hoochie Coochie Man'. By this time Keith Fenables was also smiling.

Half an hour later it sank in – I was playing with the Originals. I dreaded to think how it sounded, but after a few songs I felt brave enough to glance at the crowd. They were looking happy and a little shell-shocked. Who the hell was this wonder kid? Where was Nipper, the one-and-only, local Hank Marvin? The audience got louder as the night went on, and everyone had a bloody good time. At the end of the night, Keith introduced me to the crowd: 'Let's hear it for the new kid on the cuh-tah, ladeez an' genelmen!'

Keith was deliriously happy. Never again would Nipper Rogers dictate to the Originals: here was a readymade and impressionable new player they could call on, unencumbered by girlfriend or job. The position of my hero Nipper as the top dog was gone after one Sunday night in the King's Head. I was the new kid in town. Nipper never once called me out for taking his gig. Not only that but he was the single influence among all the great guitarists who made me believe I could pick up a guitar. Thanks, Nipper.

The bonus that night was that I got paid! Thirty shillings, a pound note, a 10-bob note and a baguette sandwich to take home. I could sense things were about to change – this was a turning point for the very young BM. I was hired for the regular Sunday night Originals gigs and the Hofner Colorama paid for itself many times over. I practised hard, improving the guitar parts on the songs and gaining in confidence. All my earnings were put aside at home for a Fender Strat and amp, and my mum found the savings one afternoon. There must have been the best part of a hundred pounds, a hell of a wad for a teenager. She and Dad sat me down to ask where I'd got the money from. It was only fairly recently that my dad admitted they thought I might have been a robber. They never expected I was paid to play. My dad's face lit up although dear old Mum seemed a little sceptical. I soon acquired my own Burns Orbit amplifier.

We played most weekends, mainly in pubs, working men's clubs and at wedding receptions and I got my first taste of fame. I loved it. I became quite a draw at the King's Head, a local guitar hero. People treated me slightly differently – most were positive, although a few were jealous and some were unable to accept that this young kid could play the guitar at all. Women who were years older than me loved to hang out with the band, regardless of their marital status. Some weekends I was invited to a female fan's house for a drink. I got to know a lot of them and I must have been very different to their husbands who had to be at work the next morning, mainly because I had to be back at school.

By the time I was 15, I was in my room so much, playing guitar, that I had become a bit of a loner at school. I did have a few good mates: Richard Bernert, Steve Wheeler, Derek Knee and Mick Hodgkinson, but even then it was the common love of music that connected us. I'd often go to Richard's and mime to the Small Faces' first album he played at maximum volume in the living room. I was Steve Marriott, of course, and Richard was Kenney Jones knocking the crap out of a cake tin and cushions with a knife and fork.

Music also played a background role in a job I did with Derek and Richard. We worked for a local chicken farmer, feeding thousands of chickens, collecting eggs, and cleaning out the cages. It was pretty well-paid for the time. The henhouse was an inferno of squawking, but we had a very loud radio pumping out Radio Caroline or Radio London from an eight-inch Fane speaker. The first time I ever heard the Stones' 'Jumpin' Jack Flash' was on Radio Caroline. The opening line really grabbed my attention.

Pirate radio was so important. I got to hear fantastic records one after another, and maximum volume in the henhouse made them sound so much better. The radio reception was unpredictable: some days our area was good, but I was likely to lose the guitar solo just when I was ready to learn it!

I didn't want to leave school at 15, so I stayed for another year, not knowing what I wanted to do in terms of a 'proper' job. The only clear path I had in my mind was something involving guitar. And, boy, was I playing a lot of it by the time I reached my final year …

At the start of the year there was mass excitement because of the arrival of a new 22-year-old French teacher, Elizabeth Rees. She was a great-looking girl, about five foot three, long, black hair, glasses on the end of her nose, short skirt and high-heeled shoes. I think she could tell she was near enough every schoolboy's fantasy. She stopped me in the corridor to ask why I had opted to take history instead of French. As she smiled at me I asked myself the same question. She said that she would make sure I worked hard and I went to the school office and promptly dumped history. I never did learn much French, but she did teach me one hell of a lot about life.

Elizabeth had heard me playing with the Originals and said she was astonished by my playing and I would be famous one day. This was a revelation – she was the only forward-thinker in the school, heading for the Seventies with the same attitude as all the kids who were stumbling towards that decade of change.

Despite my passion for the guitar, music had never been a favourite lesson. I didn't know or care what a stave was – tiny black squiggles on five straight lines did not seem like music

– but I enjoyed the playing side. I remember one lesson I was playing to some girls when music teacher Mrs Gwen Clark arrived. I put the guitar down.

'Don't put that thing away just yet,' she said with a hint of sarcasm. She passed me a handwritten sheet music. 'So, can you play that?'

I looked at the paper – black squiggles on a stave. I couldn't decipher it. She was making a point about my sight-reading ability.

'Now listen and learn,' she said. She played the first notes on the piano. I recognised the tune, the theme from *Z Cars* on TV. The girls in my class looked on. I picked up the guitar and played the *Z Cars* melody almost instantly, Mrs Clark was looking a little vexed. I then played the guitar intro to Chuck Berry's 'Johnny B. Goode'.

'So, can you play that?' I asked her. There were more than a few giggles. Mrs Clark was furious and, to contain her embarrassment, she left the room. I laughed, but she should have taken pleasure in seeing one of her own students playing this way, as an untrained natural. I am still irritated by the way that people with obvious talents were disregarded. If I had listened to my teachers I would never have left Buckingham, and never have tried to make it as a guitarist. It makes me wonder how many potential writers, musicians and artists there were in those dingy, soulless schoolrooms during the Sixties who were ridiculed for having such dreams.

I needed a practical music education. Enter my cousin John Keeley, three years older than me, who visited from Liverpool. He sang and played harmonica in a band, which impressed me a lot. I told him that I could play the guitar, which didn't impress him, but he did listen to me playing along with record-ings by Gerry and the Pacemakers and the Searchers, before instructing me to throw the records away. He told me to get LPs by Howling Wolf, Sonny Boy Williamson, Muddy Waters and Buddy Guy – but I did refuse to give up the Beatles. John had seen Williamson at the Cavern with the Yardbirds, and allowed me to keep my live Yardbirds LP featuring the young Eric Clapton. The blues hit me like a hurricane.

I became obsessed with all things Eric Clapton. I even bought Tuf town shoes because I read he wore them – I read any Clapton magazine article and I paid close attention to his influences. I soaked them all up – I was a musical sponge. If Clapton mentioned a player in an interview, I went straight down to the local shop to order that record. Some were so obscure, some on American labels with strange names: Chess, Federal, Sue and Pye International with the red-and-yellow labels. Artists such as Freddy King, Otis Rush, T. Bone Walker, and more. I slowed down the records to 16 rpm on the radiogram, making it a little easier to learn the guitar parts.

It wasn't always straightforward to find this music. A folk guitarist first suggested I should listen to BB King. The folk player had a really good fingerstyle and liked the way I played, saying it was a very different approach. I was lucky to get a UK Ember label 45-record by mail order of 'Rock Me Baby', BB King's great song. When that Ember record arrived, that was really it. I later found King's UK Stateside releases, the European versions of the early BluesWay/ABC. *Live at the Regal* is the one liked by most guitarists, but for me it was *Blues is King*. Both were recorded in Chicago in the mid-1960s with a small band, and BB is on great form vocally and his guitar playing still motivates and inspires me.

If asked today, I might most often say that the music of The Beatles was the source of my musical career. But, if I am really honest, the blues music went on to inspire and motivate me most of my life. I had already been aware of Big Bill Broonzy, his name fascinated me, but I never really knew what blues music was. But, once I had heard the Yardbirds and John Mayall I was looking for their source material. I searched for

BB King, Leadbelly, Big Bill, Brownie McGhee and Sonny Terry, which led me to Freddy and Albert King. I was given a Louisiana Red album when I was about 14 called *Low Down Back Porch Blues*. I liked it a lot, although I didn't really understand what it was about.

At around that same age, I saw Lightnin' Hopkins, Sister Rosetta Tharpe and Muddy Waters on TV. I was mesmerised. There is some quite phenomenal footage from 1964 of Rosetta Tharpe tearing it up with a white Gibson SG Custom at a railway station platform in Cheshire. It sounds crazy but it is a fact. Try and find it! This was the music I wanted to play. I bought a 45 of Howlin' Wolf, 'Smokestack Lightning', which featured a fantastic guitar player on B-side 'Goin' Down Slow'– this was Hubert Sumlin. Hubert played with both of the great Chicago blues players, Muddy Waters and Howlin' Wolf.

I was soaking up all this music. Gone were all my records of UK artists, even The Beatles and The Hollies were at the back of the pack when it came to the bluesmen. 'Boogie Chillen' by Hooker fascinated me, and still does. The guitar part is so weird, but I loved it and tried to play it. I didn't know about capos or tunings then, but I loved the sound. I found that I could reproduce some of Sonny Boy's harmonica parts on the guitar. That inspired me a lot. Just a tiny fraction of this music was developing my own style and, even though I was fully aware that Eric Clapton and Peter Green had already got it down, I did persevere.

When Cream themselves played Aylesbury in February 1967 there was nothing that would stop me seeing them. My pal Alan Clarke and I hitchhiked to a venue which was heaving with the largest number of people I had ever seen in one space. And then Cream were there: Jack Bruce, Ginger Baker, and 'God' himself, Clapton. Their Marshall amps towered on the small stage, Eric playing his Gibson SG Standard and I heard the 'woman tone' in person. I watched in a kind of dream state as they opened with 'N. S. U.', and played 'Sleepy Time Time', 'Sweet Wine', 'Born Under a Bad Sign', 'Cat's Squirrel', and a devastating 'I'm So Glad'. They were magnificent.

I was jolted into the real world in a surprising way. I felt a sharp prod in my back, and turned around to see Elizabeth Rees, the new French teacher. She was in a very good mood, looking really good, and had a definite twinkle in her eye. She straight away said she would take us back to Buckingham after the show. She was with a friend, a nasty little piece of work named Drew, who taught history. How pissed off Drew must have been to take us back on his date. Alan and I were just grateful not to walk back the sixteen miles.

Outside Buckingham town hall I thanked Drew for the lift, he eyed me with some contempt, and I got out of the car. To my surprise – and Drew's shock – Elizabeth also said 'Thanks' and 'Goodnight' to him. Man, he must have been livid. Alan walked back home while Liz invited me back for a coffee at her flat in Well Street, a minute's walk away.

I was still filled with the excitement of the Cream gig, until it slowly dawned on me that I was alone with my French teacher in her flat. She was calm and chatty, and we discussed the show and our musical interests: all very grown-up stuff. Liz had liked that I played 'Hoochie Coochie Man' at the pub. She went to her bedroom and came back with an album to play on her Dansette record player. It was *The Freewheelin' Bob Dylan*. I had never bothered with acoustic music, unless played by black musicians. The only folk music I was aware of was by the likes of Wally Whyton and the King Brothers on the radio show *Family Favourites*. Bob Dylan was so radical. I was quite stunned.

'Listen to his words,' she said. I still listen to them today.

She told me I could be like my heroes and that if I practised, worked hard and, above all, dedicated myself to being a musician I could make it a career. She pointed that neither Bob Dylan nor Eric Clapton had ever seen the inside of a university, and that the old USA blues players that I worshipped were lucky to get any schooling at all. I really listened to her. Academically, I was way behind, but in learning about life I was taking a huge step forward.

I spent a lot of time at school with Liz Rees, and rumours were rampant, particularly as my French was not improving. Liz was a bohemian free spirit, just the person a young lad of fifteen years of age should stay away from. I was infatuated, of course: she did exactly as she pleased and didn't give a damn about authority.

Something had to give and, halfway through my fifth year, it did. I was called for a meeting with headmaster Gerald Banks. I expected a loud barrage of abuse, but he was very cool and professional. Mr Banks was a good man, and I now see how he turned out to be more of an influence than I realised. Miss Rees was not mentioned by name, but we both knew what the talk was about. He was astute enough to realise and could see that I was a very grown-up fifteen-year-old. I knew what I wanted and I think he knew I would get it. I had no fears about the future, exam results were of no real interest to me and I certainly didn't give a toss about other people's perception of my relationships.

As the summer of 1967 approached it was obvious that my French exams were never going to happen. Liz even rang me at my home telling me to stay away from the oral examination, given that I couldn't really speak a word of French.

There were rumours that Liz been asked to leave at the end of the year or that she might have been sacked. I think she would have resigned long before they could have fired her. I went to her flat to be greeted by a bloke of about 22. She introduced me to him, he was in a band from Birmingham called the Ugly's. She had met him at a gig that weekend. Liz

Rees was with a man, I was mortified, but didn't really know why. Now I know, of course, that I was jealous. She was spending time with him and not me. She could sense my distress, smiled and put her arm around me. He made us all some coffee.

After a few days sulking, I went to see her again but her housemate Eileen Marner told me that she was gone for good. I must have looked terrible because Eileen was extra nice and told me I needed to get over her. Liz had been my guru and I as a young boy I was totally smitten. Her outlook on the importance of enjoying life and take-it-while-you-can attitude struck a chord deep within me. She said that I could do it. She was right, wasn't she? Thanks, Liz, wherever you may be.

I did glimpse her briefly once more, years later. It was the early summer of 1974 and I was on my way to play with Wild Turkey at the Marquee Club. I waited for a tube, dressed in my four-inch, wooden-heeled platform boots – black-and-white stars and stripes all over the leather – orange-and-yellow loon pants with twelve-inch flared hems, a psychedelic tie-dye shirt, accessorised with long necklaces, rings and my hair long and very curly. I also had a long, off-white Afghan coat – well, it was 1974. I spotted an attractive woman in her thirties, reading a book. She smiled back at me and as the train pulled out, she mouthed, 'Bernard?' Liz! But she was gone, and I have never seen or heard anything of her since. I thought again about those long discussions we had – not for the last time.

After that brief summer of love, the guitar always came first. I was dumped by girls many times, but I never gave it a second thought. In any case, I struggled with girls my own age, having discovered older women. A lot of the venues the Originals played had female managers who would ask the guys to 'send that young one that plays the guitar for the cash'. The band would giggle as I would often be met by a buxom, mid-thirties stunner in seamed stockings, black underwear and high heels. The rest of the Originals would be waiting for my reaction.

I vividly remember a lunchtime bowling alley gig in Bedford; the manager was a miserable old sod of about 40, but his more than attractive wife was the lady with the money. She was a wonderful tease, running her hands along her legs, smiling at me, saying how young I was to play so well, flattering me and watching my reaction. Giggling and flirting outrageously, she gave me a sexy look and put the two ten-pound notes in her very considerable cleavage. She added that if I could retrieve the cash without using my hands she would add another five-pound note. I played along, burying my head in her bosom and using my teeth to get the notes. I was young, naive and, of course, enjoyed the whole thing very much. She told me she was bored in Bedford since moving from London where she had been an exotic dancer, whatever that meant.

'Check these out,' she said. 'I was a bit of a catch when I was younger.'

She passed me a few photos of her naked or wearing very little. I was shocked, really, holding full-frontal pics with the very lady in them standing next to me. Her husband arrived at that point. He grabbed the pics from my hands, threw them in the corner and told me to fuck off. She laughed and gave me a cheeky wave. I had the gig money though, safely in the back pocket of my Levi's. The band asked whether I'd gotten the £25. The extra fiver had been a ruse.

4.

WELCOME TO THE REAL WORLD

I finally left school in 1967, without any qualifications, but also without any misgivings. I did feel a little sorry for myself though and found myself kicking my heels around the town. School done, Liz Rees gone – I supposed I'd have to go to work, then.

To my folks' relief I found a job, at a ladies' hairdressing salon in Bletchley, about ten miles from Buckingham. I commuted on my scooter, on which I had painted bright coloured flowers – 1967 was, after all, the year of the hippie and of having flowers in your hair (or painted on your Vespa). My treasured Hofner guitar was similarly adorned. What a sight I must have been, a long-haired kid zooming down the A421 Buckingham to Bletchley road every morning. I got a lot of stick for it but all I cared about was making enough money to buy a Fender Strat and eventually, in my dream of dreams, using that Strat to earn me enough money to buy a white MGA sports car.

The reality of my first proper job soon hit home. Adam of York was in Brooklands Road and the owner was a small bald man, certainly not Adam, but maybe he had come from York. His wife was a first-class battleaxe, a Margaret Thatcher lookalike who called her husband 'Mr Derek', and I disliked her from the start, though she was fascinating. She was prim, very self-assured and loudly northern, but affected a posh speaking voice, accented by her heavy Lancashire twang: 'Madam's 'air lewks loovly – very classy 'air,' she would say. 'That'll be two-poun' ten, please, lady.'

'Mrs Derek' seemed incredibly old but was probably only forty. She was a tyrant and treated all the staff like shit. She obviously believed that she owned people if she paid their wages. I heard 'I pay the wages around 'ere!' many times. I should thank the sad old bird, really, because she cemented my desire to be my own boss.

I washed around fifty heads a week. My hands were in and out of hot and cold water every day, sores and splits began to appear and they even bled. I applied tins of Atrixo cream, but the pain was still excruciating. The final straw for me came with Mrs Derek's point-blank refusal to let me watch Chelsea and Spurs in the FA cup final of 1967. This was the only live football game of the year. I snuck out of the salon at three in the afternoon and watched a bit of it in a local TV shop, before moving next door, to the Jim Marshall music shop but my northern ogre knew where to find me.

'Get back to work, you little sod!' she screamed from the doorway, her face contorted.

I was making three pounds and a few shillings a week from this waste of time. It had been my folks who, understandably, thought I should have a real job. But I hated it so much. I returned to the salon one last time. 'Just stick your job Mr Derek, and your awful wife. I've got a gig to go to,' I said, feeling rather good about myself.

Mrs Derek was furious because she had wanted to sack me first. What a sight she was – eyes bulging, tongue out, spitting out words and looking at Mr Derek for support. He gave none. The older girls laughed, loving the fact that the old bag was getting it from the youngest and lowliest employee.

I walked out, never to return. My folks took it well but were keen to see me employed somewhere. It was not to be with the

Originals. I had been feeling very stuck with them, sucked into music I didn't really want to play. I was a lot younger and had younger ideas. Time to find another band but, as it turned out, they found me.

The Daystroms were the biggest local group in the area, even touring outside Buckingham with their own vehicle – a Ford Thames van. I'd heard a lot about them. They took their name from a Swedish company that produced home kits to make amplifiers. Mac Stevens was their bassist and Tony Saunders was on drums. Singer Dougie Eggleton called the shots and, most importantly, owned the van and PA system. Dougie had seen me with the Originals and decided I would be better off in the Daystroms. I didn't argue – I wanted to be in the biggest group in the area.

Lead guitarist Alan Rogers was Nipper's cousin. He was a cool guy; tall, slim and, I noticed, he had very long fingers. I thought this was essential for a guitarist – I looked at my own fingers and inwardly frowned. But even with longer fingers it became obvious in those early rehearsals that 'the kid' was already some way ahead of Alan as a lead guitarist.

The group practised in the drivers' room at Buckingham's milk factory. It was small, stank of smoke, and was not at all suited for the job but it was free and I loved it. I didn't love the material much. Even at this very early stage I knew I couldn't play 'Silence is Golden' by the Tremeloes for very long. I was still super-keen to be playing, though, and endeavoured to learn all the rhythm parts. I also knew most of the lead guitar parts, and Alan Rogers was very aware of this as he struggled to play them.

My first performance with the Daystroms was at Whitchurch youth club. Alan Rogers didn't show up and Dougie Eggleton was panicking. 'Bernard, you will have to play lead and rhythm guitar, I know you can do it.'

I knew that I could do it, too, and even if I was a little over-confident everything went well. Afterwards, in the dressing room, Dougie announced that I was to take over on lead. Nobody uttered a word in protest, and I breathed the rarefied air of the lead guitarist.

Over summer we changed our name to the more modern-sounding the Clockwork Mousetrap, and the Ford van became a kaleidoscope of colour. On stage we played 'San Francisco' by Scott McKenzie, 'Massachusetts' by the Bee Gees and still bloody 'Silence is Golden'. Despite my reservations about the material, I played a lot of shows, including my first bookings at any distance. We travelled to Northampton, Bedford, Aylesbury and even into Cambridgeshire. It wasn't exactly a world tour, but for a 16-year-old it was an amazing experience. I was at the annual Buckingham Carnival parade, playing with the band on the back of a lorry. We also played the town hall that night.

I built a musical reputation yet, to a fair few, I seemed like a 'right little big 'ead', with an ego. But I was simply growing in confidence because I knew I could play. Most of the criticism came from people who would so have loved to be able to play the guitar. Bitterness is a horrible trait.

We played just about every local village hall twice – or more. We also had more prestigious bookings, like the officers' clubs of Upper Heyford and Croughton US air bases. The crowd reacted differently to UK audiences. Maybe seeing a band playing American songs reminded them of home, thousands of miles away, as did the drinks and homemade snacks that I had never heard of before: cold Budweiser beers, Hershey bars, and the infamous product of one Mr Jack Daniel. I looked forward to the interval, when I could listen to their great soul records, including Wilson Pickett, Eddie Floyd, Otis Redding, Aretha Franklin, James Brown, and Marvin Gaye. I was soon hooked on soul. After the break I'd have to get up and play 'Silence is Golden'. I really wasn't impressed.

One GI became a huge factor in my subsequent career. He was a black officer at Heyford and a guitarist, who had seen me struggling with a few parts. He approached me one Friday night during a break. He had a rich, southern accent, somewhere like Alabama. We had been playing our average versions of Stax material, probably 'Soothe Me' or 'Hold On I'm Coming' and he asked if he could play my guitar. He was good – very good. To my shame I only remember his first name, Bobby, but I've never forgotten his help.

He showed me the correct way to play the great rhythm guitar parts and brought his own Fender to the club. Between sets he taught me to play all sorts while the others were usually having a drink. Bobby explained in great detail where and how to shape chords and told me about fret positions. He kicked me into advanced playing by really emphasising the importance of rhythm guitar when I had previously been of the mind that lead guitar was of prime importance. Bobby spoke about 'the feel', over and over again. He told me that 'the feel' should be the very first and the very last thing I think about when learning a song. That tiny but monumental piece of advice stayed with me throughout my career.

We enjoyed our weekend partnership for some three months, during which time he even gave me records from Stax, Motown, Atlantic, and King and then he told me at one Friday night gig that he was leaving the air force and I was devastated. He had been the first real guitarist who actively nurtured my ability. He had turned me around and the advice he gave me formed the bedrock of the way I played from then on, the way I would write songs and, most of all, it ensured I would never do anything other than play the guitar for a living. He was a game-changer. He even joked that I would become famous one day because of his help. Well, what can I say? Thank you, Bobby. Wherever you may be.

I made a return to the Cream gig venue, but this time it was to be me on the stage. When the Clockwork Mousetrap played the Assembly Rooms in Aylesbury, I made sure that I stood as close to the spot where 'God' played and I went into my own zone. I still do that today at certain gigs – nothing really changes. On the stage in white paint in capital letters was a warning: 'NO AMPLIFIERS IN FRONT OF THIS LINE'. I smiled to myself that night. I was sure that Clapton's Marshall amps went well over that line.

About half an hour before the show Dougie had produced some grey, flared trousers and horrendous pink, polo-neck acrylic sweaters for each member of the band. I looked at him in disbelief and refused point-blank. The other members of the band began to get dressed and Dougie looked at me. What none of them understood was that I didn't really care. If I wasn't in that band I would surely be in another. I won the showdown, of course. What could he do? To fire me would mean cancelling the next few weeks' gigs. My outfit stayed in its plastic bag although, with the others dutifully kitted out, the Clockwork Mousetrap looked like a very bad acid trip under the questionable stage lights. I would always have a problem with stage clothes. I have never really been interested in image, perhaps to my detriment but all I ever wanted was my next pair of Levi's, a T-shirt or maybe a denim shirt and a leather Levi's jacket. Rory Gallagher was always going to be my sartorial role model.

I was stonewalled by the band on the way home but the power of the lead guitarist had been established, and I used that little trick for some time, if not for long with the Clockwork Mousetrap. We parted company shortly after the 'pink sweater affair', but Dougie, Mac, Tony and, especially, Alan should be credited: they moved me forward a lot. I think they knew the time had come: I was on a totally different wavelength, with a whole new musical world emerging.

It was a guitar player from Seattle, America, who provided the real reason for me deciding to leave the band. I suspect Jimi Hendrix broke up many other bands as well. I saw the unknown guitarist on *Top of the Pops* performing 'Hey Joe'. I had never seen anything like him – I suppose Presley accomplished the same thing for the previous generation. Jimi did outrageous things with the guitar, such as playing with his teeth. I was mesmerised – what a sound he created. No pink sweaters on this boy.

I knew I had to form a three-piece: guitar, bass and drums. Everyone I knew was reacting to the Jimi Hendrix Experience and Cream. I was getting tired of being 'the kid' and I wanted to be respected as a guitarist. This was a big dream for a 16-year-old from rural Buckingham. I formed the James Watt Compassion (I have no idea why I called it that), with Paul Sandman on bass and Charlie Hill on drums. We settled on tracks by the Bluesbreakers, Cream, and Hendrix, playing them exactly the same as the records – or so we thought. As the other two were both from Bletchley and none of us had a vehicle, we rehearsed over the phone, which was not great preparation for shows. We believed we were the business, but we were just about average, and it was the material that carried us through. We lasted less than six months but I knew it wasn't working and the others agreed. At the final show Paul's girlfriend chinned me for encouraging him to leave his previous band. Good girl.

The audience that night also included two members of the best young group in the area, the Hydra Bronx B Band from Brackley. They were there to offer me a new job, not knowing that I was just out of a band. Ian Dysyllas and Ray Knott said I could have the use of a Marshall 50 amp and speaker. A bribe, yes, and I took it with both hands. They even had their own rehearsal room at Ian's house in nearby Turweston, packed with amps, guitars, microphones and a drum kit. They also had a coffee machine, which was all new to me.

They were more of a soul than a blues band and they did play some great stuff: 'Hold On I'm Coming' and 'Soothe Me' by Sam and Dave, 'Sweet Soul Music' by Arthur Conley and the brilliant 'Soul Finger' by Bar-Kays. The crowds loved their Motown.

Ian 'Dizzy' Dysyllas played drums and Ray Knott was on organ. Then there was Tom Kemp on bass, Ian Smart and Cyril Southam on saxophones and the dynamic Chris Adams on vocals. I replaced Graham Smart as guitarist. The band wondered if fans would still come out in force with the change but we won them over from the start. Ian and Ray could hardly stop smiling after the first show. We went back to Turweston and got pretty drunk on cheap Justina wine. For the first time I was playing the music I wanted to. The discipline in the band was very good for me, and Dizzy was organised in running rehearsals and making proper musical arrangements. It highlighted my rapidly improving playing.

The band slimmed down to Ray, Dizzy, Chris and me, playing proper rhythm and blues. There were more changes. I suggested to Ray, 'Why don't you play bass guitar? You are so rubbish on that organ.' Tact has never been my strong point. We drove to London the following weekend and swapped the Vox organ for a vintage Fender Precision bass. Ray still plays bass today. Now going under the name the Skinny Cat Blues Band – I was a fan of Black Cat Bones with Paul Kossoff and Simon Kirke so I think that's were the cat came in – we set about building on the Hydra Bronx crowd. I was really enjoying myself. The Daystroms had never had a musical direction, but Skinny Cat did.

I thrived on watching other talented people play. I always tried to emulate them even if I often failed. The Skinny Cat guys picked up on this almost immediately and I gained their respect. Guitarists who were years older than me started to come to Skinny Cat gigs, while we would open for other local bands and promptly steal all their fans. That is how it was in those days.

Banbury will always hold a place in my heart, as it was the first area away from home to adopt me, as a musician, openly taking to my talent. I had gone to a new blues club there and asked to play a song during the interval, as I thought I was better than the featured band's guitarist. Unbelievably, they agreed and the player in question, Ron Prew, even had the decency to loan me his treasured Gretsch guitar. The promoter somewhat reluctantly introduced me, I sat on a stool with this alien guitar, and played Eric Clapton's version of the Robert Johnson song 'Rambling on My Mind'. The audience, players and fans alike, knew the track backwards. Most only dreamed of playing the solo, but I could – note for bluesy note. For good measure I threw in a couple of extra lead breaks of my own. I was rewarded with an edgy silence and so, wincing mentally, simply said, 'Thank you for listening.' The place erupted with applause. A few days later Skinny Cat was booked into the venue which more usually featured pro bands such as Chicken Shack, Jellybread, Duster Bennett, and the Aynsley Dunbar Retaliation. We were in good company.

We continued to play the venue with our following increasing all the time, although Chris Adams left the band as Ray, Ian, and myself were so tight. Yours truly became the singer, but then 'Dizzy' left to get married. The Skinny Cat line-up of eight was now down to bassist Ray Knott and me. Mick Bullard, the drummer with another local band, was given the job. He was used to learning songs from records but we were having none of that. Ray and I wanted to jam and find our own groove, to see where it would lead us. Mick agreed to join us even though we had no money coming in and he had to leave a band whose wages contributed toward his young family. The three of us cut the name down to just Skinny Cat to avoid being pigeonholed by the 'Blues' and in September

1969 I went into the studio, with the group, to record for the first time.

We booked a Saturday afternoon at Shield Studio in Kettering, at something like £5 an hour. It was a lot of money for us. The engineer, Derek Tompkins, was from another era – a total boffin with sound but about as musical as a candle. Roger Taylor, later of Queen, recorded his first band's demos there as well.

I had my much-anticipated Fender Stratocaster by then. I acquired it in 1968 through a *Melody Maker* ad. It was a straight swap for a Grimshaw guitar. When I met the swapper and took my guitar out of the case, a pick-up dropped out and my heart fell out with it, but luckily the guy loved the guitar and while Ray Knott shook his head in disbelief I had a 1961 three-tone sunburst Fender Stratocaster. Dreams do come true if you wait. One of the best guitar deals I ever did.

I arrived at the recording session feeling a little panicked, having been writing rather average songs for about six months. I wasn't ever that bothered about lyrics for my songs and tended to have a solid chorus with verses made up as I went along, which was difficult in the studio. I asked the others in the band to write lyrics, but they were not remotely interested.

Feeling insecure – maybe my songs were rubbish after all – I decided to record one of our stage favourites, 'When You Say You're Sorry', by American band Rhinoceros, also recorded by Rod Stewart. The B-side was a very standard twelve-bar blues, along the lines of, 'I left my baby this morning …' you get the picture? A very rare 45-rpm disc indeed, I still have the one and only copy! The photos from this session are better than the record.

We returned to the studio about ten months later, now driving a brand-new white Ford Transit. These later sessions produced a much better tape of four original songs, and the band was tighter and eager to record. Mr Tompkins's input was actually invaluable. The songs were a little better and this time I actually had written out lyrics beforehand. I heard the four-track acetate again in 2016. There is a diabolical version of 'We Can Work it Out' by the Beatles that I had erased from my memory. Nonetheless, I remember our local fans all loved the demos.

I took the tape to London visiting agencies and record companies. At Blue Horizon Records I saw Fleetwood Mac producer Mike Vernon. I was excited to be so close to Peter Green. Mike said he liked my voice and that the guitar was very good and, credit to him, he did come to see us live: many wouldn't have done so. He wrote that he had enjoyed the playing but the material was 'not strong enough'. I still have the letter somewhere. Not strong at all, Mike, you were very kind!

I had no luck anywhere else. I went to the label run by Dick James, the Beatles publisher, in New Oxford Street. I had been waiting in reception all morning when I recognised Elton John coming in. He was dressed in denim with fabric badges sewed all over his jacket and jeans. He looked pretty flamboyant, even at that early stage in his career! He had a great record out at the time called 'Lady Samantha'. He seemed pleasantly surprised that I recognised him and asked if I'd like to join him for a coffee – probably the first real cup I ever had. He was a very nice guy and with a grin insisted he paid for the coffee, as he'd get the money back from expenses. We returned to the office and there was still no sign of the man I wanted to see. I had other appointments and Elton John said he would get the tape copied and leave it for my contact. What a lovely gesture and although I never heard from the label about the Skinny Cat tape, I'm not surprised, thinking back. The songs were not exactly John and Taupin. I had missed my chance

– it could have been Bernie Marsden, not Bernie Taupin! Dream on, BM.

The main feedback I got from my visits was to concentrate on the guitar – meaning forget my band. It was the right thing. The truth was I was trying to run uphill all the time. Skinny Cat were a great live band, but the material was nowhere near good enough. As much as I wished we could go as a group, I knew that I would have to make the move to London on my own and I began to look for audition adverts in the music press. Mick Bullard had small kids to bring up, and Ray was always meant to take over the family car business in Brackley. For the time being, I continued to enjoy myself with Skinny Cat. We remained semi-pro, determined to be the best in our field, and that we were. I have some great live recordings with a fantastic level of energy.

We all particularly enjoyed the summer ball gigs organised by our management for the colleges in Oxford. We called them 'penguin balls' as we'd never seen people dress up in white ties and tails. We opened for bands such as Trapeze, Osibisa, and Dada, featuring wonderful singers Elkie Brooks and Robert Palmer. They evolved into Vinegar Joe and we opened for them many times. I talked to Robert Palmer a lot – he was so cool in those days but always very approachable and chatty. We lost him too soon in 2003, but he left us some fantastic music. Elkie Brooks was simply stunning. The first time I watched her perform I was completely mesmerised by her outrageous clothes, cowboy boots, stage manner and incredible voice. She sang like a dream and there was the bonus of the pairing of her voice with Robert Palmer.

Vinegar Joe guitarist Pete Gage took me under his wing. He played a Gold Top Les Paul, wore a cowboy hat, and was married to Elkie Brooks – I was green with envy. I later had the extreme pleasure of playing guitar for Elkie. I received a phone call from her asking me to cover for Geoff Whitehorn for a few gigs in 2005 and, well, a few gigs turned into about six months. After all those years I spent worshipping her and her voice as a young man, she was now singing better than ever and with me playing guitar by her side.

5.

TO THE CITY

Alan Upward was one of Skinny Cat's roadies and he lived in Oxford. He was quite a character. It was Alan who introduced me to a commune near Buckingham at the end of 1969.

Some people he knew had moved into Chetwode Manor, a very large rambling mansion, close to dereliction, but the crazy thing was that the electricity and water were still available. A group of Oxford hippies had discovered it, and Alan knew them well. I became a weekend hippie, the band rehearsed and played there, and it was fun. I wanted Skinny Cat to move in. Ray said that he had to go to work, but I did move in as I was between jobs (I still took washing home for my mum to do).

One evening a girlfriend of one of the other guys who lived there returned from work at an Oxford teaching hospital and passed around some pills. I have never been much of a drug-taker. I've never smoked cigarettes or indulged with weed very much. I was a little sceptical but I swallowed one of the pills. I had watched the others' reactions on a previous weekend and they seemed to be fine. I waited for about two hours. Alan had also dropped a tab and we both looked at each other and shrugged. Nothing was happening.

When somebody else said they were going into Buckingham Alan and I jumped in the Land Rover. That's when things started to happen in my head, things that I didn't really under-stand, and our driver gave us very strange looks as we arrived in the town centre. Cars floated around me in a stream – no longer a street. We tried to walk towards the market but the sand was too deep, and we didn't mind. I tried to talk to Alan but my voice was a loud gun going off in my head. We reached the market, and a group of people came to talk to me. Alan pleaded with me to be cool. Cool? What was that? We were close to a pub and people were asking me about Skinny Cat. Their speech slowed down until their mutterings became one extremely long word.

What on earth was wrong with them? I thought.

The sand shifted beneath my feet.

I looked up and everyone had the head of a fluorescent, brightly coloured animal: a rabbit, a cat, a dog, another rabbit, a cascade of colour and noise. They were all speaking, all shouting, all at once. I was terrified. I stood in that wet sand while everybody else went absolutely mad. I knew I was the sane one. Frantically, we tried to get back to the Land Rover, and one of the locals grabbed my arm and asked if I was OK, with genuine concern. Me? I was obviously fine. He had the problems.

I never took LSD again.

Skinny Cat opened for Fleetwood Mac, thanks to a booker we had met at the Oxford Polytechnic. I'm sure this is a fact very few people know. The gig was in Headington in Oxford. Although there was no Peter Green, I did talk with Danny Kirwan and John McVie. Mick Fleetwood was around but I didn't get a chance to speak to him. Kirwan played brilliant guitar on his black, three pick-up Les Paul Custom – the very guitar he would smash to pieces before leaving Fleetwood Mac only a year later. I took some old photos with me that night. They were from an early Fleetwood Mac gig in Windsor. John McVie looked at them with great fondness, especially the two single shots of Peter Green. I remember his face and exactly what he said: 'It'll never be like that again.'

I didn't really take his words in at the time, but I do now. He was reflecting upon the loss of Peter Green in the band and couldn't imagine they'd ever be the mammoth success they became and still are today without him. I will always remember John's face as he looked at those old photographs. At the time, mainly because Peter Green wasn't there with Mac, I didn't really realise the momentous thing it was for Skinny Cat to open for them. I hugely respected the others in the band, but Peter Green was my idol. It's only really writing this all down now makes me realise how big a deal it was to open for the one and only Fleetwood Mac, with Peter Green or without.

Towards the end of that year, 1970, Skinny Cat gigged all the major venues in London, including the Temple at the Flamingo Club, the Marquee with Audience, the Acid Palace in Uxbridge with Blonde on Blonde, the 1860 Club in Windsor with Argent and Eel Pie Island with Hawkwind and Stray.

In October we opened for the brilliant Irish guitarist Gary Moore with his first band Skid Row at the Haverstock Hill Country Club, near Hampstead. Skid Row were sound-checking when we walked in. Within seconds, my mouth was wide open, not only because of the utterly astonishing guitar playing of Gary, but the sheer power of the band: Brush Shiels on bass and Noel Bridgeman on drums. The frenetic style of the music and the sheer speed at which they could play really brought home the differences between the pros and semi-pros. Gary had a woollen bobble hat, drainpipe jeans, a tank top, and the trace of a beard. He played a red Les Paul with P90 pickups. He was sitting on the drum stool, playing 'Rambling on my Mind' on guitar, bass drum and hi-hat – a one-man band. This was the very same song I had played back in Banbury; needless to say I didn't play it that night!

Gary and I got along very well. He admired my newly acquired Gibson SG Les Paul, the same guitar I loaned him many years later. We were almost the same age, but I could see how much I needed to improve. Gary Moore at that time would have been a real eye-opener for any guitar player. I liked him best when he played slower and bluesier things. He soon became a treasured friend, and he played at my wedding in 1980.

The venue had one poky little dressing room but Skid Row insisted we share it. I took note of their attitude. DJ Bob Harris introduced the bands that night and we are friends to this day. He is an extremely well-read person in music, and his knowledge of country is fantastic. He still remembers those brilliant days at the Country Club.

We also opened in London for performance art collective Principal Edwards Magic Theatre and prog band Van Der Graaf Generator, who were both more than snobby backstage. Slade, by contrast, had that whole skinhead thing, and really did look very intimidating. They were actually quite scary with their very loud Midland accents. They put on quite the most foul-mouthed act I had ever witnessed. I was quite disgusted, even at 19. But any negative first impressions dissolved after we chatted and found they were actually really decent blokes. Noddy Holder told me that all the effing and blinding was part of the show and the crowd loved them.

Seeing the different sides of genuine people in bands as I did with Skid Row and Slade made me think about my future. It had dawned on me that the music business was a very broad church and could accommodate both Gary Moore's obvious genius and the basic honesty of Dave Hill's guitar playing. It was a real eye-opener for me, as were some of the dirty tricks played by headliners to make their support acts look bad.

One of these was Stray, who had a record deal. We were pleased to be on the bill with them. We thought we would be able to use the in-house PA system, but Stray didn't allow it. We had to bring in our little Marshall PA system, and then Stray's road manager didn't like the space it was taking up on the stage. It was an unpleasant feeling to be treated so shabbily, and I made a mental note to myself that if I were ever in that position, I would know how to act. We played the gig and went down fairly well, but I never forgot their antics.

As Lowell George sang with Little Feat's 'On Your Way Down', you might meet again with those you misused on your way up. That was true for Stray, I'm afraid. They never really made it, and what went around did indeed come around. Just a few years after that night in London with Skinny Cat, Stray were the opening act for the chart-topping Cozy Powell's Hammer in the splendid Blackpool Opera House. It was 1974, and I was the guitarist in Hammer.

There were problems fitting Stray's gear on the stage because Cozy's kit was very large, and Hammer had a lot of backline. Was this time for my revenge? No, because I didn't want to stoop to Stray's level, but I was quietly pleased when our drum tech got in a heated discussion with Stray drummer Richie Cole. He looked at me sheepishly. He knew who I was and he knew we had met before but couldn't quite remember where. I asked the tech to move Cozy's legendary red Ludwig kit so the Stray lads could get their stuff on for their gig. Those Stray boys taught me that the stage belongs to all musicians.

Skinny Cat were not going to make it either, that much was clear. We continued to gig, but for me the goal remained getting myself a pro gig and moving to the city. While I enjoyed playing in such a strong regional band, I was also on the lookout for promising auditions. There was a newspaper kiosk at the end of Charing Cross Road and Tottenham Court Road in London that had the first London issues of *Melody Maker* by Wednesday lunchtime. Musicians gathered to see the 'wanted' ads a day before the rest of the country. The ads would promise a record deal and would give a number. You rang, and rang, and rang, and then finally got through to someone on the other end of the phone who gave you a day the following week to go to a rehearsal studio somewhere in London. You'd turn up, usually not having a bloody clue what band you were auditioning for.

But I did spot a *Melody Maker* ad for the Bluesbreakers, still the gig of gigs for any aspiring or established pro player. I called Miller Anderson, the guitarist of the Keef Hartley band, who helped me out after Skinny Cat had opened for the band; a good guy. Miller knew Mick Taylor who, it was rumoured, was leaving the Bluesbreakers. I was confident enough to think I might audition. It sounds a little crazy with hindsight but it shows you just how confident I must have been. Miller called Mick Taylor to see if I could skip some of the audition scenario. There would have been scores of guitarists looking for this gig with John Mayall. Miller arranged for me to meet Mick in London and also asked him to put in a word for me with John Mayall himself. Thinking about it, it made total sense. Mick Taylor had only been 17 when he joined the Mayall band himself and he would understand.

Mick lived in a flat in Porchester Road, Paddington. I rang the bell feeling nervous: Mick was a huge name, alongside Eric Clapton and Peter Green, but he was a quiet, studious kind of person and made me feel at ease, although I couldn't help but wonder to myself where his guitars were stored in the flat. We had a conversation over coffee, and he soon enough shared some devastating information. While Mayall's management had run the ad in *Melody Maker*, John had decided he wouldn't be taking on another electric guitarist. I think Mick felt a little awkward, but I was not at all put out. I was thankful for information that had, after all, come from John Mayall himself.

I headed home, admittedly feeling a little deflated. Mick was not much older, but he had so much more experience and was already a tremendous blues guitar player. Of course, he also knew at the time that he would be joining the Rolling Stones in the near future. He didn't tell me then, but when the news was announced I was excited – I knew a Rolling Stone! The holy trinity of Clapton, Green and Taylor – was it ever better than that? What a time to be playing the guitar.

I finally got to play on stage with Mick Taylor in October 2016 at a Jack Bruce memorial gig in Shepherd's Bush. We stayed at the same hotel and I told him about the time we first met. He didn't remember any of it, why should he? I had been the kid from nowhere back then. At last we finally got to perform together and he played some truly beautiful stuff. It may take years but music always brings you together.

Another disappointment followed my first encounter with Mick Taylor. This time it was with Alan Clarke of the Hollies. He drank in the same Hampstead pub as my dear uncle, Ken Gotts, and said that he was putting a band together. He had left the Hollies, and Ken duly mentioned his talented nephew. There was a lot of excitement at home when Ken called my mum to say he had arranged an audition. Dad drove me to Watford and gave me the money for the train. At the hall near Belsize Park I waited in the hallway for my call, my guitar case clutched tightly, excitement and nerves building. Alan shook my hand as I introduced myself as Ken's nephew. Then, disaster. The sight of my guitar emerging from the case was met with awkward coughing from the others.

Alan was auditioning for a bass player.

I didn't blame my uncle Ken. Not only was he always a bit deaf, but he probably wouldn't have realised there was any difference in putting the 'bass' before guitarist. I made my apologies for wasting their time and got ready to go. Alan Clarke told me not to worry. He passed me a bass and I had my audition after all. How nice was that? I hung out with him and the band for the day, making tea and coffee. Alan gave me a huge injection of confidence when he told me I could go all the way with the guitar, and I thank him for that.

I had another non-starter, at least first time around in April 1972, with UFO, a band who didn't mean that much to audiences in the UK. I had never heard of them before I auditioned but they had enjoyed success in Japan and Europe. They were certainly a bigger band than Skinny Cat. A hippy girl with pink hair answered the door at what I thought was the audition. 'Name?' she said. No greeting. 'Wait here.' A few lads, presumably guitarists, were waiting in a small room. There were guitar cases everywhere. The pink-haired girl ushered me into a small office to meet manager Mark Hanau, who was in a yoga pose, wearing a thin woollen sweater, and sporting cropped, spiky hair and a good layer of makeup. He looked at me without saying a word. I was almost 21, had long, thick, curly hair and was wearing a denim shirt, jeans, and desert boots. I wasn't exactly Ziggy Stardust. 'Bernie Marsden?' he said, looking at his list, not me. I just wanted to know where I should set up and play.

Calling me 'my dear' a good few times, Mark said that UFO was his vision and I would by no means fit that vision. I could be the best guitarist in the world, but I had turned up to an interview rather than an audition. I was straight out. What a twat. I thought that was the end of that.

Late in the autumn a green envelope arrived emblazoned with the logo of a fairly new company, Chrysalis Records. Wilf Wright was UFO's new manager and he was inviting me to an audition – yes, a proper audition, in a rehearsal room, with a Marshall rig. I was working at that time for a Buckingham builder, and took the day off work. It was a case of second time lucky. I got the gig. Time to be a rock star.

Skinny Cat had built up a very good following but I knew the band would never scale the heights. Mick Bullard and Ray Knott were very supportive and said they had known I would be gone at some point. I only have fond memories of my Skinny Cat days. My folks were pleased for me but, understandably, a little apprehensive. They had read about bands and musicians in the press: womanising, hard drinking, drugs, overdosing. I did my best to reassure them that I would be OK.

My girlfriend, Frances Plummer, was a fashion buyer at Harrods and we got a tiny bedsit in Shepherd's Bush. This was it – the life in London that I had dreamt of and that we were now living together. We didn't earn much, but we got into a wonderful London routine: jumping on buses, hailing black taxi cabs, taking the tube, exploring markets with spicy foods and foreign ingredients, and visiting Greek, Chinese and Indian restaurants. Fran's career advanced rapidly and I would go away a hell of a lot on tour but she understood. She knew that me being a pro guitarist wouldn't be easy but she too had her work. I was extremely lucky to have her by my side.

I soon realised that, by coincidence, the guitarist from Hawkwind lived on the top floor of our house while Mott the Hoople guitarist Mick Ralphs and his wife Nina rented the large basement flat. Mott were veterans of multiple US tours, despite Mick being a notoriously bad flyer. I watched the tour manager and band members carry him from the flat to the car for the airport on many occasions, full of sleeping tablets for anxiety.

It was while we were having one of our regular tea breaks in their flat, Mick fiddling with a newly acquired Gibson 335, that he passed me a cassette to play. A fan of Mott had sent the band a demo of a song he had written. It was called 'All the Young Dudes' and the fan was David Bowie. Mick really rated the song and thought it would be Mott's last shot at the real big time. It was, indeed, the breakthrough at last, followed by 'All the Way from Memphis' and 'Honaloochie Boogie'. I was lucky to get to hear these as rough mixes. Suddenly Mott was a hit. Fran and I watched Mick on *Top of the Pops* on our new tiny colour TV in the bedsit. I felt happy for my neighbour, it was a massive deal and a dream of mine. I thought one day maybe it could happen for me.

The UFO manager, Hull-born Wilf Wright, was good to me from day one. He may have felt a little sorry for me, because he knew there was a slight tension from the off between the rest of the UFO boys (Phil Mogg, Andy Parker, and Pete Way) and me. Partly this was because the others were all from north London, and I was the lone country boy. They let me hire one roadie and so I was always grateful to have Chelsea Dunn from Skinny Cat with me. It really did help in those early days to have him around: he was my only ally. The band only ever seemed to play one-chord boogies; there was nothing particularly challenging about the music. Still, it was good to be playing in a headlining act – I was now in the first division.

My first pro gig was at the Marquee Club on 3 November 1972. Other bill-topping acts that week were Chicken Shack, Patto, Beggar's Opera, Stackridge, and Nazareth – even Screaming Lord Sutch. Fans were queuing to get in along the street and past the Ship – this was the Wardour Street pub to be seen in, if you were a musician. Once I used to be in those lines myself and now others were waiting to see UFO.

I injected a few bluesy things into the setlist, 'Move Over' by Janis Joplin and 'Back In The USA' by Chuck Berry, but that was the extent of my musical input at this early time. Andy Parker was a powerful and very loud player, although he could not play a straight drum roll. Pete Way, in my opinion, wasn't the most naturally gifted bass player I'd ever worked with. He wasn't that fussed about technique or sound, and rarely locked in with Andy – which is vital for drums and bass: the rhythm section always needs to be together. He was always more concerned with his stage clothes than his playing.

A pattern emerged very quickly. Phil Mogg had a tendency to 'Baby, baby' after almost every line he sung and it irritated me intensely. The first line of 'Move Over' is, 'You know that it's over, baby', and even that was followed by 'Baby, baby'. I found myself stifling an irritated grin every night. Phil and I were on a collision course from day one, really. He never passed up the chance to exert his position as number one, not that I ever wanted it, but I did ask more questions about running a band in that first month than Andy or Pete ever had. I wanted to learn about this business of being pro, and fast.

I soon gathered a following, much to Phil's acute annoyance: we played about five shows a week and I received £15, increasing to £20 when we were in Europe. Doing a gig almost every day of the week undoubtedly hardened my character. I was becoming very resilient. It wasn't long before I realised the job was much more than playing the guitar.

My first trip abroad – my first-ever flight – was on a Lufthansa plane to Frankfurt, Germany. We played the Zoom club, the Frankfurt equivalent of London's Marquee. I was amazed when the audience really took to me. Everything made sense that night – my decision to join had been vindicated. Here was a whole new audience for me to conquer: goodbye north Bucks, hello northern Europe. I never underestimated all the hard work UFO had done in Germany, which helped me to build my own name. We were headlining for audiences of up to a thousand a night and thousands more at festivals. It was a far cry from the couple of hundred fans I might have seen before. I appreciated that, still do today.

We got to play alongside If, with Geoff Whitehorn on guitar, a great player; the Scorpions, Klaus Doldinger, Hackensack, Supertramp, Climax Chicago, Can, and Atlantis. It was wonderful to meet so many great musicians from different countries. I did a lot of reminiscing about Skinny Cat – it seemed a very long time ago, particularly when I was experiencing avant-garde bands such as Can. I liked their guitarist, Michael Karoli, as a person and, as a musician, well, I thought he was a quiet genius. He was the David Gilmour of Germany, playing a white Stratocaster and using an Echoplex tape-echo machine with loads of distortion pedals. Everything I never had. I'd watch him as he stood right in the middle of the stage for about fifteen minutes just playing a single chord with effects pouring from his army of pedals. I was totally fascinated by his approach. I had never been exposed to music like theirs. I realised that being a pro guitarist was a long-distance race rather than a sprint.

The other UFO boys were totally incredulous. Phil Mogg thought it was demeaning for the headliners to watch the support. Sod that! I watched everybody I could. Posters began to appear in Germany that promised, 'UFO featuring Bernie Marsden'. I'm quite confident it would be a good thing for most people, but not UFO. Phil Mogg ended up screaming at the promoter. I just couldn't understand what the problem was – wasn't I in UFO? The others resented my growing fan club and I couldn't help but wonder if the same thing had happened to my predecessors Mick Bolton and Larry Wallis. Sometimes I had to fight back both verbally and physically. Chelsea had to pull Mogg and me apart. We laughed it off, but there was an undeniably negative vibe.

The beginning of the end of my relationship with UFO was a double-headliner with Supertramp at the London College of Printing in 1973. UFO opened and Supertramp guitarist and writer Roger Hodgson watched in the wings. I didn't have a guitar tech and when one of my guitar strings broke I quickly put down my Firebird and switched to my spare Les Paul Junior. I felt something hit me in the side of my face. The lights were in my eyes and I presumed somebody had thrown something, until I saw Pete Way laughing. My suspicions were aroused.

Mogg looked at me with a grin on his face, 'Try to be more professional, country boy.' He had indeed just slapped me on the face onstage. I lost it, big time.

I flew across the stage as Phil caressed his mic stand and hit him squarely across the back with the very solid 1956 Gibson Les Paul Junior. He staggered forward still holding the microphone stand and managed to carry on singing.

Cue pandemonium.

Phil charged with the mic stand swinging in my direction. I parried with the guitar, Pete Way soon joined in, and Chelsea came on stage, trying to break it all up. Drummer Andy Parker just kept playing, blissfully unaware that anything unusual was happening. The crowd thought it was part of the show.

Roger Hodgson was still in the wings, open-mouthed. He later asked if that was a regular occurrence. I said it wasn't usually so violent.

I saw Supertramp a lot in those early days. They were a very good live band and all really nice people – unlike UFO. I began to get familiar with some of the new songs Supertramp were playing, most of them not yet recorded. I liked them a lot. I heard 'Dreamer' and 'Bloody Well Right' in very early versions. The entire world now knows those songs and I feel lucky to have heard them in development. They released *Crime of the Century* in 1974 and became a worldwide success, selling millions. I smile every time I hear the harmonica intro of 'Crime' on the radio or 'Dreamer'. I always feel a connection with Supertramp. Good days.

As for UFO, Wilf Wright had practically vanished and this was a major factor in what was a looming break-up. It was a shame: I had enjoyed recording demos at Rockfield Studios in Monmouth with Dave Edmunds. He was a kindred spirit, a fellow blues-orientated guitarist. Unfortunately, but not surprisingly, the others instantly hated him because he was a), Welsh and b) very famous. Some of the basic tracks later appeared on *Phenomenon*: 'Rock and Roll Car', '16', 'Oh My' (songs that I had written with Skinny Cat) and an early working of 'Doctor Doctor'.

I got to meet the Schenker brothers, the guitarists in the Scorpions, through gigging with UFO, and I was immediately impressed with Michael's playing. I thought he was everything UFO could do with. I told Phil to check him out. He, of course, refused. Back in England, band relations worsened and I soon realised I wasn't happy at all. My dream of turning pro wasn't quite living up to my high expectations. I hadn't imagined I would be considering quitting my first pro gig, but I was dreading my shows.

I called Wilf and told him I couldn't face another tour in Europe. I don't think he knew how serious I was. The guys left the UK and I didn't follow. For years the official story was that I missed the ferry because I lost my passport, which was utter rubbish. I didn't want to go and it was the only time in my entire career that I have missed gigs. Michael Schenker took over on guitar while Wilf and Chelsea persuaded me, rightly, to finish off the tour. I eventually arrived to find I was not the most popular person in the dressing room. I was petulant, unprofessional and ego-ridden, but I had been the odd one out for too long.

Those final gigs were filled with tension, which only eased towards the very end. We made a deal – an extremely strange deal. We just didn't like each other and so I denied ever having been in UFO and they denied that I had been in UFO with them, despite the fact thousands of fans had seen me playing with them on stage between November 1972 and July the following year. This crazy 'secret' lasted until the Whitesnake days.

I knew that Michael would be approached to have the gig on a permanent basis, which was exactly what I had suggested without any response a few weeks before. In no time Michael became a bona-fide guitar hero, and that still makes me proud. The moment I saw him, I knew he was bloody good and he only got better and better over time.

I now realise that those gigs with UFO across Europe made me the musician I am today. I still think the music I inherited from the former guitar players was crap and that UFO improved in leaps and bounds with Michael Schenker. But the experience for me on a personal level was invaluable. I took the baton with both hands and I'm still running with it today. Phil, Andy, and Pete, I wish you well.

6.

DANCE ON
THE WATER

I met Gary Pickford-Hopkins, the excellent lead singer with Wild Turkey, in Berlin, when I was still with UFO. Doug D'Arcy of Chrysalis managed the band which had been formed by bassist Glenn Cornick after he left Jethro Tull.

Gary told me that their guitarist, Tweke Lewis, was leaving to join Man and to speak to Glenn. Where could I find him? Gary pointed up to the sky. Glenn was in a lighting tower 40 ft above us. I climbed up to make a pitch for the job.

'Yes, that all seems fine. I'll see you next week, old chap, rehearsals in Richmond, ask Gazzy for details.' And that was it. I was the new guitarist in Wild Turkey.

The band played bluesy, hard, melodic rock, and their songs had clever chord progressions. They had a strong UK and European following and were growing in the USA, mainly because of Jethro Tull. It's hard to put it into words but I felt that I belonged in Wild Turkey, a feeling I never had with UFO. The music was so much more to my own taste, and working with Mick Dyche on guitar was a joy. It was the first time I'd worked professionally with another guitarist which, on reflection, totally prepared me for Whitesnake.

The guys in Wild Turkey were all very good players and interested in their own musical development. Glenn Cornick had been a big influence on Jethro Tull's music – listen to the bass parts of 'Living in the Past' and you'll see why. Wild

Turkey had recorded two albums for Chrysalis Records by the time I joined and I was thrust into heavy touring.

We went off with two roadies, a three-ton truck, and six musicians on the payroll. We covered some ground, that's for sure. At the 76 Club in Burton Upon Trent, the dressing room was in the next-door chip shop and we had to get changed for the gig in the window that looked out onto the high street. Nobody cared, it was part of it all and the gigs were always a joy to play. Chrysalis had us out almost seven nights a week. The gigs were endless, usually followed by a curry or fish and chips in the car on the way back to London. We saved money by staying out of hotels when possible.

This was the turbulent time of the three-day week: power cuts, strikes and heavy petrol restrictions had been imposed on British industry to conserve power supplies due to the miners' strike. Oil had quadrupled in price, there were new speed limits to curb fuel use, and petrol was rationed to £5 per person. This was awful for everyone, but it was hopeless for bands. We had a very thirsty Chevy and would plead with the petrol station owners in hope they'd let each of the six of us have a fiver's worth. Thirty pounds of gas was a lot in 1974. The queues were huge, but we never missed a gig.

When we did stay overnight it was usually in some of the worst places you can imagine. There were damp beds and walls and landladies literally pulled us out of bed at 7.30 a.m. in the morning for some breakfast (a dirty mug with a hint of tea). But staying in anything better, such as a proper hotel, was still a bit of a thrill for me – waking up in a strange room as a pro guitarist was a good feeling. We encountered some magnificently busted ladies in their forties and fifties who'd create the biggest breakfast on Earth as they told us how Arthur Askey, Norman Wisdom or the Troggs had stayed with them. They were rough and ready, but they were very motherly towards us wretched-looking lads.

Glenn Cornick would fire up the Chevy each day and he never stopped mid-trip unless we absolutely begged. He once drove from London to Madrid only stopping for petrol. His taste in clothes is also worth mentioning. Glenn used to go to fabric shops to find material for suits that would depict the tales of Robin Hood, the Lone Ranger, or the Battle of Britain. He also had magnificent thick, black hair down to his waist with a matching headband, a Zapata moustache, and red cowboy boots. You get the picture.

The rest of the band were talented guys – apart from Mick Dyche there was Steve Gurl on piano, Gary Pickford with vocals, and Jeff Jones on drums, who lived for his brilliant solos. I felt encouraged to write. All this was new territory, and I loved it.

Chrysalis booked a double headline gig in Germany with UFO, which I knew was bound to be interesting. Chelsea told me that Phil Mogg was determined that UFO would blow Wild Turkey off the stage and had even specially rehearsed John Lennon's 'Cold Turkey'. As it turned out, the only thing UFO blew away that night was their reputation. We went on first and Glenn played a fantastic bass solo while Gary sang his heart out. It was one of those special nights. I was astonished by how much I enjoyed being with this band.

Phil Mogg tried every trick he knew to upstage Wild Turkey and it all failed. Michael Schenker grinned at me from the stage as I watched from the side. He came up laughing afterwards to say Mogg was going completely crazy in their dressing room.

We had a friendlier experience with Yes, who asked Wild Turkey to open for a short tour of Germany in April – a truly mystifying package, but it worked. I had garnered a good following in Germany and Glenn Cornick was very pleased to hear the roar when Gary announced my name. After a gig near Stuttgart we ended up in a very crowded steam room in a Holiday Inn. Steve Gurl, Yes bass player Chris Squire and members of the Turkey and Yes crew were drinking beers with a host of very pretty and naked German female fans. It was all pretty innocent really, the men wearing small towels.

Gary Pickford arrived in a pretty drunken state, his customary plastic bag of fresh fruit and nuts to hand. He would always have an apple and then light up a Marlboro. 'These things won't hurt ya,' he'd say. When he lit up in the sauna there was uproar. The girls ran out coughing and spluttering and jumped into the swimming pool. Gazzy looked very confused, Chris Squire was very amused and a watching Rick Wakeman cracked up.

Rick was very down-to-earth and hung out with the support band although he was a big star. I can confirm the legend that he really did order and eat curries during the gigs – washed down with a nice bottle of wine. His band were always pleasant and I realise that I was fortunate to be on the road with them.

Wild Turkey found life in General Franco's Spain was a lot less easy-going. Driving from Zaragoza to Madrid we were unknowingly trailed by police and the military. The dictatorship viewed us as the worst kind of influence on the youth of Spain. I didn't know the history then but the very fact that a British rock band was on tour in the country still amazes me.

As usual, Glen didn't want to stop but it got so hot that we had to beg. We pulled into a roadside taverna and six of us piled out, dodgy-looking and long-haired. Mid-drink, soldiers appeared, shouting at us in Spanish. A younger soldier explained in English that we could be in trouble for drinking on the roadside. We were sobering up fast until a local policeman saw Glenn and shouted, 'Living in the past!' A Spanish dictatorship Jethro Tull fan. We were free to go and were given a high-speed escort. To this day whenever I gig in Spain, someone will talk about that Wild Turkey '74 tour. I always enjoy that.

The band split on our return. We had no management and Chrysalis had not signed a new album. Endless gigs were the future and none of us wanted that. With them, I'd had my first sessions at BBC radio, Maida Vale and we had been the last touring band to play the original Cavern Club in Liverpool. I still remember the smell – old beer, body odour, cigarettes and Dettol. It sounds disgusting, but it was fabulous. Gary Pickford and Glenn Cornick passed away in 2013 and 2014. They were both wonderfully talented and good-natured individuals. Both very much respected and missed.

I moved on from the bedsit in Shepherd's Bush as Fran and I took a basement flat in Paddington that we christened 'The Dungeon'. It was shabby without the chic, but we were very fond of it and the location was fantastic. I was keen to find a new band and I didn't have long to wait.

I had first met Cozy Powell in his dressing room at Manchester University after a Wild Turkey and Bedlam double-header. We immediately got along. I loved his can-do attitude. Here was a truly phenomenal player who had played in the Jeff Beck Band and yet he was much more interested in talking about football and racing cars. He said Bedlam was falling apart, Cozy's hit record 'Dance with the Devil' having a negative effect.

Cozy called me at The Dungeon some weeks later to ask me to join his next band, Hammer. I was over the moon. I think it had upset him personally that his solo success had caused a problem. I said that I had experienced something similar with UFO, and he revealed that he knew all about that. He had been checking me out …

He was signed to Rak Records, owned by super-producer Mickie Most, and the new band would comprise singer Frank Aiello from Bedlam, Clive Chaman from the Jeff Beck Group on bass and Don Airey as keyboardist. Don was a classically trained musician with little experience on the road with a rock band but when he arrived at the rehearsal room, everybody's face lit up. I heard a Mini Moog for the first time that evening and Don was already a total master, bending single keyboard notes the way I could bend a string on a guitar. It really was something else. His solos would scream just like a guitar.

Cozy's double red Ludwig kit, shining in the centre of the room, looked ominous even before he sat down at it. Hearing him play was a real eureka moment, totally unlike experiencing him with other bands or on record. He held the sticks in the traditional way and could be very subtle with his playing but then the power of those bass drums would knock me for six. I was blown away by his timekeeping. I had to keep myself together with this man.

Our set opened with an instrumental, 'Super Strut' by Eumir Deodato, an old bluesy song by Elvis Presley, 'Trouble', a couple of Cozy's hits – 'Dance with the Devil' and 'The Man in Black'– the Clive Chaman song 'Who's That Girl' and a couple of songs I had written, 'Hold On' and 'Keep Your Distance'. A Marquee gig was heard by the likes of Queen's Roger Taylor and Brian May, along with Cat Stevens, Brian Auger, Max Middleton, Suzi Quatro and Jeff Beck. Clive was quite unbelievable that night. 'Super Strut' had me open-mouthed at his dexterity. Cozy eventually leaned over to Clive and whispered, 'Clive, listen, I know all your famous mates are here, but do you fancy playing the next fucking song with the rest of us?' I was in hysterics!

Football would become almost as loved in the band as music. We played at any opportunity – in rehearsal rooms, outside gigs on the car parks. The mere sight of goalposts on the way to a gig would result in a stop-off. 'Surely we can spare twenty minutes for a kickabout?' Cozy would say.

We carried our kit everywhere, Powell in bright-red Swindon Town gear, Don with his Sunderland stripes, Frank in Arsenal away kit, and Clive in a gold Brazilian shirt. I looked more like Dave Mackay after too many nights in the pub. We were late for a Swansea gig after stopping for about an hour in the heavy mud of a Welsh field. Don was injured in a filthy Aiello tackle. He hobbled to the venue entrance, moaning and groaning, the rest of us covered with mud. The Welsh doorman was having none of it. 'Fuck off yew lot, I've got Cozy Powell and the Hamsters 'ere in 'alf an hour.' We explained that we were indeed the Hamsters.

Here is some inside info hardly anyone knows about. Cozy put a team together to play in the showbiz league, with members of the Average White Band, Humble Pie, Hammer and David Gilmour (a fine footballer). Cozy was a raiding winger, fast and dirty on the right. Don Airey played in midfield and was dreaming of and trying to channel Jim Baxter. Frank Aiello, on the inside right, was a real nuisance to opposing teams. Alan Gorrie was our superb goalkeeper. Hamish Stuart, a powerful centre-forward, was brave beyond the call and headed any ball. Jerry Shirley never stopped swearing. Dave Clempson was a fast and brilliant forward.

As Hammer, we even played indoor football during rehearsals for Mickie Most's revue, 'Rak Rocks Britain'. The Arrows were to be followed by Hammer and then Suzi Quatro. Mickie had us travel in one tour bus to keep the costs to a minimum. When we weren't playing football we would be taking the piss out of the Arrows or looking at Suzi's bum in her tight leather trousers. But the 1975 tour was a flop, with the kids not getting most of the songs we played. The halls were at best half-full or – as Mickie pointed out – half-empty. The press said the revue presented a mismatch of artists, pop music and heavy rock and I had to agree with most of the constructive criticism.

But it was a good gang of people to be out on the road with, and I did enjoy myself. We were playing in Sunderland once when Don Airey's folks invited us all for tea. There was only one request from Don – don't swear in front of Mum and Dad. This was completely fair enough, although not a particularly easy task with Frank Aiello in the band. Mrs Airey, a very nice lady, had made her speciality dish for us – meringue. We ate in the parlour, our meringues on china plates and hot tea in china cups. We made polite chat about Don, his family, and our respective musical backgrounds, sitting like good little boys in their splendid room. At length, Cozy gave me a prod and said that it was time for the soundcheck. We all got up, gave our thanks to the Aireys, Frank being the final one to say goodbye at the doorstep.

'Thank you, Mrs Airey, and those meringues was fucking lovely!' Oops. I thought Don was going to pass out. Mrs Airey never heard the words though.

We went into the studio with a new song called 'Na Na Na', by composer John Cameron, who also hired me for a lot of sessions. It was a straight-ahead rocker and the first time I had been in the studio with Cozy Powell, let alone the legend that was Mickie Most.

I was surprised to be greeted by a very large live PA system in the studio, until I learned that Mickie and Cozy used this to get the incredible drum sound on his records. I was sworn to secrecy from that day on (until now). Microphones on the kit sent the sound to the PA system and both sources were recorded simultaneously. I watched the pair work to get the drums up and running, totally swept away by both of their abilities. The sound in the control room was breathtaking … enormous … devastating. I couldn't wait to start recording.

Mickie wanted a B-side and in his office had passed me the Gibson J-200 that Jeff Beck had used for 'Greensleeves' on the famous tour album. I played a tune that I had been playing in

The Dungeon. I was pleased when he liked it. He made a few suggestions before we put it to tape at Morgan Studios. We had a B-side. I thought no more about it until I saw the back of 'Na Na Na'. The tune now had a name, 'Mistral', and was credited to Michael Hayes – Mickie Most's real name. I had a real lesson in the art of writing songs – for somebody else! I didn't hold it against him. I learnt more from Mickie Most about recording than anyone else.

I had just bought my treasured 1959 Gibson Les Paul, and Na Na Na' was the first recording I made with it. It's now, of course, universally known as 'The Beast'. Cozy was the one who gave the guitar its nickname during that session. The resulting single sold over 150,000 copies in a week, was a UK Top 10 hit and No. 92 in the Top 100 songs of 1974. I was more than pleased with that.

I soon went on to do sessions for Mickie, including recording for Hot Chocolate. I never knew which songs they were as I worked on the backing tracks but bass player Patrick Olive told me that he thought I played on 'Emma', 'Disco Queen', 'You Sexy Thing' and maybe 'A Child's Prayer'. I do remember playing on 'Heaven is in the Back Seat of my Cadillac'. I was pretty good with a wah-wah pedal in those days.

I'd often go to Mickie's house in leafy Totteridge, north London. The RAK mobile recording studio would be parked up in his grounds, usually with Mike Bobak engineering. The first time Mickie picked me up in his gold Rolls-Royce and telephoned ahead to his wife. A telephone *in* the car (remember this is 1974)! I don't think I believed it was actually happening. 'I'll be home for dinner later and Bernie will be with me.'

We went straight into the mobile to record and later into Mickie's house where a butler greeted us and showed us into the magnificent dining room, its heavy ornate table and chairs, shiny silverware and candelabras with huge, scented candles.

The butler announced the arrival of Chris and a vision of beauty floated down the wide staircase. Chris had high heels and a gold chiffon evening gown, and her elegant styling was topped with a small, twinkling, studded tiara. I glanced down at myself in a T-shirt and some ripped Levi's as she asked Mickie for a private word. I heard a huge laugh from both outside the room and when they returned Chris explained that the only Bernie she could think of when Mickie called her was Sir Bernard Delfont, the great theatrical impresario and brother of Lew Grade. She had been expecting Lord and Lady Delfont for dinner – and got me. Even the bloody butler cracked up.

I drank far too much red wine and later walked into a plate-glass door that was so clean it was virtually invisible, despite having been warned about it. Mickie and Chris were both in hysterics by the time I returned from the toilet with a great welt on my forehead. I stayed the night – Chris felt more than a little sorry for me. You should have seen the shiner on my forehead in the morning. I did many more sessions for Mickie Most but some mysterious reason I was never invited for dinner again.

As part of the Hammer line-up I played on *Top of the Pops*, a real career-defining moment. I knew that there would be people watching back home in Buckingham, the people who laughed at my dreams, who would see me on the biggest music show in the UK. On my first programme I saw the fabulous Pan's People dance troupe, probably the sexiest thing on television at the time, except in rehearsal, when there wasn't a leotard in sight but rather sweaty old tracksuits. They were all working very hard and very noisily; the flesh would be revealed later. I watched their run-through, dress rehearsal and just about every move the gorgeous Cherry Gillespie made. Perhaps they considered me a bit of a stalker that day, and probably rightly so, but you had to be there – it was fantastic.

At another rehearsal one Wednesday afternoon, Cozy and I got into the lift with none other than the Three Degrees. Lead singer Sheila Ferguson's ample bosom valiantly tried to escape her low-cut yellow dress. I was a few inches from her, the lift was extremely small, and my face was even closer. The other girls and Powell took great pleasure from the awkwardness as I stood motionless under the stern gaze of Ferguson.

'You're closer to me now than my old man gets, young fella.'

I felt like I was thirteen years old again, going redder and redder. Powell was in hysterics and to this day, if I see an old clip of the Three Degrees, my heart still skips a beat for Sheila.

I had an even less welcome experience of confined transportation when we flew to Belgium to do a TV show. We had to share a cramped flight with a new Scottish band called Pilot – bassist David Paton and gifted guitar player Ian Bairnson, Stuart Tosh and Billy Lyall. Our flying pilot was an old chap, who looked like a true relic from the Second World War, replete with a handlebar moustache. Jerry, as we nicknamed him, had a private plane but it was nothing special – a very sorry-looking aircraft with two propellers.

Powell sat next to Jerry in the front and neither of them ever stopped talking or laughing. As soon as we took off, Frank Aiello, the bastard that he was, started singing Buddy Holly songs. Powell roared along in the front seat. We shook our way to fifteen thousand feet and I looked behind me to see the petrified looks on Pilot's faces. The show took just a few hours but as we prepared for the return flight Jerry was less relaxed. He said the weather conditions were changing quickly and he wanted to get us all back as soon as he could.

The return flight was like a scene from a 1940s' war movie. The plane juddered all over the sky. Don, Frank and I drank duty-free whisky in hopes of laughing it off, but it just wasn't funny this time. Co-pilot Powell poked his head out of the sliding window, apparently looking for the white cliffs of Dover. There were lots of sudden drops in height and straining from the engines. Nobody was laughing this time except our glorious leader, co-pilot Powell. And Aiello, who started into 'Peggy Sue'.

'Can you see the white cliffs, squadron leader Powell?' I asked.

'No, Bowler' – Cozy's nickname for me – 'I can see fuck all in this fog!'

I tried to look out of the windows but they were frozen on the inside. When Cozy pulled his head back into the cabin the front of his hair had frozen solid and he looked just like Donald Duck. Jerry, to his credit, never looked remotely flustered. In a posh voice he asked if us 'chaps' were all all right. Cue a pathetic 'Yeah' from Frank and me – nobody else made a sound. Perhaps all the other mouths in the cabin had frozen together.

We arrived safely back at Gatwick and Powell was brisk. 'What a fucking load of old women you bastards are,' he said. He had never at any moment looked nervous. No wonder he loved to race cars: he had no fear. If we had all been around in 1939, I'd have followed him anywhere.

By October 1974 we were expecting to be given the schedule for recording a Hammer album but instead Mickie Most said the deal was over. We weren't pop – his speciality – and he thought we would be better off with another label. We carried on gigging for a while but there had been a major change in the vibe of the band and Cozy decided to call it off. I was upset on a personal level more than a musical one but I'd learnt that there was always another gig to go to. Mickie Most had decided not to record our album and that was that. Most died in 2003. He had always been really friendly to me and I remember him with great respect and affection. He changed my whole approach to professional musicianship.

I stayed in contact with Cozy Powell and recorded his solo album *Over the Top* in 1979, when he also gave me a huge mental boost. He had hired no less than the utter genius that was Jack Bruce from Cream to play bass. I think Cozy had more confidence in me than myself. We ran through 'El Sid', the song I'd written for Cozy, and I tried to be cool but this was Jack Bruce. I kept making small mistakes and Powell, never the most patient of recording artists, said, 'Listen – I am playing the drums, Jack is playing the bass, you are playing guitar on your own song, I am recording it because it is a great track, and so are you, now get on with it!'

My insecurity was instantly banished. There was the real Cozy Powell for you. Having said that though, he could destroy you in seconds if you cocked something up enough times. After a few failed takes he'd start to give me 'the stare' and it wouldn't be long until I heard him shout, 'Will you bloody get on with it Marsden, and stop fannying about with those chords!' Cozy and I went through a lot together and many years later we even spoke about forming a band again with people from Rainbow, Gary Moore, Deep Purple and Whitesnake – we joked we would call the band the Ex Files.

It was the last time I saw him was at Buxton Opera House in 1997 for the Rory Gallagher memorial concert. Cozy was as happy and relaxed as I had seen him in a long time. He wanted to record a solo record and told me to 'sort' some tunes for him. I asked if he was coming for a drink. He looked around the room, full of male musicians and most of them his mates. He smiled and nodded toward his new girlfriend. 'No, I am fucking not, not with you ugly bastards, I'm going to my room! Do you blame me, mate? I'll see you at breakfast, Bowler.'

My dearest of friends and my mentor, Cozy died the following April. He went out as he had lived – in a fast car and on the road. Sometimes now whenever the phone rings at home I have a very quick thought that it might be Powell. It was his habit to ring out of the blue as if we had spoken just the hour before. His unmistakable voice would say, 'Abbey Road, studio three, 5 o'clock, be there.'

I had lost a best friend, and you don't have many of those.

In the immediate aftermath of Hammer in 1975, Steve Gurl, my old mucker from Wild Turkey, asked if I would be interested in joining his band Babe Ruth.

He had been with them for about a year and effectively kidnapped me on the day, picking me up in his treasured gold Vauxhall VX90 from The Dungeon for a rehearsal. Steve said that the girl singer was a cracker and they would be going to Canada soon and a tour of Japan was in the pipeline. I was told it would be £65 a week – £25 more every week than I'd ever earned. Big money. I didn't audition and didn't realise what I was getting myself into.

Singer Jenny Haan was delightful. Her boyfriend Dave Hewitt played bass, Ed Spevock was on drums, and Steve on keys. They had a structured team behind them, Johnny Jones and John Michel from Evolution Management, and a deal with EMI's prog label Harvest, which soon finished and the band became the first in the UK to be signed directly to Capitol Records. We had pictures taken at 20 Manchester Square, made famous by The Beatles' first album.

Being connected to EMI was a boost. There were frequent lunches with journalists and head of press Charles Webster took me to the Park Lane Playboy Club. Not four years had elapsed since my day job had been building the new fire station in Buckingham, and there I was having lunch opposite Bruce Forsyth and Sean Connery, being served by bunnies. Surreal. Cozy was pleased for me and said he always knew it wouldn't be long before I found a new gig. 'Get those songs on a bloody album,' he said.

Babe Ruth had booked the Roundhouse Studio, Camden, and Steve Rowland was our producer. I turned up as quite the rock star, in my first-ever car – a sporty bright-yellow Lotus Seven two-seater. I pulled into my reserved studio car space and felt very much that I belonged. The *Buckingham Advertiser* sent a reporter to shadow me and document the local boy in the big city recording studio.

I brought along a couple of songs for the album *Stealin' Home* and stacked up my Marshalls in the giant live room with the Beast in my hands. Ed had written a good funky song called 'Fascination' with a long guitar solo that gave me a chance to let rip and show the Babe Ruth fans that there was a new guy in the band. It still sounds pretty damn good today. My songs, 'Winner Takes All' and 'Say No More', had both been written for the Cozy Powell album. But while the recording sessions were pleasant, they were underpowered. I felt a little uneasy. I knew it could be better than it was, hell – I had had it with Hammer. Had I made an error joining, or was I just missing the Hammer boys' musicianship?

Further problems were apparent in tour rehearsals during that hot summer of 1975. Johnny Jones was always there and I'd never had a manager instruct a band. He'd tell Jenny how to sing, where and how to stand, and what to say between songs. I found it bizarre. When we did play live Jenny had to put up with constant calls of 'Show us your arse!' or 'Get yer tits out!' If I spotted an offender I'd invite him on stage for him to get his bits out. That would only be fair, right? That soon shut them up. Jenny coped with it well; she was a really sweet girl.

I never really felt settled. After the power and musicality of Cozy Powell, Clive Chaman and Don Airey I couldn't help but think I'd taken a backward step. It's near impossible to describe the feeling you get when you are playing with exceptional musicians – it's like a natural high. It wasn't fair to compare Babe Ruth with Hammer but it just didn't feel the same. Still,

I had to look at the positives and I decided to focus on song-writing.

In January 1976 we recorded a new album. Capitol Records had done a decent job with our debut but as we worked on *Kid's Stuff*, Babe Ruth split into two camps. In Group A was Steve Gurl, Ed Spevock and me and Group B consisted of Jenny Haan and Dave Hewitt. I had voiced concerns about the pair. I just couldn't see the band progressing with them. Jenny saw herself as the British Janis Joplin – I did not. Yet it's important to remember that none of this was ever personal. Ed Spevock said we should see how the session went. He was right, a wise man.

Steve Rowland was the producer again. One day I was about to start some guitar overdubs when a friend of Steve's arrived, a vision that I immediately recognised. It was actress, sometime singer and Page 3 girl Luan Peters, who became well-known as a busty guest in an episode of *Fawlty Towers*. Pictures of her had adorned two of the walls of the tea hut on the building site I'd worked on and now she was here, in the room with me. She made herself comfortable in the studio, was naturally cool, and watched what I did with the guitar.

'You are very talented,' she said.

I was still seeing those pictures in my head and mumbled something like, 'So are you, Luan.' Useless.

When Steve offered to take her home I said I would go with him. Three people getting into Steve's Lamborghini was not easy, but I was determined. When she got home I said, 'Goodbye,' with a sigh.

'Did I make a fool of myself, Steve?' I asked.

'Oh, yes!' he laughed.

I had been encouraged to write for the new album and had almost all of the songs ready. I was becoming the reluctant leader of this Babe Ruth line-up, which Dave Hewitt was not happy about. I took a much stronger line on the composition of the album and stayed long hours in the studio for the mixing. By the end, Dave Hewitt had been fired. I wasn't surprised as I could always tell the management didn't like him. Who likes a perpetual moaner? Jenny quit soon after. I can only assume that Dave had in his turn tried to have me fired. I'd imagine it was, 'Either Bernie goes or Jenny and I go.' Well, that backfired. Camp A found itself in the studio with a finished album, but without a singer or bass player. Hmm … now what?

Neil Murray and Don Airey came in to rework some of the tracks. I called up Ray Knott, my old Skinny Cat friend, and asked him if he wanted to audition to play bass. I never told the others of our shared past and he got the gig on his own merit. Now came the hard part – getting another girl singer.

Sydney Foxx – how she came to the office I still don't know – was an American who sang and looked great. A former singer with Tina Turner's Revue, she told me she had been the first white Ikette. For the first time in a long time I felt very positive about Babe Ruth, until I learned that Sydney was married to former Yes guitarist Peter Banks and was also still a member of his band Flash.

We settled on a singer named Ellie Hope, and I mixed the album at studio 3 at Abbey Road, where The Beatles had recorded *Revolver*. During breaks I used to go to the tape library to go through EMI masters that included monitor mixes on quarter-inch tape. I listened to unreleased mixes of The Hollies, The Shadows, Pink Floyd and, to my wonder, The Beatles. It was a treasure trove and such an opportunity would never arise today. Magical.

We got *Kid's Stuff* out on time and went on the road to promote the album. I felt settled for the first time in a long while. By this time Cozy Powell was with Ritchie Blackmore's Rainbow and invited me to their gig at Wembley. Ritchie didn't go back out for the encore, resulting in pandemonium and hundreds of chairs thrown onto the stage. It was rather exciting and only built Ritchie's reputation.

It was a little after the gig that Cozy told me that Deep Purple – Jon Lord, Ian Paice, Tommy Bolin, Glen Hughes and one David Coverdale – had broken up. Cozy had heard the gossip that Jon and Ian were starting a new band and recommended me. I was at home with some time off touring when he phoned me about the gig.

'How did you get on?' Cozy asked.

'Get on with what?'

I had no idea, having been on tour. He gave me the Purple Records office number. 'Call now, Bowler, and let me know what goes on!' he said.

A posh-voiced woman named Pam was very pleased to hear from me. 'Oh, so you *do* exist,' she said. Pam was manager Rob Cooksey's PA and the new band was Paice Ashton Lord. I had an audition the next day at Manticore Studio, belonging to Emerson, Lake and Palmer. I'd heard that Jon and Ian had seen the best part of a hundred guitarists and bass players. I suddenly wondered why I was even going. I didn't know any Deep Purple songs apart from a couple of riffs that everybody could play (a certain 'da da daah, da da da daah', for one) although I had known about Ian Paice for a long time. As teenagers, we lived in council houses just 12 miles apart: Buckingham and Bicester. We didn't meet back then but I knew his sister, a girlfriend of the drummer in The Jokers in the mid-Sixties. Ian was three years older than me and had been in a band called The Shindigs, who were well-known in the area. Some of the older guys in my early bands would rave about them. Cozy Powell later told me he also held Ian's drumming in high esteem. He wanted to know how much Ian practised (never) and if he really wore high-heeled boots on stage (yes).

There were about ten other guys waiting to audition, guitars on their laps being played or being cleaned. In the corner was an old friend, Cosmo, a Scot I knew from a band called the Heavy Metal Kids, who'd been signed to RAK. He smiled and stood up and announced to the room, 'Gentlemen, to save time and sorrow might I suggest you take your guitars and leave now. This man is Bernie Marsden of UFO, Wild Turkey and Babe Ruth and he is about to become the new guitarist with Jon Lord and Ian Paice.'

I laughed, but about half of the guys did exactly what he said: they picked up their guitar cases, shook my hand, and left. It was one of the strangest things I ever saw.

I was last on the list for the day. Cosmo's words had instilled a certain amount of confidence but, to be honest, the thought of having to face Powell without having secured the gig was much scarier.

John Ward arrived, Ian Paice's assistant, nicknamed 'Magnet' for his miraculous ability to attract fantastic-looking girls. I'm reliably informed that it was Robert Plant who christened him. John took me to meet Jon Lord and Ian Paice for the first time. I didn't know that the irrepressible Tony Ashton was also involved but he was no Deep Purple-type of player, and I could see this was going to be different. Jon oozed charm and Ian was cool and detached. I was impressed as you can get a bit jaded after hundreds of auditions. We played a jam in G, then 'Ain't No Sunshine' by Bill Withers and I suggested we might play the brilliant Paul Carrack song 'How Long'.

Ian Paice asked me if I knew any Deep Purple songs. I had to be honest. I saw him glance at Jon as he sat back down at his drums. I racked my mind and said that I did know 'Dance on the Water'. Jon Lord rolled his eyes and Ashton giggled behind his Hammond organ on the other side.

'I think you mean "*Smoke* on the Water",' said a smiling Jon.

'Er, yes, that's the one, Jon, but I only know the riff.'

We didn't play it. I was quite nervous. We played 'How Long' until Jon waved his hand and the music stopped. I thought that was it and that I was out of there. Jon asked me to show him the passing chords in the middle of the song. The crew had been running a betting book and I apparently then became the hot favourite. They had never seen Jon ask anyone about a musical matter before.

Tony Ashton, who I will adore for ever, came over to me and said, 'You are a fucking breath of fresh air, mate,' and asked if the office had my number. I said that I bloody hoped so and saw Paicey hunched over his silver Ludwig kit, cracking up. I liked these people and, man, could they play. We had been together for an hour and I felt as if my life was about to change. Jon Lord was such a master of the Hammond organ that he made it seem simple. Ian Paice is funky, rocky, subtle and had it all, but was there only playing at about 40 per cent. Tony Ashton was a totally different player to Jon, with a jazz-orientated core. He was clearly a lot of fun. It was plain from that first day in Manticore that I had travelled up the musical ladder to a considerably higher rung.

Rob Cooksey called that night. 'We would like to offer you the gig,' he said. 'Cozy Powell said you were good, we have to thank him.'

I called Cozy right away and he was delighted. 'Welcome to Deep Pockets – the bottomless pit,' he said. I wondered what that meant.

Babe Ruth were great about it. Ed Spevock was in awe of Ian Paice, as most drummers were. Steve Gurl was really pleased for me and, as for my old friend Ray Knott, well, he simply smiled and said 'Good luck' – he had been here before. Babe Ruth had been a really decent gig. It had given me two albums for the CV and introduced me to some really good people who looked after me. I think the two Babe Ruth albums should be rereleased and I still have the master for the lost Jenny Haan version of *Kid's Stuff*. Jenny, Dave, Steve, Ed, Ray and Ellie – thanks for the memories.

7.

PALS WITH DEEP POCKETS

Paice Ashton Lord were off to Munich, to the famous Musicland Studios, in no time and I was going with them. This was the recording home of the likes of ELO, Deep Purple and Queen.

I was very excited, but nervous too, at first, but the recording and writing would go very well. Ashton made me feel particularly welcome. I think he rather enjoyed having somebody less well known to work with as, make no mistake, Lord and Paice were both huge names in the rock world of 1976.

We stayed at the Arabella House Hotel. It had two restaurants, a cocktail bar and a swimming pool and gym on the top floor. My suite on the twenty-third floor had an entrance hall, living room, fitted kitchen, sitting room with TV and plush furniture, and a balcony. The view of Munich was breathtaking. I sat alone in the suite for about fifteen minutes, just soaking it all up.

Jon phoned me to invite me for a drink downstairs in the bar. He was alone and celebrating quietly – Bill Reid, the mastermind accountant behind Deep Purple Overseas Ltd, their company, had informed him that he was officially a millionaire. Cozy Powell's words about the 'bottomless pit' were starting to make sense. He was talking about DPO Ltd, which was their own offshore management company. Both Ian and Jon were tax exiles, living in Spain – and anywhere they wanted to be.

Jon was incredibly cool and I was totally gobsmacked. I drank the champagne cocktail rather too quickly and another one soon after. Jon was always easy to be with. He said he was looking forward to the new project and couldn't have been more encouraging. He wanted ideas and said that while the band might be called Paice Ashton Lord, I was also crucial. That meant a lot: I was already in awe of Jon Lord. Fair to say he was one of the most important man I ever worked with, hard though it is to come down to one name. I had never been drawn to keyboard sounds before I met him but was always a giant to me, not only in ability but physically, too, well over six feet but carrying himself with great elegance. He had an infectious laugh and a commanding yet very gentle voice.

He remembered playing at Buckingham town hall with the Flowerpot Men and I was fascinated to hear it, although, to be honest, I was entranced by anything he said. I lapped up his stories about Ritchie Blackmore and what it was like touring America with the fledgling Deep Purple at a time when I was still at school. His knowledge of German was impressive and I loved to drive in his Rolls-Royce with him, asking him so many mundane things that he should have thrown me out of the car, but he never did.

Creating the one and only PAL album, *Malice in Wonderland*, was a wonderful experience. I would take the elevator from my room directly down to the studio in the basement – it was all just brilliant. The nights in the studio moved into the days and at one point I realised I hadn't seen natural light for about ten days. Recording on location really brings a band together – getting to know fellow musicians is the best part. I soon became familiar with another side of these rock legends: Jon's good and gentle nature, Ian's subtle humour and his legendary thriftiness, and Tony Ashton – who was without doubt one of the funniest men I have ever known. Tony had many comic phrases and catchwords and would drop his trousers down at

With The Jokers, 1965. Roger Hollis and me cradling my precious Colorama again.

Playing with Skinny Cat at a University of Oxford May Ball, 1969.

On stage with UFO,
Frankfurt 1973.

Playing my first
Les Paul with UFO,
Folkestone Tofts, 1973.

Wild Turkey in
Germany. Gary with
his bags of fruit
between his legs!

Cozy Powell's
Hammer.

Babe Ruth
publicity shot.

BERNIE MARSDEN

Official PAL shot
for the album, 1976.

PAL in Munich, 1976.

Me and Jon Lord.

With the King. Me sat with B.B. King in his dressing room at Birmingham Odeon, 1978. Look at my face!

The Alkmaar Festival,
Holland, 1978. Pete Solley
was on keys.

David Coverdale on stage at
The Royal Latin School, 1979.

Whitesnake, Liverpool Empire, 1979.

Early days with Whitesnake.

any time, in any place, for no reason at all. I'm told he even did it when there was nobody else in a room. He always had a mad laugh, a beer in one hand and a ciggie in the other. Bass player Paul Martinez was a really interesting character. He had been in a band called Stretch, but was most famous for being in a bogus version of Fleetwood Mac in the early 1970s, formed by their ex-manager with not one of the original members among them.

I soon heard the rumours in the studio that there were naked women on the roof of the hotel and decided to check them out. I took my swimming stuff and went into the sauna. After a few minutes a woman in her late thirties with blonde hair sat down beside me, stark naked, and wished me a good afternoon. After my pathetic attempts at conversation, she lay down on a sunbed, stretching out her very long and very tanned legs. Welcome to Germany.

I decided to have a swim, calm myself down a bit. Another man in the pool, about my age, was moving quietly through the water as we both did lengths. I gave it my best attempt at breaking the language barrier and he smiled and responded with heavily accented English. 'You *schwimm gut.*'

'*Ja, I schwimm gut!*'

We had a broken conversation about our lives which concluded with his offering, 'Zere is too much of zis English rock music in Chermany!'

Cheeky sod, I thought. We got out the pool and my new friend stuck out his hand. 'Hello,' he said, 'you must be Bernie Marsden. I'm Martin Birch, the producer, and I'm very pleased to meet you, mate.'

I could have drowned him on the spot; he had done me already. This was the first of many funny battles in a long and highly amusing war. Martin Birch was already a legend: he had produced and engineered most of the later Deep Purple work and he'd worked one-to-one with my idol Peter Green on all the classic Fleetwood Mac greats. He had some pedigree, that's for sure. Martin Birch is one of the wittiest and funniest guys I've ever worked with, a brilliant engineer and an extremely perceptive producer. We were to enjoy a long working relationship over the years.

Ian Paice and Martin made a very good team in the studio – they really understood one another. Watching Paicey at work was a revelation for me. During rehearsals he'd not put in more than about 50 or 60 per cent of his ability. Cozy had treated a small rehearsal room the same as he would a huge concert hall; but Ian never did. But when he was on stage – look out! I never missed one of Ian's drum solos. His favourite drummer was Buddy Rich and there was a lot of that great man in his playing. Ian could be very direct, did not suffer fools, and didn't do small talk. I'd happily admit I have followed his example.

Ian also seemed to be very together when it came to money and was affectionately known as 'Tight Wallet', 'Small Pockets', or 'The Bank of Paice'. Yet he lived in style. Magnet once drove Jon and me to see Ian's fabulous new home in Oxfordshire. A high gate sported carved eagles either side and a long drive took us to a house set in twelve acres that once belonged to actor Richard Todd. They asked me what I thought.

'Oh, I've seen houses like this before,' I said airily. Jon and Ian looked a little surprised. 'From the side of the road, that is.' They both cracked up. I think that they liked my attitude after all the sagas of Deep Purple.

Musicland Studios were then owned by producer Giorgio Moroder, and our engineers were Mack and Hans. The recording days started around midday with Ian, Paul Martinez and myself. Tony would then arrive after a couple of beers – this I would get used to – but where was Jon Lord? I have never been the earliest of risers, but Jon was a past master of not getting up. I found this very refreshing and decided to follow his example, which I do to this day. Thanks, Jon.

Birch got this massive drum sound through the Harrison mixing desk, and the backing tracks were mainly done by Ian, Jon, Paul and yours truly. We began with a song of Tony's; the haunting 'Arabella', written about the hotel with its reputation for suicide jumpers and the hookers in the bar every night.

I was amazed at the number of people around while we worked. There was a full film and sound crew making a documentary, road crew, tour managers and managers, record company people and publishers, lawyers and accountants. It was obvious that was going to be a big band. Nothing was spared. Deep Purple had been huge and with two of its original in this new group, how could it fail?

Rehearsals for our live show were equally grand. Back in the UK in the autumn of 1976, the recording complete, we took over a soundstage at the magnificent Pinewood Studios, Buckinghamshire. Filming was then under way for *The Spy Who Loved Me* and I had to park outside the 007 stage. Finding a space wasn't easy as there were loads of Lotus Esprits everywhere. A very smart man was in front of me, peering through the door.

'Excuse me, could I get in, please?' I said.

Roger Moore, in full James Bond gear, turned around, looking apologetic. 'I'm sorry, am I in your way?'

I introduced myself and invited him inside. He was fascinated by all the equipment and I gave him a tour of my amps, and Ian's shining Ludwig kit. He was most taken by my red, double-necked Gibson guitar.

'How do you play that?' Roger was genuinely interested in what we did. After he'd looked around, he thanked me and invited me to visit the Bond stage. I accepted his invitation with relish!

When the band began to rehearse together, I was tasked with picking up Tony Ashton on the first day. We met at his pub in Hampstead, London, at lunch, which was packed with creative people including veteran actor Ronnie Fraser, Slade drummer Don Powell and *Minder* creator and writer Leon Griffiths. I finally got Tone away and into my TVR. He told endless jokes and filthy stories about his mates – musicians, actors, writers – tears rolled down my cheeks all the way. It probably counted as dangerous driving. Tony got out a cutting he always carried around from a 1963 Blackpool newspaper: BLACKPOOL'S FIRST TWIST VICTIM. This was the tragic tale of one fifteen-year-old Anthony Ashton, taken to hospital after injuring his back dancing the twist. I could hardly keep the car on the road I was laughing so much.

We drove through the imposing gates of the studios – very late – and I was ready for a rollicking. Jon merely smiled and said he was surprised that we were there at all. Mission accomplished, I now I had the responsibility of getting Tony to work every day. I'd turn up at the pub to be greeted with a chorus of boos from the crowd. Ronnie Fraser, pissed as a rat usually, once said in his inimitable tones, 'You really are the most disagreeable little fucker, are you not? Taking Ashton out of here every fucking day in your little red car. I really don't care for you at all, old chap: you are a shitbag.' Nice.

TV producer Paul Knight was another regular but never abused me. He had made *Black Beauty* and *Robin Hood* and was working on a show set in working-class London, called *The Crezz*, about a London street market in a crescent road. When he commissioned Tony to write the theme music, Tony asked me to play guitar. The session included the massively talented Simon Phillips on drums and Dave Peacock (who was the Dave in Chas and Dave) on bass. All we needed was Tony and Tony's demo. He arrived hours late direct from Steele's, wobbling into reception. Oh dear, oh dear, oh dear … he was not well at all. I took him to the cafe next-door for black coffee and kept him away from the others in the studio. I asked him for the demo.

He looked at me with that wonderful grin and slurred, 'No demo, no piano, no nothing!' and started to roar with laughter. 'Bernadette – Bernadette – you can handle it, can't you?'

I bollocked him about being a pro and told him not to let Paul Knight down. Some chance of that, I thought. Tone smiled, his woollen hat on the side of his head, scarf at a random angle.

'No problem. Listen to me,' he whispered. He started to sing, hum and whistle a tune in my ear, all the while stinking of cigarettes and Scotch, and then slumped on my shoulder. 'All right, Bernadette?'

Back in the studio, Dave Peacock roared with laughter at my news (David had worked with Tony before) and Simon Phillips, ever the pro, just smiled. Dave and Simon grooved so well that the track almost gave birth to itself and was, astonishingly, exactly like the tune that Tony had managed to pass on. The man himself sobered up enough to add the piano part. Listen to the theme now and, after one musical break, you can hear Ashton groan, 'Crezzzzzzzzz.'

Tony and I went on to do music for ads, including the 'thirst-quenching, lip-smacking' Pepsi campaign, set to Eddie Cochran's great song 'Summertime Blues'. For all of this I was paid the union rate, about £125, and have since watched that bloody commercial in cinemas, on television and heard versions on the radio all over the world for years. That one ad should have made a fortune for Tony but, of course, it didn't.

As the PAL rehearsals intensified I could see that Tony was becoming increasingly nervous. He was drinking more than usual and was not at all himself. Ian and Jon put it down to nerves. I thought that there was more to it but, being the new kid on the block, I decided to keep my mouth shut. I also had questions about the developing sound of *Malice in Wonderland*. It was great, but a million miles away from Deep Purple and I wondered how the Purple fans were going to respond. Martin

Birch thought they would be fine but did mention his own concerns about Tony to me. We never discussed it with Jon or Ian which, in hindsight, was maybe a mistake.

There was a true showbiz launch party for the album at the Pinewood soundstage, including BBC DJs, producers, pop stars, film stars, and celebrities. The odious Ronnie Fraser came up to me with a fake, sickly smile and told me that he loved me really. He waddled off to the bar to meet the rest of the pub drinking club, who were loving every minute of it – mainly the endless free booze.

We played about five songs to rapturous applause. Tony was fine that night; he looked relaxed and wasn't drinking very much. To be honest I wanted to hug him, I could see how hard he was trying to hold it all together. I'm certain it would have been much easier for him to get totally blotto with his mates from Haverstock Hill but on this day, Tony was a real pro.

As the tour drew nearer, we had a planning meeting in December 1976. It was interrupted by an upset secretary who whispered into Rob Cooksey's ear. Rob looked ashen and addressed the room. 'I have just been told that Tommy Bolin has been found dead in Los Angeles.' There was a gasp in the room at this news on the Deep Purple guitarist. Jon was very shocked and upset, Tony Ashton looked suitably down, and Paul Martinez hung his head. Tommy had been just twenty-five years old, three months younger than me, and that hit home as well. I didn't see much reaction from Ian. A moment of silence passed, he shuffled papers on the table, and looked at Jon.

'What about these truck costs, then, while we're on the road? Ian said.

That was it. The meeting resumed as if nothing had happened. The demise of Deep Purple had hurt Ian very deeply and it's my theory that a lot of the blame was laid at Bolin's door. I resolved there and then never to cross Ian.

We were to begin touring with European gigs planned for March 1977 that were to glue us together as a live band. These would be followed by a live, simultaneous BBC radio and TV *Sight and Sound in Concert* show. But in a sign that storm clouds were gathering, the first four dates were cancelled. In no time at all, all the European shows were not just postponed, but cancelled. This was major: cancellations had been an unknown word in the Deep Purple camp.

The tour now consisted of just five shows in the UK, and that wasn't all – the BBC live show would now be PAL's first-ever gig. No warm-up in a club or small theatre could be arranged in time: disaster loomed. Tony Ashton did not take this news well and, for the first time, he confided in me. He was genuinely quite terrified and in no condition to go on television at all, let alone do a live television show. But we had no choice. Ian and Jon were both steely and professional about our situation.

'Can you cover, Bernie?' Jon said. I knew what he meant and I glanced at Tony. I really could have cried for him. He looked terrible and I thought I couldn't have been the only one to see his distress. Ian shared my concern.

On Saturday 10 March we were driven to the BBC Golders Green Hippodrome to play the show. Tone was nervous, had a drink, and because he then got drunk, he became more nervous. Our rehearsal was cancelled due to technical problems and the BBC men in white coats only got everything fixed with a couple of hours to go. Tony went to the bar in the meantime but reappeared looking pretty much OK.

The band managed to be amazingly tight, and I enjoyed it, although I watched Tony like a mother hen the entire set. For a first gig I think the performance was quite brilliant. Just listen to those horn arrangements and see how magnificent Jon and Paicey are. BBC producer Jeff Griffin made a good job with the recording and that still stands up forty years later. We thought that if we could get through something like that, then we could cope with just about anything. Positivity is good.

The five UK dates went ahead as planned and all went well until the last night. The fans' loyalty to the Purple guys was astonishing, although they must have found the new direction confusing. We had eleven musicians on the stage, wonderful staging and great lighting. I wondered what I had missed by not seeing Deep Purple in their prime. I was the unknown element, but the fans seemed to take to me, and I was singled out for high praise from the music press.

Our final gig was at the Rainbow Theatre, Finsbury Park. Tone had fixed it so that the odious Ronnie Fraser would introduce the band although, as far as I know, he had not informed Ian or Jon. After our tour support, Bandit, had played, the spotlights went up on the small middle-aged man holding a skull under his arm: Ronnie Fraser, ladies and gents. He looked sheepish while trying, in vain, to appear confident. Wearing a black cloak and brandishing the skull, he went into a speech from *Richard III*. Nobody knew or cared who he was and within a few moments the shouts and boos began.

'Get off, you old fucker – off! Off! Off!' the crowd chanted.

I looked at the crowd and could tell it was going to kick off.

'Now then, fucking listen, you horrible bastards,' said Ronnie. Believe me, it's never a good idea to speak to a rock'n'roll crowd like that. He was whisked off the stage by two of our crew, I suspect on the orders of either Jon Lord or Ian Paice, and rightly so. That bloody skull went missing as well, for which Ashton later received a bill. I thought of all of those nasty little scenes with Ronnie in the pub and decided that it was karma that had fucked him up that night.

At last, the lights went down to a tremendous roar, dry ice and flashing lights. Jon's clavinet fired up 'Ghost Story' and we were off for the fifth and what turned out to be final time.

Abruptly, Jon's clavinet riff in the song ceased, I kept playing with Ian and Paul until the lights came up to reveal Jon Lord in the orchestra pit looking up at me. He was mouthing at me to sing. He motioned to his left where I saw, to my horror, Ashton, lying face down on the floor of the orchestra pit. For a second I thought he was dead. He had tripped and fallen six feet down into the deep orchestra pit, headfirst, and he hadn't even been drunk. Frank Zappa had done exactly the same thing on this very stage.

The intro restarted and I watched Tony being picked up by the crew. To my considerable relief he made it to the stage position, hobbling. I could see he was in considerable pain. During one of Jon's solos Tony went off to have a painkilling injection.

We completed the set to the same brilliant reaction we'd had all along but nobody even bought the bloody album. It never charted, and was not featured on the radio, even after the live BBC concert. This was a spectacular bomb. I presumed that the whole thing would be over but, no, within a few weeks we were all back in Musicland, recording the follow-up album.

There was a key ingredient missing this time. Martin Birch was now producing Ritchie Blackmore's Rainbow in France. I became apprehensive without him, but I bear no animosity towards Martin as it was the most sensible move for him. It was strange to be recording again as if shows hadn't been cancelled and the first album hadn't died. David Coverdale, who lived about an hour away from Munich, dropped into the studio. He had already worked with Tony on Roger Glover's *Butterfly Ball* and I had quite a long chat with him in the studio. I liked him immediately and he said PAL had talked about him joining but he was working on his second solo album. Who knows what might have been if David Coverdale joined that band? His powerful voice would have made the difference we needed, with all love and respect to Tony Ashton.

We recorded about a dozen pieces of music in all, mainly backing tracks with few vocals. I was still on my retainer when we returned but I was concerned as nothing happened for months. Rob Cooksey eventually called to say it was over. I was never told why, but I suspected money was a major factor. Ian and Jon must have put the best part of quarter of a million pounds into PAL.

Malice in Wonderland is a very collectable record these days, which tells you that not many were pressed first time out. The end had been no real surprise: without Martin Birch things soon started to unravel. I believed at the time, and still do today, that he was the real heart of the band. Yet playing with Ian Paice and Jon Lord changed my outlook. Tony and Paul were fine musicians, but Jon and Ian had bitten me and I was sad to not be a part of their team. They were simply in another class, and it was a class I wanted to remain a part of.

So, it was time to move on. PAL sax player Howie Casey told me that my old friend Jimmy McCullough had left Wings and Howie recommended me to Paul McCartney. There were promising discussions at the McCartney office in Soho Square but I didn't get to meet the man himself, who was out of the country. During the lengthy period I spent waiting to see if Wings would come to anything, I went to the Rainbow Theatre to see Frankie Miller. Although never that well-known, he was a bloody great songwriter and vocalist. He and I were both working-class boys and got along very well from the first time we met. If you search out his albums you won't be disappointed.

It was then 1978 and Micky Moody was playing guitar for Frankie. As I walked into the Rainbow foyer I met David Coverdale who was forming a new band and asked if I would help at the auditions for bass player and drummer. Micky also came along to the rehearsal studio the next day and we instantly formed a pretty special understanding. David

Coverdale was keen to get me in with Micky but said he didn't have the kind of money that Wings could offer. I pointed out that there had been no offer of any kind as yet. We played together the following day and the three of us had a small celebratory beer – without a bass player or drummer. The next day I called McCartney's office to be say I was very thankful I had been considered for the gig, but could I now be unconsidered as I was forming a band with the singer from Deep Purple. They were surprised, to say the least. McCartney's 'Mull of Kintyre' was top of the charts at the time. I was told later that Paul had been at his home in Arizona most of that time and it was a real possibility that he had, and still has, no idea of any of this story. Ever since then I've been questioned about turning down Paul McCartney. I never turned down Paul McCartney. I turned down the chance to be turned down by Paul McCartney. That's true. In any case, 'Mull of Kintyre' would hardly have been a good fit with my style of playing at the time. Who knows?

8.

WHITESNAKE

'Well, what shall we call it then?'

I was back at the Halligan and Heape rehearsal studio, the day after joining forces with David and Micky. We were there to reduce more drummers and bass players to tears. One drummer, called David Potts, resembled Cozy Powell so much that it was a bit odd. After a few beers in the pub he became over-confident, slurring, 'I'm better than Cozy Powell, you know.' Goodbye, Mr Potts.

The next one, John Shearer had the best opening line of any audition. 'Good afternoon, gentlemen, I'm John Shearer and I have the biggest drum-kit in the world.' Mr Shearer didn't get in but he did go on to open the biggest drum shop in Islington.

Auditions are strange affairs. Ability is obviously important but you want to know more about how they will act after three months of touring than how well they play a drum roll. After four long days, David Dowle, of Brian Auger and Streetwalkers, got the drum gig. I told David Coverdale about the bass player Neil Murray, who played really terrifically with David. He was in, too. It was February 1978 and we had a rhythm section, the best singer I ever worked with and two guitar players.

We still needed a keyboard player and Tony Ashton asked if he could see David, to my surprise after all the problems of

PAL. We had a jam and David looked delighted. 'BJ, you're a genius!' he said, 'Bringing Ashton down will be fine, let's offer him the gig straight away.' But Tony had other ideas.

'No, no, no, no, Bernadette, not want gig!' Tony said as he became eight years old. 'I'm just enjoying m'self and havin' a beer.' After all the pain, stress, and physical hardships of PAL, Tony felt he would continue to write and play jazz music, which he did brilliantly. He later became a very fine painter and a couple of his works hang on my walls. We lost dear Tony, still laughing, in 2001. He's someone I could never forget.

The next day we settled on keyboard player Brian Johnson. He had played with Thin Lizzy and had played with David Dowler in Streetwalkers. Brian was Scottish and seemed a nice wee feller.

We met to write at David Coverdale's flat in Langdon Park Road near Archway. We worked on new songs at a very quick rate, with 'Come On' the first. We would play songs from his solo albums, and from Deep Purple and work in our new material. It was raw, bluesy, and loud – all you ever need for a real rock'n'roll band. I could see that we were onto something special.

It was in the flat that the David Coverdale Band became Whitesnake. We had already talked a few names over and I've frequently read that we settled on ours because of David's liking of snakeskin boots, but that's not entirely correct. I had brought up the fact that his debut solo album was *Whitesnake* and said that would be great. He was very insistent that his own name was not to be in the title but both Micky and I told him that he was the singer from Deep Purple and it was inevitable that his name would be up on the posters. A compromise was made – we would be David Coverdale's Whitesnake.

David's manager was John Coletta, owner of Seabreeze Management, and through his own record label, Sunburst, they had negotiated a deal with EMI International, a subsidiary of the mighty EMI Records. Coletta wanted us to sign contracts immediately. Micky was already signed to Quarry Management but, as for the rest of us, the buzz was so good that I think we would have signed an agreement with the devil which, looking back now, I think I actually did. After the failure of Paice Ashton Lord I had become a little cynical about the prospects of the business. The idea that a band might generate vast amounts of money didn't enter my head and it never occurred to me that we wouldn't get paid correctly. This would prove to be a massive oversight, and signing that contract would haunt me for the next few years. The rollercoaster ride had begun, and what a ride it would turn out to be.

We rehearsed for about three weeks before changing venues, only stopping for lunch at the White Horse pub in Market Road, Islington. The landlord was former darts champion Joe Hitchcock. He would regularly ask one of us to stand against the dartboard with a cigarette in our mouth. He would then take careful aim and throw a six-inch nail to knock out the cigarette. I still recoil at the memory of it. It was quite something to see twenty-six-year-old David Coverdale positively shaking in front of that dartboard. Joe and his wife became great friends of the early Whitesnake.

In March 1978 David Coverdale's Whitesnake took to the road for our first-ever tour. We played 'Come On', written by David and I, Deep Purple tunes 'Mistreated', 'Lady Luck' and 'Might Just Take Your Life', and a song I had long admired by the superb blues and soul singer Bobby Bland – 'Ain't No Love in the Heart of the City', written by Dan Walsh and Mike Price. I thought it would be a perfect vehicle for David's voice, a real blues song that was a long way from the Deep Purple stuff. We wanted something to make it our very own version and Micky Moody provided that in the form of the guitar riff which he got from, of all things, 'Come Together' by The Beatles. We slowed it down and played it in unison and that opening became one of the most famous of the Whitesnake intros. Across the tune is a haunting keyboard phrase and a lovely melisma from David.

I have heard that many bands do the Whitesnake version, thinking it was our own song. I can now also explain why the lyrics in the Whitesnake version are so different from the original. David didn't know the song and I never took the album into the studio because I thought I knew the words – which it turned out I didn't. The simple truth is that I got into the studio, I mixed up the words from the two bridges and that's the version that Whitesnake put out and the one that everybody knows these days. When I play live I sometimes sing the right words and get accused of singing the wrong words. My fault.

In March 2000, I had the pleasure of meeting Bobby Bland backstage in Brighton. His son, Richard, was playing drums and turned out to be a rock fan. He knew who I was and all about Whitesnake. The impressive Bobby shook my hand. 'You are one of the Whitesnake guys that recorded "Ain't No Love in the Heart of the City"?' he asked in his great Tennessee drawl. 'You done made a shit load mo' money than I ever did!' He thanked me for doing it. He was a charming man.

Whitesnake's first-ever gig was at the Lincoln Technical College for between 250 and 350 people. It was a solid opening but marred by a blow-out on the M1 on the way back to London. The next gig was almost sold out and the crowd included Don Airey. The following night was at the cramped Lafayette Club in Wolverhampton where Ian Paice was watching. David thrust his fist upwards in true rock style and put it straight through the tiled ceiling which reduced me to hysterics. But we were becoming ever more powerful. Neil and Dave were really tight, Micky and I were developing an almost telepathic guitar understanding, and David was simply magnificent.

We added 'Breakdown' to the show and we began to rehearse 'Trouble', which David and I had written together. A Basingstoke Technical College gig was watched by Cozy Powell, who said that he was tremendously impressed with the band (praise indeed from CP). We knew that the first report would now go back to Ritchie Blackmore. The next night we were in London at the Music Machine, and I think we almost sold out with a crowd of about 1,200 people. They made a hell of a noise and that first gig in London was a marker of things to come.

I took time out to go to a rainy Silverstone for a *Daily Express* trophy race, got soaked through and drove back to Chetwode in Buckinghamshire, where Fran and I now had a delightful old school house. I had a shower before driving on 200 miles to where I thought we had a gig in Newbridge, Wales. I couple of nasty and very angry-looking men came up to me in the club.

'And what the fuck do you want?'

I stood with guitar case in hand, looking at the stage, where I could see none of our gear. About an hour before I arrived our tour manager, Steve Payne, had cancelled the gig due to the stage being too small and the venue's lack of facilities. I made my apologies on behalf of the band and said I had driven hundreds of miles myself, which seemed to appease their fury. I promised faithfully to return and have never been to Newbridge since. Not for nothing did Steve get the nickname 'Pull 'Em Out Payne'.

The dates we did play continued to be packed to almost dangerous levels. At the Outlook Club in Doncaster David Coverdale attempted to perform a miracle. With the whole place swaying and sweating, David demanded that every single person stand up at the end of the gig. He meant absolutely everybody and gestured to a group of people at the front left side of the stage who didn't seem to want to move. We left to a great ovation and in the dressing room, David was very enthusiastic about the crowd, only taking issue with 'the sad bastards down the front'. I quietly pointed out that they were all disabled and were mainly in wheelchairs. Moody was in hysterics. To his eternal credit, clothes still soaked in sweat from the gig, David immediately went to apologise for his mistake and asked the security people to let the group stay for a drink with the band. The image of those fans, looking at David Coverdale with such reverence, has never left my memory.

We headed north for the Coverdale homecoming gig at the Redcar Coatham Bowl, Yorkshire, a cavernous 1960s' structure with poor sound quality but a great gig. This was also a local gig for Micky from Middlesbrough. You always feel a certain amount of trepidation with a local crowd, no matter how famous you are. David introduced me to a pretty decent roar after which he went into a long and protracted story about an important person without whom he'd not be in the music business and have this great new band. Moody was busy preening himself and smiling in preparation for his big moment.

'Ladies and gentlemen,' David said, as Moody stepped forward, eyes becoming moist, 'please put your hands together for ... my mum, Mrs Wyn Coverdale!'

Our great and momentous return to the north-east was complete. The members of the band were becoming very tight, very fast, with one exception. Brian Johnson just didn't fit into the band and we were always a little uncertain about him. The end came after a Plymouth gig when we were driving back to London. A very drunk Johnson had shuffled across to sit next to David in the van. Moody and I jumped in the back row to sit with Murray and Dowle and watch the pair interact.

'Hey, Davy,' said the jolly Scot, leaning into Coverdale's face, 'this band is fuckin' great.'

'Yes, I am quite aware of that,' said a brooding DC. Most people called him David, very rarely Dave – but never, ever Davy.

Cue much eye-rolling and muzzled, schoolboy giggling from the back row.

'We should write the songs, Davy.' Brian was totally brandied up.

'Really ...' said David. He was revving up.

Brian carried on sipping the brandy and then fell on his sword. 'Hey, Davy. Your missus is lovely.'

'Thank you, Brian,' David said, very coolly.

'And she's got great tits.'

The back row held its breath. Time stood still.

'Stop the van!' David's voice boomed, 'And get him out of it, now!'

I can still see the bewildered face of Brian Johnson, gig case at his feet, next to a bus shelter in North London, waving the almost empty bottle of brandy in his hand as we drove away.

'Davy – new keyboard man then, Davy?' we roared from the back of the Mercedes. I never saw Brian Johnson again.

Our first tour was over. The music press had been very good to us, the audiences were much larger than expected and we had only lost one of the members – a result! We began our first recording sessions in Central Studios in London in April. My mate Martin Birch was producing and I was thrilled.

We put out an EP of four tracks, 'Snakebite', and weren't told until much later that this was all EMI had been prepared to do. If David knew he never told anybody. Our first song was 'Come On', which was apt as it was the first song David and I wrote together. The backing track was done in about three takes; it has a great live feel. David had a new song, 'Bloody Mary', 'Ain't No Love' was already incredibly solid and fast becoming a stage favourite, and 'Stealaway' was already going down better. We also recorded 'When You Go Down for the First Time'. It was a gospel-type blues song that remains unheard as the masters for the sessions have been lost.

Micky solved the keyboard problem with a call to Procul Harum's Pete Solley. None of the rest of us had met Pete but he came to rehearsals and seemed like a decent guy and was a very good player. With Pete on board we continued touring and in May began to record *Trouble* album with Martin Birch producing. The new songs included 'Don't Mess with Me', essentially by Micky and me with David writing lyrics more or less on the spot. This song was a band track. This meant that any publishing income was split between all members. I had always wanted to cover The Beatles' 'Day Tripper' in a funky style. Dave Dowle loved the idea and his drum style was perfect for the arrangement. I got to use my voice box to good effect on the track and people still ask me about it. I didn't imagine I'd be explaining it to George Harrison only a couple of years later.

We took a short break before playing our first festival in Alkmaar, Holland, in June. It was a major success and was recorded for Netherlands radio, which did us a huge amount of good in Europe. This must be where the bootleg LPs came from.

We performed 'Bloody Mary' on *Top of the Pops* in June with Black Sabbath, Thin Lizzy, Brotherhood of Man, Heatwave featuring Michael Jackson's writer Rod Temperton, Legs and Co and Bob Marley and the Wailers. That's how *Top of the Pops* was in those days. Also on that bill was Andrew Lloyd Webber, Rod Argent and Don Airey wearing sombreros and playing 'Argentine Melody', the World Cup theme that year. It was pretty bizarre. The rest of Whitesnake showed little interest in Marley. David quite rightly told me that I should leave Bob alone. But I stalked him all over the BBC, trying to catch his eye. He was taller than I expected and oozed charisma. His entourage smoked huge joints all day at the BBC and Whitesnake followed them on stage. I vainly tried to get Bob to notice me with my guitar. Bob sang 'Satisfy My Soul' in a blue denim jacket and red shirt and played that odd Gibson guitar he always used. To my delight, he put his Fender amp on my Marshall cabinet. I was beside myself. Finally, I got my chance and and shook his hand.

'Bob, I love your music, your spirit, and it's an honour to be on this show with you.' I was a mumbling mess. He slowly rolled his eyes all over me and my guitar, and looked at me deep in the eye for what seemed like an age.

'I know, man, I know!' he said with a grin. That was it. BM spoke to BM. I was so happy.

I took Fran for her first experience of life on the road at the end of that month. Unfortunately, it was a washout festival in Belgium. Torrential rain had punished the site for two continuous days and washed away some of the staging. Instead, we enjoyed a night in the local disco and Fran said watching Moody dancing like John Travolta was the best part of the trip.

EMI senior management were beginning to take an interest in the band and were there to see our triumphant return to the Lyceum in London's Strand. About 1,500 people packed the place and we were then moved from EMI's International to United Artists/Liberty Label. These business moves largely passed Whitesnake by. We simply picked up our pay packets each week and focused on song-writing. This was the pattern for the next eighteen months. We followed the itineraries and knew nothing of deals, agreements or projections and never really saw much of John Coletta. Only David Coverdale had been in a successful band before, the rest of us were simply solid gigging players. We were all behind him one hundred per cent and if he trusted the management, then who were we to question that?

I was simply enjoying being in the band and I knew I had already come an incredible distance from my Buckingham days, although I did go back briefly in July to play a gig for the

Royal Latin School. This was a favour I was doing for my home town and I assumed David wouldn't be particularly interested so I asked Neil Murray, David Dowle and Don Airey. We set up and sound-checked before having tea at my parents' house and went back to see the support band from the school. While we played one of the kids pointed to the side of the stage where I saw, to my surprise, one David Coverdale watching and smiling.

I had never dreamed of asking the singer from Deep Purple to play for free, but for his part David had only been waiting for the request. He decided to join us and travelled alone to Buckingham from London by train and taxi, and stopped a passer-by in the town to ask him directions to the school where he said he was going to surprise a guy called Bernie Marsden.

'Oh, our Bernie! The boy from the Buckingham Pipers!' said the man, according to David. I'm quite sure he said 'papers', because I used to have a delivery round, but David Coverdale still maintains that I had been a member of some marching band in Buckingham in the Sixties. He always found it hilarious and would say on stage, 'Ladies and gentlemen on guitar, the boy from the Buckingham Pipers!'

The school audience were every bit as gobsmacked as I was to see the guest star. I was deliriously happy when David took to the stage and really went for it. Having played the Deep Purple California Jam for 300,000, David was now in front of a crowd of 300 in my home town. It was a special gig. The kids in the audience – now very much grown-up – still stop me on the street to talk about it. If I had needed any convincing that I'd done the right thing not to pursue Wings, this gesture showed that David was the real deal. The school gig formed a solid bond between us. We both came from humble beginnings on council estates and were both only children. That night each of us gained a surrogate brother. I think.

Whitesnake was becoming a tight ship and very few would gain access. Pete Solley was the next to leave, just a couple of weeks into August. He was a great player, but I never really felt he was properly in it. Jon Lord, who had been to a couple of shows, heard the rough mixes of the album and said he wanted in. We all enthusiastically agreed. Whitesnake became a fixed six-piece band for the first time. Jon told me he was genuinely happy that we were working together again and I felt brilliant about that.

Pete Solley's playing was wiped from the recording and Jon Lord went into the furnace of Central Sound and reheated the place. The studio shook under that Hammond organ power. The old team of Birch, Lord, Coverdale and Marsden was reunited – add Moody, Murray and Dowle into the mix and you had a band in a strong position with a real identity.

The *Trouble* tour opened in Newcastle in October and ran on into November. We walked out at Newcastle's city hall to a tremendous roar. It all worked naturally and without any real effort. Micky played his slide solo, he dropped the famous Geordie folk song 'The Blaydon Races' in for good measure: the cheering was amazing, I can still hear it today. Jon looked at me on the side of the stage and just smiled. This was going to be one hell of a tour.

Our first and only weekend break from live work was used to film our cover of 'Day Tripper' and 'The Time is Right for Love'. The resulting film was called *Rock Faces* but I have never seen it: a lost Whitesnake chronicle.

Back on the road we were booked into the Copthorne Hotel for an Ipswich gig, along with the players in the West Bromwich Albion football team, managed by Ron Atkinson. We ran into players such as future England legend Bryan Robson. I encouraged some of the boys to come to the gig, even though they were supposed to be tucked up in bed that Friday night ahead of a game. A few of them did sneak out of the hotel. They enjoyed a great show, came backstage, leaving before us to get back before we did. I was later told that Mr Atkinson went nuts when he found out they had gone to the gig. Even so, West Brom won that game 1–0.

Years later I faced my reckoning with Big Ron himself. I was at the Oxford United vs. Manchester United League Cup match in December 1983, when Ron was managing Manchester United. Oxford won 2–1 and I was invited to a post-match gathering by Oxford's Jim Smith where I was introduced as a former member of Whitesnake. Ron was a big guy, and although he'd been enjoying a jovial evening he instantly glared at me. 'Are you one of the bastards that took my West Brom boys out of the hotel?' What could I say? I was guilty, but Ron's stern face soon turned into a big smile when I reminded him of the result. 'Better than tonight's fucking disaster, then!' You have to love the original Big Ron Atkinson.

After the Ipswich gig we carried on to Portsmouth and Cardiff. The show in Cardiff was held up for nearly three hours due to Welsh nationalists telephoning a radio station and falsely claiming there was a bomb in the building. The crowd loyally waited for us to start at 11.30 p.m. The vibe was something else in the room. The people in that crowd were to me the true nationalists.

Promoter Adrian Hopkins would introduce us at each gig with his best Monty Python voice – which was not very good at all: 'Ladies and gentlemen, welcome to the Liverpool Empire, you've got *Trouble*, you've got Whitesnake!' At the Victoria Hall in Stoke-on-Trent a few of us were held up in traffic and an unknowingly Adrian walked out from behind the heavy stage curtain and began, as usual, 'Ladies and gentlemen, you've got *Trouble* …' He was interrupted by Jon Lord on the other side of the curtain. 'No, Adrian, it's you who's got trouble, mate. Coverdale, Marsden and Moody aren't here yet.' Adrian almost choked, and waddled off stage.

A gig at the New Theatre in Oxford was close to my family and I arranged to meet my folks and some other friends at the Red Lion pub nearby. Whitesnake fans wanted autographs and a chat. I signed as many as I could and excused myself to get back to my family. Then, just like a scene from a cowboy movie, the room was very quiet. Jon Lord had walked in. I can never really explain the presence Jon Lord exuded. A tall man, shock of grey hair, wonderful smile, his stature with the fans was something else. Sure, I was well known, but Jon was from Deep Purple, worthy of another level of fan worship.

Jon waved at me to join him where he was, surrounded by the fans. As ever, he shook my hand as I approached – this particular handshake became a bit of a Whitesnake thing, greeting each other with this gesture, passed down from Deep Purple. When Cozy Powell later joined the band he referred to Whitesnake as 'Handshake'.

Jon, without any preamble whatever, said, 'Bern, I don't think you have met George, have you?' He turned, big grin on that face – he knew what he was about to do! And there stood George Harrison, with a smile, shaking my hand.

That classic Liverpool drawl, 'Nice to meet you, Bernie.' No wonder the bar had suddenly gone silent. Jon Lord, yes, but having George Harrison at his side was something else.

I was speechless for a moment, but he was charming and insisted on meeting my parents too. We made our way through the pub.

'Mum … this is George Harrison,' I said, hardly believing it myself.

'Hello, Mum,' George said.

My mum was never fazed by meeting famous people, but I could see she was moved. 'Well, it's lovely to meet you George. It's all because of you and those Beatles that he plays the guitar y'know!'

George laughed out loud. 'I better plead guilty, then.'

He shook my dad's hand and kissed my mum on her cheek when we left. She talked about that for years.

I could see George in his seat from the stage while we were playing. I was transfixed. I hoped it wasn't too loud for him, and that he could actually hear what I was playing. He told me later that he enjoyed it very much and that he heard a lot of Eric Clapton in my playing. He also mentioned that my mum had reminded me of his own late mother. George was a lovely man.

I later got to socialise with George and even spent time at his awe-inspiring home, Friar Park in Henley-on-Thames. I had planned small talk around racing, as I knew he was a massive Formula 1 fan, and he did ask me about Silverstone as it's very close to Buckingham and I told him I had been there as a kid on many occasions and even saw the great Juan Manuel Fangio. He got very animated about that. He went on to say I was fortunate to have been in so many different bands as a professional, and pointed out he had only ever been in The Beatles.

'Well, you did OK with that group, George,' we laughed.

He took me for a walk in his extensive gardens, about which he was very knowledgeable. I also got to see his studio, where the guitars included 'Rocky', the psychedelic Fender Stratocaster he used on the *Magical Mystery Tour* album. He said I could pick it up – I didn't! I was totally immersed in the day. I saw his *Sgt. Pepper* suit, usually kept in a trunk. I found it utterly surreal. He then opened a door to a large room containing only silver, gold and platinum discs. Hundreds of them, in rows, back-to-back on the floor. It was a day of wonder really, it was like being a child again.

George referred to himself as 'Geoffrey' when we talked on the phone and when we met at parties he would always tease me about my obsession with the band he always referred to as 'The Fabs'. He asked me if I really knew the serial numbers of Beatles' records and I had to admit that I did.

He was at the huge party Whitesnake threw in Jon Lord's house after headlining the 1980 Reading Festival, when the band was reaching its musical peak. The party was suitably lavish, complete with exotic dancers (the less charitable people might have said strippers!). One of the girls noticed George Harrison on the sofa. She and her friend danced their way over and popped themselves on George's lap. The entire room instantly burst into singing, 'She Loves You' – I might have instigated that. It was truly an unforgettable moment, and George positively reddened in the face.

We were later queuing to use a bathroom next to the room in which the girls were changing after their act. We looked at each other, feeling a little shifty. Then George smiled. 'We must look like a right pair of stage-door Johnnies here, Bernie. C'mon, let's go and have a drink.'

The following year I ran into him at the Grand Prix at Silverstone. I had just seen some Buckingham people I knew, who had obviously been drinking. One of them, who I knew had never liked me, sneered, 'We have just seen a real rock star, Marsden. No less than George Harrison – top that, Buckingham boy.' The others in the group looked a little embarrassed. I spotted George a little later, about to go inside the enclosure of Nelson Piquet's trailer. George was waving to the crowd when he saw me.

'Nice to see you, Bernie, I thought you would be here.' There was sudden hush all around. 'Come in and meet Nelson.' The crowd parted like the red sea as a security guard let me in and – this is the best bit – I could see the Buckingham party. The gobby idiot stood with a lost look on his face, totally incredulous. I made sure he knew I could see him.

'Topped, I think.'

Thanks, Geoffrey, you will never know how good you made me feel that day. We last met at an Indian restaurant in Henley with Joe Brown and Dennis Waterman. The place was busy and we got a few glances our way – in that company, I was the one nobody knew! But it was quite normal at the time, simply four blokes from the entertainment business telling stories, laughing, and chatting. I wish now I could remember more about what we said. In 1986 I started an autograph book and George Harrison's is the first signature: 'To Bernie, the pudding was wonderful', and features a small drawing of a guitar. Not a bad start for my book. The quote? Now, that's my secret! When we lost George Harrison in 2001, we lost so much more than a Beatle. He was a family man, a wonderful songwriter, an innovative guitarist, a spiritual champion, but most of all – he was a genuinely nice man. I am so proud to have known him.

The final gig of Whitesnake's first tour was at the Hammersmith Odeon and was recorded for a live album for the Japanese market. This provided half of the *Live in the Heart of the City* album in 1980. By the time we finished that gig we had covered almost all of the country and played to almost 35,000 people. It was a triumph. *Trouble* charted and the EP was still doing well. The band was almost getting too good too soon but the camaraderie was amazing. We played hard, partied hard and fooled around a great deal. We were also starting to write some great songs such as 'Take Me With You', 'Trouble' and one of my all-time favourites, 'The Time is Right for Love' and 'Nighthawk (Vampire Blues)', all really good stuff.

It was around this time that I got to meet one of my all time heroes. I had made some good friends at Anchor Records in Wardour Street, including publicist Charles McCutcheon, who asked me if I wanted to go on the road with BB King. I had recently been given a copy of BB's album, *Midnight Believer*. Charles was working on its promotion, and his great idea was simple – up-and-coming rock guitarist meets his blues hero, goes on the road. In a nanosecond I said, 'Yes.' Charles said the music magazine *Sounds* were very up for running the piece and they arranged everything with BB's management. I never told anybody in Whitesnake!

Charles and I took a black limousine to the Birmingham Odeon, and a great day ensued. BB's band were sound-checking as we arrived. At the gig BB's amp was on stage, a LAB series combo. I was told that BB didn't do sound checks and his famous guitar, Lucille, was nowhere in sight. The guitarist was still in his dressing room and, smiling, shook my hand, and greeted Charlie warmly. He was already the coolest guy I had ever met. I don't think he ever knew I was in a band, and probably thought I was just another journalist.

As BB King offered me a drink, out of the corner of my eye, I could see 'Lucille' sat on a chair, and then he told me about his upbringing in Mississippi, and about the Chitlin Circuit. This was the name given to venues throughout the southern US states that were set aside for black musicians in those days. BB told me about some pretty dark stuff that went on at their gigs.

He also told me how there was a fight at a Mississippi gig of his in the 1950s, and a fire broke out. Everybody ran but, to the horror of the rest of his band, BB King went back into the building to get his Gibson guitar. He and his guitar were both unharmed and he later learned that the fight that caused the whole disaster was over a girl called Lucille. From then on, every guitar he owned became Lucille.

He talked of his great love of Blind Lemon Jefferson, Lonnie Johnson, T Bone Walker, and his personal favourite, Belgian jazz player Django Reinhardt. He picked up Lucille and played some Django – man, it was something else. Since then I've always heard Django in his playing, something I hadn't really noticed before that day.

During a quick break, Charlie told BB I was actually a musician. The guitarist seemed to warm to me more after that, and became much more relaxed and friendly. I asked him about *Midnight Believer*, an album I still love today. He told me how pleased he was with his collaboration with the great jazz funk band The Crusaders, and then, mid-conversation, he passed me Lucille.

'Why don't you play me something, Bernard?'

I felt about twelve years old again in the presence of the great man, cradling his black Gibson guitar. In my awkwardness I have no real recollection of what I produced. I do remember my surprise at how light and how close to the fretboard his strings were, which meant, when I played, that the strings often buzzed against the frets. Yet there was not a single buzz when BB King played – I still wonder about how he did it.

Bebop, King's long-serving assistant, had been eyeing me the whole time I held Lucille, I passed the guitar to him and he took it to the stage. It was getting close to show time and we had been chatting for about an hour. He signed my *Best of BB King* album, 'To Bernie, a friend, stay with it, BB King', and he gave me signed promo pictures

He was magnificent that night. I watched with tears in my eyes, not twenty feet away in the wings, as the king of the blues poured his soul into the performance. He worked in new songs from *Midnight Believer* and played 'Night Life', '3 O'Clock Blues', and 'The Thrill is Gone'. The audience lapped it up, me included. I was so emotional. I had seen a hero play, and now we seemed to be friends. I returned to his dressing room, to see BB look very relaxed, sweat still on his brow, but now a glass of wine in his hand. He was wearing a fresh shirt and a comfortable suit. 'Bernard,' he smiled.

He asked me what I thought of the show. I was gushing, but he was cool. He had enjoyed playing the show and suggested that we carry on with the interview. I asked him about his old guitars, but he said that his instruments would be stolen on the road or broken so frequently that he simply replaced them as needed.

We were getting along famously for about twenty minutes when Bebop entered with two very fine Birmingham girls. BB, ever the gentleman, immediately stood up and wished them a good evening. The two girls were in their late thirties, maybe a little older, but they looked great in short skirts, long boots, and lots of makeup, and with the broadest of Brummy accents.

'Alroight BB, noice to see yow again, great show tonoight.'

The guitarist introduced me to the girls but it was clear that the interview and the serious guitar and blues chat was over. As I left, BB King smiled and said that he would meet me the next day in London to finish the interview. Charlie and I headed for our limo, and I left on a natural high. I spotted BB in his car with the two girls, he gave me a grin as they drove away. We completed the rest of the interview at Hammersmith Odeon, and I recorded his gig with his blessing. I still have both of his Hammersmith shows on cassettes. Priceless.

I remained in touch with the great man up until his passing in 2015 but last saw him at a BB King/Gary Moore gig in 2006, in Bournemouth. He was now eighty and sitting down at gigs, but still very much the king of the blues. I felt a tear rolling down my cheek as he played 'Key to the Highway' and sang the line, 'I'm gonna leave this town, and I won't be back no more.' I could see that this really was the truth, although he still took the headline spot at Glastonbury in 2011. By then it was the turn of the next Marsden generation to go and see him, in the shape of my daughter, Olivia. She said she understood everything I had ever told her about him. Enough said.

Over Christmas 1978 Whitesnake took a break before reconvening at Central Studio in the West End in January 1979 to do some work on the live tapes. David, Micky and I did a few backing vocals – we soon became known as the 'Three Piece Suite'. The search was also on for a band for us

to support for a German tour. The managers asked around –
including UFO – but nobody would touch us. We were just so
good that, for a while, it seemed nobody wanted to follow
David Coverdale and his new boys. To their eternal credit, the
great Scot rockers Nazareth did take us on. We were off at
last, going into Europe taking a very small crew, Steve Payne
and Willy Fyffe, with the addition of Stuart Wickes to man
Jon's gear. Each band member helped out as much as he could
and the Nazareth boys could not have been more friendly or
helpful. Pete Agnew was on bass, Dan McCafferty on vocals,
Zal Cleminson on guitar, and the late Darrell Sweet was the
drummer.

Both bands got on well and we played the first night to a
great ovation. Our time was just about up onstage but their
tour manger simply waved us back on stage for an encore. We
had a raft of gigs to get to and although we ran into terrific
blizzards and black ice on the roads we never missed one. We
had a small bus and a great driver called Alfred who, on
observing any lady with large breasts, would instantly turn
around and shout in a lousy English accent a phrase that
stayed with us for years: 'Whitesnakes fastly look, please!
Knockersaknockersa, *grossen* knockersa!' Oh dear.

Musically, we gave Nazareth quite a hard time. We went
down extremely well every night as an exciting new band with
some great and catchy songs. But Nazareth never cut our time
or complained. Pete and Darrell were on the side of the stage
every night watching us. We played hours and hours of cards
with them and whenever I've seen them since Pete says he
wants a chance to get his money back. I only knew them from
their hit singles but they were a seriously great British rock
band.

By the time we got back to the UK in March we were headliners in own right – and we'd been together for only a year, if
that. Not bad, really, was it? We had about a month off before

our first headline European tour began. Exciting times, if not without hiccups. We started off in Europe with a date in Paris, accompanied by award-winning *Melody Maker* journalist called Ray Coleman. The word was out about this new buzzing band and Ray wanted in. This was good news for us, but we soon saw the less welcome news as we arrived in France. Posters advertised 'Deep Purple' and, obviously, the fans knew that the band was defunct. In a stadium that held 15,000 people we had 500 at a push. But we were all gung-ho at the time and went ahead as planned. David coaxed the audience down to the very front; it took a little time but they all came eventually. We then steamed into the set and played as if we were in a club and the crowd probably witnessed one of our best performances so far. Ray Coleman returned to London to write up what he'd seen and we drove on to Spain.

Despite breakdowns and power losses along the way, we played a great run of five dates that ended in Madrid. I had a good following in Spain, mainly as a result of the old Wild Turkey tours, and I received great applause every night. I think David was pleased if not a little surprised.

Ray Coleman's *Melody Maker* review was waiting for us when we got home and it was a stunner. He never once mentioned the size of the hall vs. the tiny crowd but focused on the overwhelming power of the band. He wrote about Jon Lord's towering presence, David's great understanding of his audience, and singled out Micky and me as the 'greatest guitar pairing since Thin Lizzy', adding that he thought we could only get better and better. He described the freshness of the new songs, the audience's obvious adulation, the power of the Purple songs we played, and the potential greatness of this new band.

This review elevated Whitesnake into a different league. Ray urged that Deep Purple should be forgotten and encouraged everyone to see us. He did us proud and we never looked back.

Other writers were soon queuing up to come to shows, and Ray himself would later devote double-page spreads in *Melody Maker* to Whitesnake. We later invited him to write the notes in our tour programmes – he really was a great music journalist. Whitesnake owe Ray Coleman a debt that could never be paid.

We spent much of May at Clearwell Castle in the beautiful Forest of Dean, Gloucestershire. The site is a folly built in the style of a medieval English castle and it was a superb place to record our new album. I had been there before with PAL to rehearse the *Malice in Wonderland* tour and David knew it from Deep Purple days. We hired the Rolling Stones mobile recording truck and Martin Birch took about a month to record what would be *Lovehunter*.

There were proper banquets every night with what seemed like an unlimited supply of booze. Both Micky and I would get pretty stoned after dinner – my guitar tech, the late Barry Evans, always had access to the best grass. There was a large inglenook fireplace that the three of us would sit in – yes, *in* the fireplace – all night, passing early riser Neil Murray on the way up to bed as he was coming down for breakfast.

I played snooker with Martin Birch and we talked endlessly about his time recording Peter Green and drank enough vodka to realise that the castle was definitely haunted. Martin, who consumed most of the vodka, regularly ended up standing on the baize of the table and telling the ghosts to 'fuck off out of it!' We'd all agree and tell them to go and fuck off. David Coverdale thought of calling the album: *Whitesnake: Falling in the Vodka*.

No wonder I don't drink any more.

Even without the ghosts of the booze we were always slightly scared, being in a castle, particularly as we recorded in the crypt. More so as Birch secretly got together the sounds of smashing glass, rattling chains, wolf howls and heavy breathing. He would then play the effects through small speakers in the room or, even worse, would filter creepy noises into our headphones when we were recording. I thought it was all in my head and resolved to try not to get quite so stoned.

'Medicine Man' was the first track we recorded. It began in a rehearsal studio in London and I used my Skinny Cat Gibson SG on the backing track. We finished it at Clearwell Castle and it turned out to be a real rocker of a song. Check out 'Are You Gonna Go My Way' by Lenny Kravitz and ask yourself whether or not he had a copy of *Lovehunter*. The title track started out in the *Trouble* sessions but got left behind until the three of us came up with a real Whitesnake classic.

I wrote the music for 'Walking in the Shadow of the Blues' and played it to David in the upstairs sitting room. I suggested a couple of rough opening lines, something like 'I love my blues, it's like a story'. I played the chord changes into the line, 'And I'm walking in the shadow of the blues.' He looked shocked.

'Fuck!' he said, his eyes totally lighting up.

He ran up to his room and came back after about an hour with an almost complete set of lyrics for the song. The title had totally inspired him. They are brilliant lyrics – in my opinion, one of his best sets. David was also happy that I had written a lot of material for these sessions but I do think now a certain amount of healthy rivalry was setting in. But the result was better songs, and the three of us were only improving.

I wanted to cover 'Help Me Through The Day', a lovely song written by Leon Russell, which I knew from Bobby Bland and Freddie King. I originally played the solo on the track, but I knew that Micky could play a better one. He thought the same and independently asked me. My attempt was replaced. There was no problem whatsoever – it was the record that mattered. And that's how Whitesnake was in those early days.

We did have disagreements, though. Our first came during the recording of 'Mean Business'. I had come up with the changes, Jon added some synthesiser parts, David wrote the words and together Micky and I did some good work with the guitar parts. The problem was that I never really liked the track. I felt it was rather heavy metal, which was strange because it was me who had put most of the music together. David said I should reserve judgement until the vocal was recorded but even with layered harmonies and a great lead vocal, I still didn't like it. His face said it all: he had worked very hard on the vocals. Birch gave me one of his producer looks. We had a forceful 'discussion': I felt that we were musically much better than this particular track but I lost the argument. David even, somewhat sarcastically, suggested that I sing it myself. Oddly enough, 'Mean Business' is one of my favourites now. I think the fact that I cared strongly enough to voice an opinion suited David. We never discussed the song again, ever, and we never played it live, either, which was a shame.

David made a more serious suggestion about me singing when he asked me to record 'Outlaw'. Jon Lord helped me with a piano line and the song became the only Coverdale/Lord/Marsden credit. When Don Airey spotted it on the album he phoned me to ask if 'Lord Marsden' was at home. To his further amusement, a document referring to the credit somehow even got to a check-in desk at an airport when I was late. As a result the desk attendant was unruffled about me not being on time –'No worries, your lordship,' she said. 'We'll get you on the plane as soon as possible.'

Drummer Dave Dowle was the only member of the band who hadn't been impressed by the castle. He was a city boy at heart and a family man who didn't care for being in the country for a month. He had became restless, it was clear that he missed his family, but none of us really sympathised. Now I have a family I can see how laudable that attitude was, but at the time it alienated him from the rest of us. He was a vital part of the early Whitesnake but he really did get stranded.

He didn't spend much time with us, and I think we all felt that a change was about to happen. This was confirmed when Ian Paice showed up one weekend at Jon's invitation and loved the stuff we had recorded. I think Dave Dowle got to hear of the visit, and the rest of us knew his time in the band was coming to an end. It was inevitable that the drum seat would be Ian's sooner rather than later. Dave Dowle would go on to run a successful landscape gardening company and I hope he reads this – David 'Duck' Dowle – good man.

9.

FREE FLIGHT

Whitesnake headed back to Germany for the entirety of June 1979. We were booked into clubs, some smaller theatres and a couple of festivals. We were all on a real buzz. After thirteen shows on our own, we joined a package tour called the British Rock Meeting, playing with Dire Straits, Barclay James Harvest, Dr Feelgood and The Police, a band I'd heard a great deal about.

I knew drummer Stewart Copeland as a drinking partner in the Marquee when he was with Curved Air, but he was now with this new band, The Police, and all the talk had been of his blond lead singer and bass player. I had taken an instant dislike to Sting, my usual stupid attitude to anything different and, of course, totally misplaced. The combination of the hair, the dark glasses and the broody attitude, just did not appeal to me. But I watched them from the side of the stage and I was utterly mesmerised. They were so original, so different and just so good. Sting was unbelievable. I decided never to judge an artist before seeing them in concert. I have tried to stick to that ever since.

After the show, a large party of musicians and crew went out to a great bar with topless waitresses and a live band. It was one of those messy nights, I'm afraid, and we consumed rather too much of everything. We got back to the hotel, and headed straight to bed with our rooms spinning and sunshine already streaming through the windows. By breakfast time, the

Rhine could be seen out of the window, a beautiful sight – unlike us. Haggard and hungover, musicians were everywhere, pouring fresh orange juice down their necks and attempting to order fried eggs and bacon in German. In my confused and fragile state, I spotted my new hero, Sting, sitting in a large wicker chair. He sported a great off-white calico outfit, sandals, sunglasses atop his head and a band of cloth hung rakishly from his shoulders. He looked like a star, but a very clean one, with nice hair and a fresh shave. He was reading a hardback John Le Carré over the moans and groans of his fellow Brits, with the sunshine streaming through the windows and over him. I think of that image every time I hear or see him. I have met him a couple of times since, but never been brave enough to tell him myself.

Dave Dowle's last gig in Whitesnake was in front of almost 30,000 fans in the Munich stadium. It was sad to see him go, he was a really good bloke and brilliant drummer, but Ian Paice wanted to join, and he was Ian Paice. Jon Lord and Ian were brothers-in-law, married to twin sisters Jackie and Victoria, and Ian was always aware of what was happening with Whitesnake. It was almost inevitable he would join. The press was all over us immediately. They asked, and asked, and then asked again whether this was a Deep Purple reunion. The only reply was the truthful one – no, it was not. The inevitable follow-up question: would Deep Purple come back in the future? No. (Turned out to be wrong about that didn't I?)

It got to the point that we couldn't take it any more. So I had some T-shirts made up with the distinctive logo that seemed to say 'DEEP PURPLE' from a distance but, when you got nearer to the wearer, actually said, 'No, I wasn't in DEEP-fuckin'-PURPLE'. The Purple boys were great and laughed their heads off, but some in the press took it as the first rift in Whitesnake. Total and utter bollocks. Not true at all. Totally wrong.

Ian Paice played with us at the Bilzen Festival, Belgium, later in the summer. He slipped into the groove as if it was meant to be. We tore the place apart and, with Ian at the back, Whitesnake settled down and it felt as though we were really becoming a serious force within the rock world. We rehearsed some more, played a warm-up gig in David's home town of Redcar and then Whitesnake set out on our – and my – first trip to the USA. Bernie Marsden was going to America, at last. I was very excited, and I could see that David felt my excitement too.

We played Royce Hall on the UCLA campus in Los Angeles. The gig was a one-off and a bit of an anticlimax, serving more than anything as a straightforward showcase for United Artists, then our US label. About 1,500 people turned up, no mean feat for a new band from England, if helped by the Deep Purple tag. Ian, Jon and David were all very famous already in the US but to their credit, always kept the other three to the fore.

At the after-show party a very attractive girl with a skin-tight, all-in-one 'Whitesnake' outfit made a beeline for David, but very soon got on everybody's nerves. Well, what happened next was not very gallant – a large piece of chocolate cake flew smack into her chest area. This sparked a full-on food fight and the place soon resembled a war zone as the well-dressed guests tried to avoid the coleslaw, salads, fruit and other party food that was hurled their way. The poor girl's suit was ruined but I'm sure she probably had a Thin Lizzy suit for another gig.

I got to stay at the fabled Sunset Marquee, just off Sunset Strip. I had heard many stories about the place, which was luxury indeed. We sunbathed at the Sunset and moonbathed at legendary Los Angeles' nightspots. As members of the Deep Purple club we had VIP access to such places as the Whiskey A-Go-Go and the Roxy. Los Angeles was all right by me.

I ran into Ozzy Osbourne at the Rainbow Bar and Grill, just five minutes' drive from the hotel. Sipping my drink and glancing around the darkened room I had seen a man sat down hunched over the table, emitting a low groan. He appeared to be drunk. When he slowly lifted himself up to order another drink I realised it was Ozzy. Whitesnake had been at his house after playing a gig in the Midlands.

I went over. 'Hello, John.' He looked at me with a pair of very glazed eyes. Using his given name confused him – he had no memory of meeting me – but confirmed I really did know him.

'It's Bernie Marsden, John. Do you remember me? I used to play guitar with Wild Turkey; we opened for you on the Black Sabbath gigs in the UK.' He looked a little bewildered at first, but then his face changed and I could see he wasn't actually that drunk, just a bit down. Now he was beaming; he jumped up, hugged me and then burst into tears.

'Fuckin' hell! Fuckin' hell, ya old bastard,' he said. 'From England! How is England? I live fucking here now you know, oh, England, England. Ya bastard!' Tears rolled down his face, whether from joy or sorrow I don't really know. Ozzy and I drank far too much and were soon forming a band together – can you imagine that? He was a pleasure to spend time with.

Fellow guests at our hotel included Brand X, the band put together by Phil Collins. I was in the pool one afternoon when he came for a swim. He explained that he enjoyed being free from Genesis for a while, and playing un-Genesis drums. I was just thinking I'd never imagined I would meet Phil Collins for the first time waist-deep in an American pool when Frida and Agnetha from ABBA arrived in bikinis. The pair swam lengths as we pretended not to notice them, the Englishmen in the LA sunshine getting redder in the face by the minute. Another member of Brand X and one of Whitesnake's crew had joined us and also appeared to have nothing to say. After only a short few minutes, the girls swam to our end. Very slowly, deliberately, they pulled themselves out of the pool using the ladder closest to us, water dripping off both of them. We were trying to keep our mouths closed. Total silence.

'Bye, boys,' said Agnetha and Frida, trying very hard not to laugh.

The sunburnt Brits stood silent and blushing in the shallow end of the pool until Phil Collins piped up, 'Hard life on the road isn't it, boys?'

Autumn 1979 was spent rehearsing the *Lovehunter* tour. Songs from *Trouble* and the new album were joined by staple Purple tunes. We had no choice about including Purple songs: we needed the material. With Jon's keyboard solo and an Ian Paice drum solo worked into 'Belgian Tom's Hat Trick', we had a very good show.

We received heavy criticism for the *Lovehunter* sleeve, a painting of the rear view of a naked woman standing over a large snake. Most of the music press loathed it, mainly because it detracted from the music, and to this day I autograph it 'Cheeks, BM'. Phil Sutcliffe of *Sounds* magazine was an ally when the band had started, but even he didn't like the image. In interview the cover became the first topic. I was fairly ambivalent about it, but David defended it, excuse the pun, to the hilt.

I had a whole bank of new amplifiers intended for the tour by Lab Series of America, a subsidiary of Gibson. They were stacked up on the stage and Gibson ran big advertisements in the music papers with me endorsing them. Rather stupidly, I had done so blindly. When I plugged in at the soundcheck in Brighton on the second date, they were all over the place. They were very, very loud but did not produce the tone I needed. By the time of the gig, my faithful tech Steve Payne had reinstated my trusty Marshalls and I never used the Lab Series gear again. I do still have some of them – probably quite collectable.

The tour sold out everywhere and included two nights at the Hammersmith Odeon in October. For one encore, Mick Ralphs went on stage playing my Les Paul, while I was still trying to persuade Jeff Beck to come on with us. I had to use my spare guitar, an SG Standard, and Jeff just grinned from the side of the stage as we completed the show. The final gig was the Fairfield Halls in Croydon on 8 November and someone threw an inflatable female doll that landed at David's feet. He was so into the song that he didn't notice it, but the rest of us fell about with laughter.

The following week we attempted to shoot a promo for 'Long Way From Home'. We were naive about videos, resenting all the pratting around of so-called artistic people when we could have been writing new songs. Back then bands mostly did a straight mime to playback, but we watched crew bringing in a whole set – fake white stone pillars, vine leaves, white slabs adorned with gold, and a water fountain. We presumed we were in the wrong studio. But just as we were about to leave we were at last greeted by the director, in thigh-high boots and long, curly hair tied into a tight ponytail. He was very nervous, but had many ideas on how we should stand and pose and what facial expressions we should make. We looked at each other, quite dumbfounded and we ran through the song.

'Cut, cut,' he said. 'This is not good, we have to go again!'

This happened many times – the director was not having a good day and, as time dragged on, neither were we. Jon Lord finally asked the question we all wanted to pose. 'Just what in the world is going on here?'

The director explained that he was moving the camera to make it look as if we were travelling along a road by the pillars and vines.

'Why?' we all asked.

'Because that is the heart of the song.'

'Heart of what song?' said David, absolutely incredulous.

'"Long Way From Rome",' said the hapless director.

Unbelievable.

The shoot continued to be a shambles. Anything the director wanted us to do we wouldn't do, and anything he tried to do we made impossible. This was probably the most like prima donnas we acted during those early years, but we were all just so tired and pissed off with the whole thing. The director finally lost it, big time, and ran out of the studio, blaming all and sundry for the total mess. I don't think the footage from the day was ever cut together at the time. Looking back it was quite hilarious. But you can now see it on YouTube – in the background you can spot the white pillars.

As annoying as the video fiasco was at the time, it had no effect on to the band's reputation one way or another. Our popularity continued to rise all over the world, and we were going down so well in Japan that I was offered a solo deal with a Japanese label called Trash. I signed with them while keeping my day job with Whitesnake and before the band began work on our third album I was able to record my debut solo LP, *And About Time Too*, all done in London in the summer.

The sessions started at the EMI studio in the basement of Manchester Square, but soon moved to Central Sound. I had to pinch myself as all the guest artists came through the studio door one by one: Cozy Powell, Jack Bruce, Neil Murray, Ian Paice, Jon Lord, Don Airey, Simon Phillips and David Coverdale. I still marvel at the names today that collected in that tiny studio in Denmark Street. Cozy Powell remarked that I was the least known name on my own album, and it was true. I also had Irene and Doreen Chanter, Tony Rivers and Stuart Carvell on backing vocals. It all came together very well.

I felt particularly fortunate to have secured Jack Bruce on bass. I had first played in a studio with him on Cozy's *Over the Top* earlier in the year. His playing had been a revelation, and I asked Cozy to ask Jack about my album and, in his usual manner, he said that I should bloody well ask Jack myself. Well, I did, and seeing Ian Paice and Jack play together for the first time was a joy, and I had Martin Birch producing the album.

We lost Jack in October 2014, and I was deeply saddened. What a truly fantastic career he had, and I am so proud to have known and worked with him, particularly on his album *Silver Rails* that year. I performed at a memorial concert at The Roundhouse in 2015, playing the spellbinding 'White Room', and at another the following year I did 'Politician', this time with Pete Brown singing.

My solo album featured some songs which came out of the *Lovehunter* sessions with David. He assumed the name 'Bobby Dazzler' for the lyrics. I'm still not entirely sure why he did that – probably for contractual reasons, but I also suspect he wanted some anonymity in case the album bombed! He wrote the words for 'Still the Same', 'Here We Go Again', 'Love Made a Fool of Me' and 'You're the One'. I wrote 'You and Me' and David liked it so much he insisted it be a Whitesnake song, so we kind of re-wrote it and it ended up on both records.

My album was very well received in Japan, and I was suddenly in demand for interviews. I never anticipated that this was the start of me being a solo artist and I should thank my co-song writer Bobby Dazzler – David Coverdale was also very supportive of me doing records for myself.

After a three-week break in Kenya with Fran we returned to the UK in December and I began work with the rest of the band on Whitesnake's third album. Capel in Surrey was freezing after Kenya, and the boys had arranged a surprise for me – a yuletide stable for my entire stay at Ridge Farm Studios. Well, it was nearly Christmas, as they told me. The stable had been converted, but it was still a bloody stable. Moody remained in mild hysterics for the first few days, asking if I had seen a star in the sky yet, whether I needed any frankincense, that he could supply the myrrh and that Jon Lord could probably sort me out with some gold. I wasn't laughing.

We were in the studios where Roxy Music had recorded *Manifesto*, and it had a good vibe. It was very rural, near the town of Redhill, Sussex, on the way to Brighton, and had a nearby village, Rusper. The Plough was the village pub, incredibly old with very low ceilings. It was fine for me, but the taller boys had to bend and the 'Quasimodo stoop' soon became a regular feature in the studio.

Ridge Farm itself was a converted barn with the studios on three levels. Working down from the control room was the drum area, then our guitar area, and Jon's keys a bit further back. It was all very rustic, but produced a real and honest sound. I liked it immediately, despite my stable bedsit. This was the first time in the studio for Neil and Micky with Ian Paice. I never said a thing, but just waited and watched for their reaction. It came soon enough, that was for sure. Paicey was a total monster.

As ever, Birch was there, and it seemed that the boys had been busy in the days before I got back. There were a few good demos already knocked into shape. 'Ain't Gonna Cry No More' remains one of my all-time favourite Whitesnake songs, written by Coverdale and Moody, who plays an open C tuning: he used to play open C Willie McTell tunes. It was a fabulous sound, and I loved it from the first moment I heard it in the room. They also recorded a great tune that turned out to be an early draft of 'Ready an' Willing'. David played me a song he was working on called 'Love Man' – very apt. It was exciting stuff, although I couldn't help but wonder if I would get a song on the record. I played David a demo of some guitar riffs and changes I had made at home before the break. It was just a cassette with me playing the guitar parts, but he liked it very much and the demo became 'Sweet Talker' very quickly.

One afternoon, Birch asked me to go into the studio to mic up my guitar rig for recording. We had a bit of banter as we ate our cornflakes that lunchtime regarding material, mainly because I'd missed the start of the album sessions and a few things were already in the can. Was I being left behind? I knew that wouldn't be the case – I had a secret weapon. I unleashed it as Martin and I checked out a Marshall cabinet, newly re-coned after I had destroyed it earlier in the year. I played a strong riff I had been carrying in my head for a while, and I then put that together with another piece I had been toying with. David was soon in the studio, asking me what it was. I said it was just nothing at the moment, and he asked me to play again. I slowed the piece down a little and added the other part in with a chord change. He smiled. 'That, Bernard, dear chap, is fucking excellent.' It was the embryo of 'Fool For Your Loving'.

Micky listened to the tune and offered up a good bridge. We all worked on the song and pulled the whole thing together pretty fast. We had a song within twenty-four hours. This was not unusual with the Coverdale/Marsden/Moody partnership. When it came to the recording, Ian came up with that memorable snare drum and hi-hat pattern and we knew instantly that we had a great track.

The last track on the album was 'She's A Woman.' David had the words and a good guitar part, but I also had a different song with what I felt was a much stronger tune and riff that we could use. I was a little cautious – I didn't want a repeat of the ructions of 'Mean Business'. But I had nothing to be concerned about. I played my riff to David, he thought it was great and said to record it straight away. That's how you made a great record: teamwork and commitment.

Martin Birch was a vital element – his enthusiasm and technical know-how was as important as a guitar solo or a vocal. Martin understood exactly the record we were making, and I believe he had a clearer picture of the finished thing than any of the band did. He was sublime to work with.

Having Ian Paice on board was the icing on the cake and this line-up would go on to be recognised as the so-called 'classic Whitesnake'. Paicey's confidence was infectious, and his stylised power and accurate breaks were a pleasure to hear and watch. His playing brought great depth to the sound, and he arrived as we hit a high in our song-writing. I now knew I could write with his style in mind.

I could feel something special was happening, and I was annoyed with myself that I had been in Kenya when they began work. For one thing, it meant that I missed out on the track credited to the entire band. We had agreed from the beginning of Whitesnake that we would do one per album and Ian, being Ian, knew all about royalties, and said, 'Why should Marsden get a piece of this when he is on holiday?' David asked if I was cool with that, and I agreed. It was probably a poor decision on my part, songs are very important as income. I'm still asked to this day why my name was not on 'Ready an' Willing' – well, now you know. I'm not bitter, but it is a little strange. At least it wasn't 'Here I Go Again', that's all I have to say.

We finished the backing tracks on schedule and broke for the Christmas holidays, which ran over most of January 1980. David went to Belize in South America and I went home to Chetwode and watched The Beatles on BBC Two.

By the end of February, the album was finished and mastered. David decided on the title, *Ready an' Willing*, and we all knew that we had a great record. Cozy Powell had been into Central and heard the 'Fool For Your Loving' backing track and reckoned we had a hit with that. He was right. Considering the stable accommodation, we had produced a cracker of an album – I think it's my favourite. Not just because it was the first Whitesnake silver – and gold – record, but I just loved having Ian in the band (with no disrespect meant to David

Dowle). I think the songs and playing are very strong, Birch was totally in control and the vibe at that time was something else. By the end of March we were back together, rehearsing for our very first trip to Japan. Now this I was excited about.

Manager John Coletta was the first to leave, flying alone, business-class direct to Tokyo on Japanese Airlines. They were then the only airline allowed to fly over Russian airspace and he was there in a matter of hours. Now it was the band's turn.

We flew from Heathrow, in an old 747 with Pan American Airlines, all points east around the world, picking passengers along the way. First we stopped at Frankfurt, then Bahrain, Delhi, and Hong Kong, before at last limping into Narita Airport in Tokyo. It had taken twenty-four hours and much of my excitement had dissipated. John Coletta had been in Japan for a few days by that point, and was refreshed and free from jetlag. He had the front to meet us as we landed, looking very relaxed, with a sly grin on his face. The whole band and crew blanked him, and crawled into limousines sent by our Japanese label Polydor. John Coletta, ignored, went back to his hotel alone in a taxi.

The excitement of being in Japan revived us. The traffic was horrendous, and it seemed me that there was about a million people on every street. Polydor Japan had left a welcome at the hotel – fruit, flowers and a bottle of Suntory whiskey – but I went straight to bed.

The first gig was on 11 April at the Yubin Chokin Hall, Tokyo, and I will always remember it. To see all of these faces here, on the other side of the world from my home, singing songs I had written in the tiny English village of Chetwode, really moved me. The nine-hundred-strong crowd went crazy, even with guards knocking them back to their seats. It was a great start to the tour.

Polydor reserved a very traditional restaurant where we had to remove our shoes and sit cross-legged on the floor. Unlike more tourist-friendly places they didn't have wells to lower your legs into. The unappetising sushi starter arrived – an entire raw fish, with head intact. Micky was served at least half of the head and looked less than impressed. Winding him up, I told him that he had to eat it or the Japanese would be mortally offended

'You fucking eat it, then!' he said

We travelled on the famous bullet train to the great industrial city of Nagoya, passing the magnificence of Mount Fuji, half-hidden in frothy white cloud with its peak covered in snow. The train times were precise and the guard made a deep bow when he entered our carriage to tell us we had arrived. You don't get that on British Rail. Nagoya was a tough, busy town and the crowd were fantastic and it seemed that Whitesnake would be an instant success in Japan.

The magnificent medieval city of Osaka was pure *shōgun* country. I wondered how they built the old castle into the granite rock – the boy from Buckingham sure was a long way from home, but he was in the band that took Tokyo. We played to around seven thousand people in the capital alone and a total of twelve thousand over the eight-date tour.

I was moved by the appreciation when I tried my best to speak Japanese. A simple '*domo arigato*' ('thank you') produced huge smiles and bows from the record company people. Polydor gave us gold discs in Japan, they may not even have been for genuine sales but it didn't matter. It made us feel special, particularly Micky, Neil and myself. The success in Japan solidified the band. Ian Paice and Jon Lord were on top form and David endeavoured to make sure that the rest of us were always included. In truth he didn't need to, but we appreciated the gesture. I guess it reminded him of his first Japanese tour with Purple.

Much of the credit for our first impression had to go to Deep Purple because they had been so huge in Japan. David,

Jon and Ian were returning to former glories, but Micky, Neil and I were the new kids on the block who worked hard and found our own audience very quickly. I reflected on the trip on the way home in the old blue-and-white Pan-Am 747. It had been a real eye-opener. To be accepted by the Japanese, miles and miles from my home, had been an amazing experience.

We took a month off before rehearsing for what would be our biggest UK tour and a chance for me to reconnect with Gary. Our agent, Rod MacSween, asked me to consider his new band G-Force for the opening act. As none of the rest of Whitesnake had any objections, Gary ended up supporting the band I was in, ten years since the Skinny Cat and Skid Row gig in Hampstead with Bob Harris.

The tour opened on 1 June 1980 in Liverpool, at the fabulous Empire. It was amazing – I had never heard such a sound as I did that night at 9.15 when the house lights went down. I think half of Anfield and Goodison Park were there. The noise was incredible, and it really hit me for the first time that I was in a very big band. This was the audience response that I associated with supergroups, and now I experienced it in my own band. I had goose bumps that night, and they would regularly return for the next few months.

Throughout the tour the three musketeers – DC, BM, MM – also spent time at radio stations plugging the album, while DC would do local TV news, and there was always another journalist to talk to. We were all having a really great time together, but it wasn't so good with G-Force. Apart from Gary, all of his band were American and they were good guys, but just not a great group. Gary had taken to playing a Fender Strat through a Marshall 100-watt amp and an old Marshall 8x10-inch speaker cabinet. The sound he was getting from the rig was horrendously loud, very thin and not at all what I associated with him. Moody took me to task, having witnessed the soundcheck at Bristol. He asked if I'd done the right thing to have G-Force on the tour and if I was sure there wasn't any shit in my ears! Gary Moore could never be bad, believe me, but his sound was terrible.

The two bands still partied together. In Manchester, we all stayed in a terrific rock and roll hotel called the Sandpiper. The booze flowed long and hard and both bands spent a great deal of time jamming. Everyone sang, David took lead, Mick and I were on acoustic guitars and the G-Force singer Willie Dee, who was completely out of it, decided to be the percussionist, using a brass hood that was over a fireplace which he played with his head: you should have seen him the next morning.

I had looked forward to Newcastle city hall shows, but David lost his voice after the first one: I remember it was pretty bad. Some subsequent shows were cancelled but David recovered sufficiently to play the two Hammersmith Odeon dates, both of which were recorded to become *Live in the Heart of the City*. This album formed the very centre of early Whitesnake. It really captures the band at its peak. I think every Whitesnake fan has the double album, and I'm very proud of it. It's revered as one of the great live recordings, up there with Cream's *Wheels of Fire* and Thin Lizzy's *Live and Dangerous*.

We had played to no fewer than fifty thousand people in one month. Whitesnake really was flying, and very high. We went straight into recording the next album. Back then bands did two albums a year and toured to support both: that's just how it was. There was no real time to take a break and reflect on where we were, but all the same we were beginning to ask questions. In particular, Where was the money? At the peak of Whitesnake's success at that time, I made less than a thousand pounds a month.

The band had reached the heights that Paice Ashton Lord never had, and it was now that the contract with the management became a real problem. I just didn't fully realise it at the time. We had all signed the contract when we joined because we all wanted to work with David Coverdale and because the vibe of the band was so special. We had all been under very heavy pressure from the office and the management, along the lines of, 'If you want to be in this band, sign this contract right now.' None of us received legal advice.

So when the potentially big money came, passing it on to the band members never needed to be a high priority for the management team at Seabreeze. They only had to pay us a monthly salary, and we didn't receive any royalty statements in the first year. I hadn't known that the contract concerned all aspects of my future career and this would prove incredibly costly. It was a 'cross-collateralised agreement', meaning that all costs – touring, recording, promotion – could be deducted from our income before we saw any of it. Seabreeze Management controlled it all: the physical vinyl (Sunburst Records), and the publishing (Seabreeze Music). John Coletta owned all three of the companies.

It might appear that I was naive, stupid, and reckless to not realise this was happening, but you have to remember a simple thing. I had dreamt about being in a famous rock band my entire life, selling out concerts and creating fantastic music, but the last thing I expected was for it to happen for real. Now I was living the rock'n'roll dream, and it never occurred to me to ask how much was taken in merchandise that night, or the previous twenty nights, or where my income was for a song I wrote the previous year. The fact of the matter was that I never thought that my manager might be ripping me off – until it was too late.

10.

COME AN' GET IT

With only four days off after the *Ready An' Willing* tour, we started the new album in July 1980 at Ringo Starr's fabulous house in Ascot, Berkshire.

His studio, Startling, was a private facility in the former home of John Lennon and Yoko Ono, Tittenhurst Park. We were very fortunate to be given this chance to work where John Lennon had recorded the unparalleled album *Imagine*.

When I first saw the glass panel above the door with the inscription by Yoko Ono, 'This is not here', I got a tingle down my spine. In the kitchen I saw the very table where George Harrison, Eric Clapton, Phil Spector, Bob Dylan, Keith Moon, and Elton John had sat many times. The John Lennon film *Gimme Some Truth* shows you the object itself. I've had my breakfast in that kitchen, at that table, sometimes sharing the space with the very young Zak Starkey before he went to school. All of us had a similar reaction in those first few days at Tittenhurst: even Jon and Ian were a little in awe of the place. The rest of us certainly were.

There were still light switches embossed with 'John' and 'Yoko', among a fair few other little touches that had been retained by Ringo Starr, who had not lived much in the house since he bought it in 1973. As I explored, I found what I called the 'Imagine' room, which had featured in the video of the song and retained the famous white piano and a jukebox. It looked just as it had on screen, with its lovely bay windows and shutters. I felt a tremendous vibe and I had to pinch myself a couple of times. I came back and sat down at the piano one afternoon, attempting a version of 'Let It Be'. Jon Lord walked in to find me ham-fistedly attempting to play the legendary instrument. Finding myself on the end of an appraising stare, I slowly removed my hands from the hallowed keys.

'Get away from that piano, Mr M.'

'Yes, sir, sorry, Mr Lord, sir,' I replied. I knew my place.

David Coverdale, of course, took the lavish Lennon bedroom suite, and Micky and I shared the adjoining double room, a former dressing room for the couple. The pink corner bath in the Lennon suite was for David only. There were more than enough rooms for everyone, but Ian and Jon decided that they would commute as their houses were within an hour of the studio.

Large French windows to the rear of the house opened on to a vast lawn where we played football pretty much every day. We also went on to the grass to use orange curtain material and a plastic football that Mick found in the house. We cut the football in half and both of us dressed up in the curtains, each with half a football on our head. Neil Murray has the photos. Grabbing a tambourine and an empty biscuit tin to bang, Micky and I went onto the lawn and, George Harrison in mind, we began chanting. Except instead of 'Hare Krishna,' we invoked, 'Hare Fowler', 'Hare Corbett', 'Hare Worth', and 'Hare Secombe'. My sincere apologies go to George and John after all these years – spiritually, at least. We were just giddily happy to be at the house and no disrespect was intended.

You could walk for forty minutes or more in the gardens, alongside gigantic trees and exotic flowerbeds to a man-made lake – the man being John Lennon. I took out the same boat that you can see John and Yoko in *Gimme Some Truth*. Moody, who couldn't swim, refused my offer to row him, even though the water was less than a metre deep. He missed his chance to be my Yoko. There was a two-seater wooden bench by the lake and we used Moody's penknife to carve 'J loves Y' in one of the arms. BBC Radio 1 DJ at the time, Nicky Horne spotted the graffiti when he interviewed David by the lake for *Newsbeat* and the discovery of John and Yoko's simple love token was much discussed live on the air. Oops. Micky also half-buried an old coffee mug that he inscribed with 'John', hoping it would be unearthed years hence as an object of great reverence.

The studio itself at Tittenhurst was not very large. Ian had to set up his drums in the hallway, in the process creating a sound that became vital for the entire album, as the high ceiling created a sublime sound. It turned out to be a real stroke of genius. We would talk to Ian through our mics and headphones and that meant he never needed to make eye-contact. In the room, Jon's Hammond rig took centre stage and Birch built booths for each guitar. There was a very cosy atmosphere and it was easy to get to work. Martin immediately began weaving his magic spells, with Martin Adam, the house engineer, as his assistant. I have no idea how much Tittenhurst cost Whitesnake (I'm not sure any of us ever knew what anything really cost) but whatever it was, it was worth it.

I found Zak Starkey at Paicey's kit one afternoon. Just fifteen, he was already into drums by way of The Who's Keith Moon. 'You're Bernie Marsden,' he said.

'And you're Zak Starkey!' I said.

John Coletta was told little of our creative progress as the weeks went by. This was a deliberate decision – our relationship with management was deteriorating and, banned from the studio, Coletta relied on Steve Payne to be his inside man. We discovered that Coletta was slowly losing his mind through knowing so little about what was happening. Camaraderie within the band itself was also beginning to dwindle, perhaps due in part to Jon and Ian not staying on the premises. I don't blame them – Ian had young kids and wanted to be with them as much as he could. As soon as rhythm tracks were down Ian would be in his car on the way home.

Despite all this, we still had song-writing uppermost in our thoughts, no matter what you might read to the contrary about the band's state of health at the time. One of the first tracks to go down was 'Would I Lie to You'. I came up with verse chords, Mick added a bridge and David wrote the words very quickly. The lyrics appear to be about a girl, but the truth is that it's about our feelings for management. They were inspired by a – rare – meeting at the Newman Street HQ when Coletta gave us his usual speech about keeping costs down in recording the new album. None of us believed what he was saying and just looked at each other and grinned. When we discussed it later on the tour bus I had my guitar with me, played the chords, and sang, 'Would I lie to you, boys?' and everyone screamed, 'Yes, you would – you twat!'

It was a fine, struttin', Whitesnake love song, at least until the end, when DC moans, 'Would I lie to you, just to get in your pants?' in his inimitable style adding, after a pause, 'Mmm … I think so.' Most amusing, but EMI didn't think that the BBC would allow it, and this was a problem as the song was an odds-on favourite to become a single. David didn't like to be told what to do by anybody, let alone EMI, but I thought we should go with it. I've never had any issue with David's tongue-in-cheek words, not when he could write such quality lyrics as 'Lonely Days, Lonely Nights', 'Shadow of the Blues' or 'Ain't Gonna Cry No More'. I always knew that I was writing with a proper lyricist, with no messing, but Paicey agreed with me on this one. All we were doing was trying to have hit records, were we not?

David and I had quite an argument. It was unlike previous disagreements, which had been musical – this was business.

But we did agree on a compromise in the end: the innuendo stayed on the album and we remixed the single without the legendary speaking part. I suspect he still hasn't forgiven me, but the BBC did play it and it went UK Top 30.

The next track we laid down was 'Don't Break My Heart Again.' David was alone in the studio for hours playing the riff on Jon Lord's Hammond rig and, if memory serves, he came up with the finished article overnight while Neil Murray was trying to sleep in the room above. 'Don't Break My Heart Again' became one of my favourite of David's songs.

With its backing tracks completed, Jon and Ian went home and The Three Musketeers stayed on for guitar and vocal over-dubs. Martin Birch showed his production skills during this recording session, playing a pivotal role. He had run cables from the live room into the control room and when I was ready to record the guitar solo, I only needed to go into the live room to plug in my Les Paul and get a good sound through the Marshall. I could then return to the control room and play one-to-one with Martin in the same space. He started the track and I heard Jon's brooding Hammond organ chords, and Paicey's classic groove sounding so good. As the solo section arrived I noodled around during the build-up, and tried out a quick run.

'Thank you,' said Birch.

'What?'

'That was terrific,' he said. 'Perfect for the song, very tasty,'

'You're kidding!'

'No, I'm not.'

I was just messing about, I told him, getting a feel for the track, but he didn't agree. Martin liked that 'messing about' very much. He allowed me another half-hour to play the solo over and over and again, just to placate me, but the solo you know from the album is that very first one I did. He was right, you see – producers are like that (the good ones, anyway).

One of my other favourites on this album is a Coverdale/Marsden/Moody belter called 'Hit and Run'. I played the riff to Micky and we both thought that it should feature slide guitar. We played around with the chord changes and put together a rough demo for David to hear. He was delighted, came up with the middle-eight section and wrote the verses. He suggested I should dig out my old guitar voice-box, the one I had used on 'Day Tripper', and if you listen carefully you will hear mumblings of 'Albert Tatlock' and 'You want it, you got it'.

Paicey was fab on this track, and the way his cracking drum intro came about went into Whitesnake folklore. We had suggested that he should open up the song with one of his trademark drum-breaks. He played a few alternatives and we listened over our headphones. All of then were brilliant, but then magic struck.

'Ian, that was great, play it again!'

'Which one?'

'That one!'

'Oh, this one?'

'No, the other one!'

'This one?'

'Nope, that other one!'

'This one?'

At last! 'Yeah, that's the one!'

The sound he creates mimics a kind of 'dag-dag-dag-en-ham' and then the guitars power in. Give the song a listen and you'll hear exactly what I'm talking about. Moments like this were not unusual in Whitesnake. It was a glorious song but we never played it live.

David had practically finished 'Lonely Days, Lonely Nights' himself, another terrific song. We worked together on the early parts, just me with a guitar, but it was always DC's song. Mick and I worked very hard on the guitar harmonies and Jon's

Hammond organ tied the track together. There were great vocals from DC on this track in particular, with backing vocals by the threepiece suite.

During dinner one night we agreed that we needed a track with a particular tempo. I had the perfect song recorded as a demo but I didn't have the cassette at the studio. I couldn't remember how the song went and it began to drive me mad. Even after I went to bed it was bugging me so much I couldn't sleep. At about four in the morning I made a decision. I got up, got dressed, had a cup of coffee and drove all the way home to look for the tape. I successfully completed my 120-mile round-trip and was back in my bed at Tittenhurst before 9 o'clock in the morning, safe in the knowledge that nothing would start before at least 2 in the afternoon.

'Child of Babylon' was the result of that three-hour drive. I played DC the demo and he was very happy with it. He loved the tempo and I think wrote some of his best lyrics to date. Jon seemed to like the symphonic feel, and I love the intro he created, which was very filmic. The song was recorded within an afternoon.

'Come An' Get It' is another solid track. I love how the finished song sounds but, again, we never played it live: shame. It was written in the studio and started off as a Coverdale/Marsden/Moody song, but somewhere down the line ended as a DC song. I have an early mix in a quarter-inch, two-track tape box and it clearly states C/M/M. Ah well, these things happen.

'Girl' came from a great riff by Neil Murray. We were in the 'Imagine' room and he played me the riff on my guitar and within minutes we were in the studio with Martin and Ian. We put down the track with the dirtiest groove we could and it was a real pleasure. DC arrived in the control room and beamed. Lyrics were quickly written about the 'pretty, little, crazy, white girl' – this was a fan who had been following us on the road for some time. We hadn't forgotten the drama she created, and she was immortalised in the song.

The Whitesnake tradition of including a track credited to the whole band continued on this album with the hellraising 'Wine, Women An' Song'. David and I wrote this song in an afternoon in the 'Imagine' room and took it straight to the studio. It's a straight-out rocker, and lyrically pretty much sums us all up at this time. The song proved to be a great crowd pleaser played live.

The album closed with a cracker: 'Till the Day I Die'. I've always loved David's lyrics and Jon Lord's work on this track is outstanding, even by his standards. I look back very fondly on the Tittenhurst sessions. Zak Starkey remains one of my closest friends to this day, although I never went back to the studio itself, which Ringo sold in 1988.

Come An' Get It entered the UK album charts at No. 2. 'Don't Break My Heart Again' was a UK Top 20 and 'Would I Lie to You' was a hit as well, which made me feel a little vindicated.

In the middle of recording the album, on 26 July, I took a break because I had another gig to go to: that was the day I married my long-standing girlfriend, Miss Frances Plummer. We had our wedding in the tiny, fifteenth-century All Saints' church, Hillesden, a tiny hamlet outside Buckingham. We had to be granted a special licence from the Church of England to be married, as we were not parishioners. The certificate was an amazing example of Olde England.

It was the middle of an English July and, to no one's surprise, the heavens opened. It was so dark the cars all had their headlights on. Cozy Powell was my best man, and a cross-section of rock royalty was in attendance. Don Airey even played the organ. The small approach road was strewn with Ferraris, Porsches, Bentleys and our gigantic, vintage Rolls-Royce. All the gang showed up. Alongside the locals at the wedding were members of Whitesnake, Rainbow, Thin Lizzy, Bad Company, and Gary Moore, among others! We had a lovely telegram from George and Olivia Harrison, another from BB King and our health was toasted on BBC Radio 1 by DJs Andy Peebles and the late Tommy Vance.

Hillesden village was in shock.

The rain had just about stopped by the time we took the vintage Rolls for the seven-mile drive to our reception at Stowe school, where my mum had worked for many years. It was her idea to hold the reception there. Stowe was the original home of Viscount Cobham, had been landscaped by Capability Brown, and was later attended by Prince Rainier of Monaco, David Niven, Richard Branson and my old mate Roger Hodgson of Supertramp.

Cozy Powell and German promoter Ossy Hoppe arranged an England vs. Germany football match on the lawns as the guests dried out a little, and before long the photographs and greetings were at an end and the reception began. The room looked fabulous. My dear old mum, beaming in her blue outfit, had been instrumental in organising the event and had arranged a very memorable day. Both my new wife and I were more than grateful for all the efforts she and a lot of other people had put in.

Joe Brown, the boss of the sound company used by Whitesnake, supplied a sound system that stood overlooking the lake. With the backline ready, a veritable super session was had in the evening. Cozy was on his red Yamaha kit, Neil Murray played bass, Jon Lord and Don Airey were on keys, and the guitars were supplied by me, Moody, Mick Ralphs from Bad Company and Gary Moore. Ian Paice was there, and David Coverdale sang. It was good to have Frank Aiello from the Hammer days sing too.

The guitar police among readers will be pleased to hear we had no less than four original Gibson Les Paul guitars that day. My old mates Mick Bullard and Ray Knott from Skinny Cat were on hand, as well as numerous record and publishing guys, agents, roadies and, of course, our families and friends. The best part of two hundred people had the best night of their lives.

I remember my uncle, Sid Inns, installing a rather large transistor radio on a table so he could listen to Sebastian Coe race in the 1980 Moscow Olympics. My mum, true to form, soon took the radio away. Another uncle, Tom Inns, talked to Jon Lord about the Second World War, and my parents' neighbour, good old Tom Tranter, was still telling people about my incessant guitar practice as a youngster and how I kept him awake for years with that 'bloody electric thing'.

It was a very special day that the poor weather couldn't spoil. Fran and I had such a good time that we didn't notice the last people leave. At last we found ourselves all alone in the hall, in the early hours of the morning, with no car to get home in. The Rolls-Royce was long gone and even the PA guys with the backline and lights had left. We laughed as we looked around at the wreckage of Stowe's famous Marble Hall. Just as we had resigned ourselves to walking the four miles back to Buckingham, still in our wedding clothes, our friend Jackie Hill came back to pick up the handbag she had forgotten. She gave us a lift home, where we marvelled at that day, and got ready for the honeymoon – two weeks in Menorca.

Fran and I flew to Mahon, and I was very glad to have a couple of weeks with my new wife – away from the guitar, the studio, and any management hassle. As it turned out, the break wasn't entirely free from incident. It had been going very well and we were invited out to lunch by Bill Reid, accountant for Deep Purple Overseas, who had been invited but unable to make the wedding. He lived in Menorca and met us at his favourite restaurant, one that was also frequented by the king of Spain. We ordered some drinks and he recommended the lobster.

'Fit for a king, my boy!' said Bill through his beard.

He ordered the same as us and as he tucked in with great relish I could see that he was an expert at eating the bloody awkward things, deftly using his cracking pliers to pull the lobster apart. We all drank the cold white wine and were having a lovely time with Bill holding court. The lobsters seen off, we had some fruit and then another bottle of wine and it was at that point I began to feel a little strange. I put it down to the heat of the day, and excused myself to go outside to the harbour where I dangled my feet in the bay. I have to rely on Fran's account for what happened next because that was all I remembered.

She came out in search of me and found me in quite a state. I now know that I am severely allergic to lobster. I'm very glad Fran appeared when she did because I was quite possibly just moments away from toppling into the water.

Bill was fabulous, sussing the problem straight away, and the frantic restaurant manager and waiters poured me into Bill's car and I was taken back to Bill's apartment to wait for a doctor. By this time I was in a very bad way. My hands, arms and legs were completely closed and locked up. I couldn't move and was deathly pale, shivering and sweating. The doctor arrived, asked Fran and Bill a couple of questions, and diagnosed the acute reaction to lobster. He shot me with a huge syringe – I have a slight recollection of being extremely cold and slowly getting warmer and warmer.

Half an hour later I was driving back to our apartment; it was as fast as that. Thank you, Bill, thank you, doctor, and thank you to my brand-new wife for taking such good care of me. It was quite the ordeal for Fran, but I felt fine for the rest of the honeymoon. Phew.

We had a truly fantastic two weeks in Menorca. And Fran and I are still together, four decades later, with our daughters Charlotte, born in 1989, and Olivia, born in 1994. After lobster-gate, how could we not have lasted?

As soon as I was back in the UK again I was plunged back into the breakneck Whitesnake schedule, starting with rehearsals in Shepperton before Reading Festival on 24 August. On 27 August we returned to Startling Studios to fix some backing vocals from Hammersmith that had been recorded with some considerable distortion. In September we resumed *Come An' Get It* sessions at Tittenhurst, recording until the 18th when we decamped to Central Studios in the West End to mix the live album, which was completed on 1 October. Three days later we flew to the USA to open on a Jethro Tull tour. We did work hard in those days! But any band from that era will tell you a similar story. Did it do us any harm? I don't think so: those albums still sound great to me.

We had thirty-one dates in the USA on a tour that wasn't to be one of our most successful outings. Jethro Tull undeniably put on a very theatrical show, with Ian Anderson as ever on top form. I was and always will be a Jethro Tull fan at heart. The fact he played the flute was radical in the blues boom, but what a great songwriter and a showman he was, second to none really. The problem was that Whitesnake just didn't sit well with the prog dramatics of Tull. Their keyboard player and violinist, Eddie Jobson, got himself dressed up in a kind of spaceman outfit, complete with full helmet. Moody asked him, straight-faced, whether he had ever thought of wearing a costume on stage. I thought it was hysterical; the Tull management did not.

Tull's audience were also tough but they were very kind to us. We did kind of get a pass because we had the former Deep Purple guys, and that just about kept us cool with most of the crowd each night. More than anything, Whitesnake got away with it every night simply through the quality of our musicianship. The record company's efforts at publicity didn't help – they were really very poor. We were with a subsidiary label of Atlantic Records called Mirage and their name proved to be very apt. Hardly anybody knew that the Deep Purple guys were even in the band until we walked out on the stage each night. America would prove to be a very tough nut to crack for us and we never did break into the US market on a large scale while I was with the band. I didn't care, though. As far as I was concerned, I was on the road with the best band in the world.

Initially, we were permitted to use Jethro Tull's set, including walkways that went out into the crowd. I knew we had to be doing OK with the audiences when our tour manager, Magnet, was told that Tull were banning us from going on the walkways – aptly also known as 'ego ramps'. Moody and I would then make sure we always went as close as possible to the walkways and each place a rebellious foot on them. Looking back, we didn't really treat the headline act with as much respect as we could have done. We also sent out for kids' flutes that Moody and I played backstage very badly while Tull were about. It was mainly schoolboy humour to keep us on the right track, as we knew pretty early on in the tour that we were in the wrong place.

The second night, in Washington at the Capital Centre, was filmed, although the footage remained unseen for years, until at last beginning to leak out on the internet. It was later cleaned up and digitised and made officially available for the first time on a compilation in 2011, *Box O' Snakes*. We look like pirates, which is pretty much how I would have described us at that time, but the power of the band is beautifully captured. We play songs from *Ready An' Willing* alongside some earlier stuff.

The US dates included New York City, and my first visit to the fabled Madison Square Garden, playing in front of fifteen thousand fans. Sitting in our dressing room for the show really completed the first stage of my so-called 'rock star' years. I was so excited to be there, even though we weren't the stars. The irony was that, in Europe, Whitesnake were a far bigger act than Jethro Tull at the time.

In Cleveland, Ohio, we stayed at a great hotel called Swingo's. They had a tremendous house band with a wonderful girl singer. I jammed with them after the gig, and they were all terrific musicians. I was then told they were all semi-pros and had day jobs.

I also flew to Kalamazoo, Michigan, with Steve Payne to visit the original Gibson guitar factory. I was so excited – this was a place I had read about for so many years. How many catalogues had I ordered from the address '225 Parsons, Kalamazoo, Michigan'? Too many to count, that's for sure.

Gibson's artist liaison director, Patrick Aldworth, a very nice guy, sent a car to the airport to pick us up. Everyone at the factory made me feel very welcome, and I was given a full tour of the plant and met lots of the staff, many of who had been working there for years. It was incredible to see those beautiful Gibson arch-top guitars being made by hand. Patrick, to my surprise, later presented me with not one but two new Les Pauls.

Patrick also took me to the electronics bay to meet a lady who had worked there for over forty years. She rifled through some old wooden drawers and found some original parts for my old Gibson guitars. Steve Payne busily filled brown boxes, and envelopes with spare parts, all courtesy of Gibson. I'm so glad that I visited the Gibson factory at that time because the whole company moved to Nashville not long after. And my visit to 225 Parsons was, and still is, very special to me.

We pressed on with the tour, knowing the shows were good for us as a band although, with little record company support, they were costing us a fortune. Ian Paice was very vocal about it, and good for him. We visited towns such as St Louis, and Kansas City, places I had dreamed about as a kid. David would always scream 'Good evening' and name the city we were in.

He always got a good response. In Norman, Oklahoma, I couldn't resist getting in before the audience responded, and no sooner had he yelled, 'Good evening, Norman!' than I rushed over in the dark and, in a very northern accent, said, ''Elloo, David!' The first song became a bit of a shambles as most of the band heard me say it. I laughed so much I dropped my Les Paul and only just caught it before it hit the stage.

Another location I was very aware of before we played was San Antonio in Texas. Blues legend Robert Johnson had recorded at the Gunter hotel in 1936 and I tried in vain to find the venue, but I just couldn't. Shame. San Antonio turned out to be a great gig, and we played to some ten thousand people in the Convention Hall.

Our final set of gigs were in California and at the same time Fran was on business in New York. She was a fashion buyer for Harrods and travelled almost as much as me. We would often pass like the proverbial ships in the night, but she always understood. David Bowie was then getting rave reviews for *The Elephant Man* on Broadway and tickets were like gold dust. When Atlantic Records managed to get me a pair I caught the red-eye from LA to New York, arriving at Fran's hotel just as she was leaving for work. I slept for the rest of the day and we met up later for the show. It was brilliant, and Bowie's performance was something else. I left for the airport straight afterwards to finish the final Californian gigs. We ended the tour at a sports arena with fifteen thousand people watching us play over two nights.

We had all worked very hard, especially David Coverdale, who put his heart and soul into those gigs. I think he always wanted to overtake Deep Purple, but we really had no clear management vision at all. With no solid plan for the band from the people with the money, we failed to make our mark. It still frustrates me to this day because we were really well received by those who did see us, even though we were virtually unknown. In America, all we did was spend money, and Seabreeze Management didn't want that.

Towards the end of November we flew to Munich to record *Rockpop*, a big network showcase. We checked into the Hilton and Neil Murray soon phoned my room.

'Did you know that John Hurt is in the bar?'

I, of course, called Mick right away and we arrived at the bar in minutes. John Hurt was, and still is, one of my favourite actors. He was at the bar looking very cool. He seemed pleased to see some Englishmen and invited us for a drink. It was my round, then Micky's, then John's and this went on until we decided to form a band. We all moved to the bar's piano, Mick played the piano and John Hurt and I sang in harmony songs such as 'Summertime'. The beers continued to be delivered at the piano, while we were supposed to be getting ready for the recording. Magnet had been ringing up to our rooms, knocking on the doors, and was looking all around for us. He was not at all happy when he found us, and frogmarched us away.

I attempted to have a shave, which was a big mistake. Freshly shaved was not a good look for a TV show. Tired and emotional – and me still raw from my tussle with the razor – Mick and I passed the great John Hurt, who was slumped over the bar.

'Look at Quentin Crisp,' said Moody.

'All right, John?' I said. The pair of us were completely wasted.

As we reached the lobby doors we could hear John shout at us in immaculately theatrical tones: 'That's it, you bastards, go to the studio without me. You only have to mime – but I will have to act, later this day!' It was a brilliant moment.

Two drunk guitarists, one of them still bleeding, arrived at the studio without a keyboard player – Jon Lord was held up. We put Magnet on the keyboards, and why not? We were, as John Hurt had said, only miming. I cleaned the blood from my half-shaved face and tried to look half-presentable. Still three sheets to the wind so I decided to play bass, and Neil took my guitar. Micky was laughing his head off, and David Coverdale didn't know what to say. He had a look of permanent astonishment on his face at the state we were all in.

The recording was actually fantastic, and the studio crowd went mad. David Coverdale was in his element, revving the fans into a frenzy, and the director asked for two extra takes because the reaction was so electric. As the performance came to a close, Neil Murray – the only sober one out of the whole troupe – slipped in dry ice and broke the head clean off my lovely, cherry Gibson guitar. He was apologetic but I just thought it was hilarious. We went back to the hotel, and found John Hurt again. There hadn't been any filming for him that afternoon after all, and he had sobered up more than we had.

'Sorry about my manners earlier,' he said with a great smile.

We invited him to join us at a Chinese restaurant that evening, as the guest of Whitesnake and EMI. The wine flowed and we were all full of questions for John, who was great company, with many very funny stories. We teased him about the scene in *Alien* in which he had stomach problems. A flower seller came into the restaurant with a large basket of beautiful stemmed roses. It was his lucky night, as John Hurt bought every rose he was selling, one for each woman in the restaurant. He received a huge round of applause. What a gent: he stood up and took a bow. EMI went ballistic when they saw that the bill for the roses was added to our tab. Thank you, EMI.

After the meal we went to a club called the Sugar Shack, an old favourite that I had visited many times during the Paice Ashton Lord sessions. We drank more wine, cold beers and were soon all pretty wasted, again. I began to think the afternoon's antics had caught up with the great actor when John disappeared. There was a short panic until David pointed him out, dancing like Nijinsky – the Russian dancer, not the horse – all eyes on him in the middle of the dancefloor. Fellow dancers paused to check out his moves. He was obviously a classically trained dancer. John received rapturous applause at the end of his dance, bowed several times and then dropped to the floor.

As his new mates, Micky and I picked up John and, back at the hotel, Magnet made sure the great man was returned safely to his room. The next time we met was at Jon Lord's house, when we discreetly avoided all mention of Munich. John Hurt was one of the truly great English actors, and it was such a joy to spend that time with him. I wasn't so sure about continuing our piano trio with vocals – I think we all did well to keep up our real jobs.

Whitesnake stayed in Germany to open for the Australian powerhouse AC/DC on tour. I had some history with the guys: Skinny Cat had opened for Home, the former band of bass player Cliff Williams, and I had hung out with Bon Scott and Phil Rudd when AC/DC played their early gigs in the Marquee. Their act had been full-on from the start and I always thought they would do well, but I do put my hands up now and say I had grossly underestimated just how massive they would be by the time I saw them again.

Bon Scott had passed away earlier in the year, and this was the debut tour for Brian Johnson. I had worked with his old band, Geordie, while with Cozy Powell. Now he was with AC/DC, and was very nervous when I wished him well that first night. It's strange now to think of Brian Johnson as apprehensive, but he was. Yet Brian never let anybody down and he pulled off the impossible trick of replacing the great Bon Scott. Brian's on-stage confidence was total and his voice was perfect. My former drinking partner Phil Rudd powered away on drums, literally bleeding some nights. Their crew were fabulous, giving Whitesnake full use of AC/DC's PA, the whole light show, and as many encores as was needed. And when we were finished, well, AC/DC did … nothing.

Let me explain.

We would go off to great applause and the AC/DC tour manager would tell us we'd done a stellar job and send us back for an encore. The crowd would go crazy again, we would play one more, and exit feeling great. Normally, if an opening act was revving up the crowd so well, the headliners would get on as soon as possible, but not AC/DC. If you'd been backstage at their gigs at any venue on any night, you'd find the band relaxing in their own, specially constructed, traditional English pub, replete with beer-matted tables, chairs, a pool table, draught beer, cocktails, a dartboard and, naturally, as much hard whiskey or bourbon as you needed. This was set up the same way at every location.

I would be in their pub with them, hearing the distant sound of the crowd going mad, while the more urgent matter at hand always seemed to be that there was a darts match to finish. I'd usually pair up with Angus Young, and we'd play Ian Paice and Malcolm Young. All the while, I would hear the volume of the audience building, screaming for AC/DC, louder and louder. Brian and Angus just carried on playing and drinking. When I asked Angus, as I always did, whether we might consider finishing the match after the gig, my seemingly absurd idea would be rejected out of hand. It always seemed to take a lifetime for the game to end, when the boys would – at last! – nonchalantly grab their gear and begin to psych themselves up to play.

Angus would always get a real sweat up for the gig, and would appear at the rear of the stage, soaking wet, a sight to behold. He would be wearing his trademark school uniform and his blood-red Gibson SG would be strapped on. By then the crowd would be almost furious with anticipation, but just when it seemed a riot was going to kick off, the PA would scream into action. 'Hell's Bells' always started the show, with the ear-splitting ring of the bell. It was so powerful. The crowd would be enraptured from the first chord and go into a frenzy. I never missed a show.

We played to at least eight thousand people each night, which was almost double what Whitesnake were doing at home. By the time the tour moved to France that figure had itself almost doubled. Our European record sales took off big time: AC/DC and Whitesnake was the perfect double act and I still cannot think of a better situation. The tour returned to Germany, when we were told that orders for our albums had tripled in just ten days. Whitesnake were really firing on all cylinders – we had never played better on stage. The massive audiences gave us quite the inspiration, and must have reminded the Purple boys of their glory days. Being with the AC/DC band and crew was a phenomenal pleasure.

We played Stuttgart on 8 December, the day that John Lennon was shot four times and died in New York. Magnet had called up to our rooms as usual when we woke up, letting us know the time the bus would be leaving. I noticed something strange in his voice, and he told me what had happened. I heard the words, but didn't really take it in, until I put the phone down and, without any warning, burst into tears. Losing one of The Beatles was like losing a family member for all of us in the band. The bus had a very sombre atmosphere as we headed to the next venue and the murder was the only topic of conversation. None of us could really believe it. It was a terrible day worldwide.

That same night we played Saarbrücken, heading into the final eight shows of the brilliant tour, until David badly hurt his knee on stage. It wasn't clear what he'd done, but he'd managed to twist it somehow, and we could all see the pain he was in. Ian Paice said straight away that the tour was over, and he was right. David was diagnosed with severe ligament damage that made further performances impossible. So this, on top of the shocking news that morning about Lennon, made for possibly the worst day of my professional career.

I knew there had been talk until then of us opening for AC/DC in the US in 1981, and I am still convinced that Whitesnake would have cracked the American market at that point if we had. Maybe I'm a little biased, but I can't emphasise enough how great the band was at this time. The AC/DC tour had turned us into a very special unit – but this was the unit that was to fall apart in the not-so-distant future.

11.

LOOK AT ME NOW

We had a long Christmas break as we waited for David's knee to mend, and returned to Tittenhurst Park for the final *Come An' Get It* sessions in January 1981.

The album had taken us more than six months to complete because the management just kept on putting us out on the road. It really was relentless. It might sound bizarre that we were on the road all over the world in the middle of recording a new album, but we didn't complaint and we were finished at Tittenhurst by the end of January.

Between the virtually endless touring and recording engagements that year, I took out a three-week block to quickly record my second solo album, *Look At Me Now*, at Britannia Row Studios. My producer for this album was Guy Bidmead and we got along very well. David Coverdale had showed a great deal of interest in using the title track with Whitesnake but I insisted on keeping it, an idiotic decision on my part.

Jon Lord, Ian Paice, Neil Murray and Simon Phillips all readily agreed to come into the studio, and I would return the favour for Jon by playing on his solo album *Before I Forget*. Michael Schenker visited us at the studio and I thought I should take the opportunity to employ his musical talents, getting him to add handclaps to 'Who's Fooling Who'! Neil Murray and I wrote a song called 'Thunder and Lightning'.

But I still needed an extra track and it was Cozy Powell who helped me out. I had always wanted to record 'Shaky Ground', a song I knew from The Temptations, written by Funkadelic guitarist Eddie Hazel, with Alphonso Boyd and Jeffrey Bowen. It sounded fantastic with Neil Murray on bass, John Cook on keys and Cozy laying down a very heavy and funky beat. Cozy brought to three the number of drummers I had, which worked out very well. Guy did a very good production and the album was complete within the very tight schedule.

My debut solo album, and *About Time Too*, had only ever been released in Japan, but it went on to be the UK No. 1 import for months. Its performance had not gone unnoticed by EMI, and both of my own albums were now to be issued in the UK. Malcolm Hill, my good friend from the Babe Ruth days, was EMI label manager and asked me which label I wanted to be on. There was only one answer: Parlophone Records, but there was a snag: it was no longer in existence. Malcolm brought back Parlophone for me and in 1979 only Bernie Marsden and the back catalogue of a certain group from Liverpool were on Parlophone Records. I still have an EMI publicity picture with the label's name in bold type.

About Time Too was EMI PCS 7215 and *Look At Me Now* followed soon after as PCS 7217. The latter charted in September 1981 at UK No. 71 and stayed there for two whole weeks – the same length of time as *Trouble*. Suddenly I was a charting solo artist, and it seemed as strange as it was thrilling.

I returned to the day job in April as Whitesnake reconvened at Bray Studios, to rehearse for a European tour. I was pleased to hear that Slade were going to be opening for us, and thought back to the Skinny Cat dates I'd enjoyed with them in 1970. I was really looking forward to this tour. We played Belgium, Switzerland and Holland but our big market was in Germany. Thanks to AC/DC we had very good crowds.

Slade were very friendly and they were big Whitesnake fans. They still had the classic line-up – Jimmy Lea, Don Powell, Dave Hill and the irrepressible Noddy Holder. They played great every night, and I really did like having them open for us, mainly because Skinny Cat had done so for them all those years earlier. I'm not sure Noddy remembered our first encounter, but that didn't matter to me, I was just happy to share the experience and I often sat with him on the tour bus.

I watched Slade at every opportunity on tour. Individually they were not perhaps the best of players, but as a unit they were fantastic and they really knew how to read the crowd, not to mention that they had utterly brilliant songs. They played with us until 9 May and Whitesnake had not even a week to ourselves before we were heading out on the road again in the UK, to promote *Come An' Get It*.

Our tour agent Rod MacSween made the usual phone call to get the seal of approval for the opening act, American singer/ songwriter Billy Squier. He already had a US No. 1 on Capitol Records, *Don't Say No* – a very fine album indeed. Rod's suggestion was met by mass disinterest from the band, but I liked Billy's album and convinced David to say yes. I was soon regretting my enthusiasm. From the first night in Liverpool I felt the eyes of the rest of the band on me as Billy played his set with a great deal of posturing that might have gone down well in the US but bombed with our crowd – big time. I watched from the side of the stage as the disaster unfolded for poor Billy. The Whitesnake fans were extremely partisan and none of them knew a thing about Billy Squier. They soon chanted for Whitesnake.

I saw a gloomy Billy straight after his set and reassured him that the fans would warm to him in their own time. I suggested a few changes that he followed and he began to be an asset to the gigs. He had been pleasantly surprised that I knew his album and he and his band really did warm up and did a fine job in the end. They got so good that we invited Billy to open for us in Germany too.

By the third night, when Robert Plant was a guest at the Bingley Hall in Stafford, I got a very clear idea of just how big Whitesnake were in the UK. We had arrived in the afternoon to find thousands of people outside in the sunshine. I asked Steve Payne why they weren't in the venue and he said that the gig was completely sold out – those outside formed the overflow. I was a bit shocked: it reminded me of similar scenes when I went to see the Stones in their prime at Wembley.

We arranged a secret show at the Royal Court theatre in Liverpool, the details of which were only broadcast on Radio City the same morning. It sold out within an hour. We had the chance to perform 'In My Life' as a tribute to John Lennon, in a vocal arrangement with Jon Lord's Hammond as backing. It was incredibly emotional. I looked out over the audience and quickly realised that we were well over capacity. I could see people at the front getting very squashed and it became rather scary. But David handled the huge crowd very well, asking them to keep cool and step back. I was too preoccupied with looking for casualties to enjoy the gig properly. Almost as terrifying were two nights at the Glasgow Apollo, with the top balconies moving up and down as excited fans jumped in time to the music.

Sell-out shows followed at Newcastle's city hall, another north-eastern triumph for David and Mick – hearing 'The Bladon Races' on slide guitar was always a highlight, and the crowd would always go crazy. One of our four nights at the Hammersmith Odeon was being filmed and recorded when there were power problems and the on-stage monitors blew up, cutting the gig short. I never have seen any film of that night. Billy Squier finished off in London and we had Lionheart on the bill for the final shows of the tour.

It had been a major success – we had sold over fifty thousand tickets in all. We were rock stars, but we still had no real money to show for it, and the questions were building. As ever, though, there was no time to get proper answers. After a two-week break, we were off on our second Japanese tour, now booked into much larger halls to promote the new album. We played four nights in Tokyo, two at the Asakusa Kokusai Gekyo and two at the Nakanko Sun Plaza, and then one night in Nagoya, before finishing in Osaka. From Japan we flew directly to America.

We immediately embarked on a tour with Judas Priest and Iron Maiden that was supposed to begin in Norfolk, Virginia, on 4 July, except that we didn't get to play after serious transformer problems developed. This proved to be something of an omen for the tour in general. Each night Iron Maiden was on first, followed by Whitesnake, and Judas Priest. David Coverdale always referred to the tour as the 'heavy metal sandwich' – with Whitesnake as the filling.

The bands hardly mingled at all. To be honest, I don't think we even acknowledged each other for the first week. I got to know Dave Murray and Steve Harris, then Clive Burr and Adrian Smith, but never really got close to Maiden singer Paul Di'Anno or any of the Judas Priest guys. In fact, the two guitar players in Judas seemed to stay as far away from us as possible. Glenn Tipton and Ken Downing never spoke a word to either Micky or me. We all just did our own thing and nobody was unfriendly – apart from during one unfortunate encounter. Micky got talking to an English guy in a bar about a week into the tour. 'And what are you doing over here?' said the affable Moody.

'I'm the lead fucking singer in the band you are supporting,' said a more than miffed Rob Halford from Judas Priest. Oops.

His band might have been headlining but they just did not pull the crowds in. Venues would regularly be at half-capacity, if that. I didn't think much about tour economics at the time, but the local promoters must have been having a hard time. As I've mentioned before, our record company never exactly threw the kitchen sink into getting our name out there, but the local promoters didn't seem to help themselves – for one thing, they could have advertised the Deep Purple connection. We didn't want to rely on it, but the truth of the matter was that the legendary name would have really helped to shift some tickets. Judas Priest were themselves a bit in awe of the Deep Purple guys, and the fact that we were supporting them seemed to have an effect on the band. It was soon turning into a problem tour. I remember Rob Halford standing side-stage ready to go on with a grim look on his face. Jon Lord said, 'It can't be that bad, Rob.' A frown was the reply. It obviously could.

There were nevertheless definite highlights on the road. A gig at the Fox Theatre on Peachtree Street in Atlanta was a personal dream come true, following the Allman Brothers and Lynyrd Skynrd. That was a very good show, as The Fox audience liked Whitesnake's bluesy approach, but problems arose yet again: the next night in Johnson City, Tennessee, our bus broke down. We were stranded and unable to make the gig.

I liked playing in Memphis, and Mick and I got to walk around Beale Street one afternoon. It was nothing like the tourist hotspot it is today. We walked into a tailor's shop to be greeted by some very surprised African-American staff – I don't think they'd ever had white customers. Mick bought a Panama hat and I bought a pair of yellow shoes. The manager told us to walk back in the centre of the road, and I guess we were naive not to worry, but we never had any problems. We saw the downtown Elvis Presley memorial, took some photos, and decided to make the pilgrimage to Graceland. The house then wasn't open to the public, and we only got as far as the gates with guitar shapes in them. Unexpectedly, it all looked a little sad and run-down. There was no security and we could have just walked up the long drive to the house. We looked at one another, but in the end just got back into the cab to downtown Memphis. As we drove, I could see the Orpheum theatre. It was closed, but it was still good to see the actual place my blues heroes had played in.

After a gruelling ten-hour drive, I arrived in my hotel in Buffalo, New York. There was a terrible noise in my room – I couldn't sleep – so I rang reception and asked them to turn the noise down. I was then told that the racket was being made by the Niagara Falls. We also played Rochester in New York and we decided to make that the final night of the tour. We had talked about it on the bus at great length, and concluded the venture had been a waste of money and time. Magnet booked us tickets home, and that was the last time Whitesnake with Bernie Marsden on guitar played in the USA. It was a shame to have ended that way. We probably seemed like prima donnas to the Maiden boys, and they were genuinely surprised when we told them we were headed for the airport. But it was something that had to be done. It simply wasn't worth it.

I watched the development of Iron Maiden on that tour. They were in the US for the first time and really went for it. Although Maiden were not my particular bag, musically, I liked the guys a lot, and we are still friends today. Adrian Smith and myself wrote some pretty good songs together in the 1990s – still unreleased. But I could immediately see that Paul Di'Anno would not be with the band for long. He was very aloof from his fellow musicians – let alone us and Priest. I still smile to think that all three of those bands were on the road together for an extended period of time without sharing a laugh, or even a drink. It was a shame, really.

Back to the UK and the Monsters of Rock gig at Donington Park in August. Now this was more like it. We were once again one of the headliners. It was quite a day – AC/DC were top of the bill, with Whitesnake, Blue Oyster Cult, Slade, Blackfoot,

More, and the late Tommy Vance. A crowd of more than eighty thousand had gathered and I reckon a large percentage were Whitesnake fans – if not before, then definitely after the gig. I really think it was my finest hour with the band. Some people say it was the best Whitesnake show ever. I don't know about that, but I do know that we gave a bloody excellent show that afternoon. We were on it as a band after the American tour, even though it had been something of a fiasco. We simply banished those rotten days of driving and the cancelled shows from our minds.

Slade tore the place up, and Blackfoot were great too. I didn't see More, but I did catch a little of Blue Oyster Cult and all I can say is that catching a little was quite enough for me … Then we were on and the Donington arena erupted. The crowd gave us an amazing roar when we finished and a truly fantastic ovation. We knew that the UK was so glad to have us all home.

I saw Malcolm Young as I walked back to my dressing room: he winked, smiled, gave me a thumbs-up, and clapped his hands a couple of times. His look seemed to say that we had well and truly arrived, and once again warmed up the crowd a treat for AC/DC. I liked him a lot. He was always a quiet force, the observer, and the real heart of AC/DC.

That same afternoon one of the merchandising guys gave me an eye-opening glimpse of how well Donington was doing as a festival. With a smile, he asked if I had a minute to spare. I did, and followed him to a large caravan parked up on its own in the backstage area. He knocked and a very well put-together girl, dressed only in pants and bra opened it a little. She saw my companion.

'Oh, it's you,' she said, and let us in.

The caravan was large and had been knocked into one area. The entire space was filled with money, from the floor halfway to the ceiling. Three other, equally underdressed, girls were counting and separating notes into five-pound, ten-pound, and twenty-pound bundles. They were in their underwear so that the bosses could be sure they weren't pinching any money. What a sight it was – near-naked girls and thousands and thousands of pounds in cash. Rock'n'roll, ladies and gents. I should have asked why Whitesnake were not seeing much of that money.

The good times were almost at an end for the band, although this would have seemed a distant prospect as we began work on sessions for a new album. *Come An' Get It* had reached UK No. 2 and the promotional tours had sold out in the UK, Japan, and much of Europe. How could it all go so wrong? The answer lay not so much in what we were doing as what we weren't. We were no longer working with the seventh member of the band, its heart – one Martin Birch. He was the glue that held Whitesnake together. With hindsight, it's bloody easy to see. Martin was not there from the start of the album sessions and so, Martin Birch, it was all your fault!

Martin was not only a great and gifted engineer and producer, but also a very astute businessman. He was then producing Rainbow, and he had been involved with the fast-emerging juggernaut that was now Iron Maiden. Martin was spending more and more time with the Irons, and I suspected he had been offered a much better deal with them than Seabreeze would agree to give him for a Whitesnake album. But when we were informed that Martin would not be producing us any more, not one of us asked any questions, and shame on us all for that. We should have asked why, and we should have demanded answers.

Instead, we just gathered at Nomis Studios in west London to fire up and see what material we had for what would become the *Saints & Sinners* album. Having had a good experience with Guy Bidmead on my solo album, I told David about him. He and Guy had a good meeting and Guy became our new producer. The band talked a lot about the situation with Seabreeze, but that was all we did – talk about it. We did absolutely nothing, and we didn't address the Birch situation. Boy, oh, boy, do I now wish we had.

I had written a bunch of stuff, David had written some good things, but Micky didn't seem to have much interest in new songs, which was a little strange to me – at least, at the time. I now look back and see things more clearly. It was the beginning of the end at Nomis. Our usual spark, energy, and overall camaraderie were missing. We also weren't able to go on and record at Britannia Row for some reason and as a result Guy recommended a studio he had used in Shepperton called Rock City. None of us had ever heard of this place, much less used it, and this was another moment at which I see now we should have been asking tough questions. Yet the same band that had recorded in high-end facilities such as Tittenhurst Park and Ridge Farm said absolutely nothing.

Rock City proved to be technically fine but, to put it bluntly, none of us liked it there at all: it just didn't have a good vibe. We didn't feel like rock stars. We arrived singly, vehicle by vehicle and soon filled the cramped car park: Jon in his Porsche turbo, Ian in the Rolls-Royce, me in my first Porsche 911, David driven in by Willy Fyffe or Magnet, and Micky on the train. We moaned about how long it taken to get there and the lack of parking. The mundane details were starting to tell.

Steve Payne had set my gear up by the time we arrived, the Marshalls were present, Jon's Hammond organ was set up, and Ian's kit glistened in the drum booth. Though the sessions would fall apart quite quickly, we did manage to record the backing tracks of 'Victim of Love' and 'Dancing Girls'. We all seemed to like the sound that Guy had recorded, especially the drum and guitar parts, but we didn't feel at home. Rock City was jettisoned and we moved the whole show back to Clearwell Castle, Gloucestershire, a place we knew and loved. This was an expensive move – Clearwell was residential and we were also hiring the Rolling Stones' mobile studio. Even if we were not receiving much money, we were definitely spending it. But Clearwell did the trick, and the vibe was back.

David had a great new song that became a Whitesnake classic. 'Crying in the Rain' was most definitely a heavy-duty, very serious rock song, but its foundations were drenched in the irresistible humour that was Whitesnake at the time. We had seen a local TV news report that had us falling about laughing. A real yokel-local man, with a roll-up pursed between his lips and a flat cap pulled down over his head, was interviewed live about the mass extermination of farm animals in the area. The interviewer was being sympathetic to the plight of the innocent creatures but his subject was not quite so bothered.

'Plenty more about,' said the man. The reporter was speechless, and we all cracked up.

The next day, 'Crying in the Rain' recording began with some bluesy guitar, while Paicey thrashed his drums to cue the vocals. Instead of that huge voice coming in with, 'Black cat moans when he's burning with a fever,' David performed a pitch-perfect imitation of the man from the previous night's TV: 'Plenty more about!' Cue absolute hysteria in the studio.

We tried it again, but all we could hear was 'Plenty more about!' The session was almost ruined: we were incapable of playing for an hour and we had to bar Coverdale from the studio until the track was in the can. It's a great track and a superb vocal from Coverdale, but I cannot hear it without picturing the band falling to our knees with laughter. It's funny partly because it really is such a serious song. There is a tape of the whole piece, and I still find it hilarious. I have played the song many times with Whitesnake tribute bands, and the singers love it. If they only knew the real story.

'Rock an' Roll Angels' was a curio. Ian Paice, for some reason that still mystifies me, really struggled with this song.

He did take after take, redoing and redoing again. He would then start from scratch with another take. It was very unlike Ian, and he seemed to be very short on confidence, also a very un-Ian Paice thing. After about ten takes he sent us to the local pub and recorded the track on his own with Guy. It's not a difficult song, especially for Ian, and it must have been a psychological thing – maybe he was losing interest. Of course, anyone listening would never guess at the difficulties and he is overall undoubtedly brilliant on the album.

One song on *Saints & Sinners* literally changed my life: 'Here I Go Again'. I have a demo of it, recorded on an old Revox tape machine, and the basic ideas are already all there. I wanted to get it all sorted before playing it to David. Jon Lord was particularly taken with the song from the very start, I played him the opening chords, and he asked me to run them by him again.

'You are a clever little sod, aren't you?' he said and smiled. He really loved the opening figure of the song, and insisted he play it on the Hammond organ.

David went into lyrical overdrive at Clearwell that afternoon. Most of the song was already written at that stage, including the complete chorus, but he was very animated and disappeared to write new lyrics. He disappeared into his room much in the same way he had for 'Walking in the Shadow of the Blues' during the *Lovehunter* sessions. He went on to sing the song in a quite magnificent way, sensitive, and yet so powerful.

Neil, Jon, Ian, and I are on the backing track. At one point I thought a collaboration might help me deal with some frustration, and I asked Mick Moody to jam with me, but he said he was just a bit too busy. I played all the parts of the harmony guitar solo, and there was a nod to John Lennon's 'Woman' in the arpeggio guitar parts.

If I'm honest, I truly believed we had a big song on our

hands and David was very pleased too. But I never dreamed how big it would become.

We moved to Britannia Row to mix the album with Guy Bidmead. But even as he threaded the tapes, things were starting to move dramatically for the good ship Whitesnake. David was in talks with his lawyer, as I would shortly find out, but more immediately Moody abruptly quit the band. It was a real shock; I was pretty upset. I hadn't seen it coming at all, although I had thought it was mainly only me and David at Britannia Row, with me doing all the guitar overdubs.

Guy, David and I continued to work on finishing the album. Jon was due to record Hammond solo overdubs, but never showed. Then he and Ian would be coming in the next day, but again, they never showed. We later discovered they had been at the horse-racing at Ascot and Windsor. David was visibly disappointed and upset. I was too. Micky was gone, Jon and Ian seemingly weren't interested, and we hadn't seen Neil Murray since Clearwell.

I looked at David in the control room at the studio and uttered the fateful words, 'We might as well end all this, David, knock it all on the head, mate.' I didn't quite grasp the full effect of what I was saying. David's eyes widened. He smiled wryly as though a weight was off his shoulders. He said that he thought he was the only one thinking it. I assured him he wasn't. He explained that he had already been having meetings with his legal people in order to extricate himself from the managerial mire.

It wasn't quite over yet. We made one final, doomed, attempt to keep things going – collectively deciding to fire Seabreeze. A band meeting with John Coletta was arranged at the Newman Street office. We agreed to plan out our approach at my flat in Paddington beforehand. Everyone showed up at the Dungeon except David and, having waited without any sign of him, we left for the 2 o'clock meeting.

I was delighted to think that we would all be getting away from Seabreeze. How could John Coletta still be the manager? He had been barred from the dressing rooms in USA, barred from the recording studios, was never issued a backstage pass, and blanked completely in Japan. But I couldn't help wondering where the hell David was. We assumed that he would be waiting at the office, but he wasn't.

The rest of Whitesnake gathered around the great Purple onyx table: Jon Lord, Ian Paice, Neil Murray, and me. I was getting butterflies in my stomach. We were all looking at each other. Where was David?

'Before you say anything,' Coletta said, 'I have spoken with David's lawyer this morning, and Whitesnake is over for you lot.' He walked around the room, pointing his finger. 'You are out,' he said as he pointed at Ian, Neil and, to my total surprise and shock, he pointed at me.

I had been the author of my own demise with my comment to David about ending the band. There was a palpable silence in the room. I thought about the last time David and I talked at Britannia Row. I didn't realise but he had been advised to break up the band in order to escape the Seabreeze banner. He later told me that he thought it was the only possible way out.

Ian Paice was stoical and left the room. Jon looked sombre. Neil looked confused. I simply didn't believe it. And then came Coletta's masterstroke. He took me to one side and said that he had been in talks with Hugh Stanley Clarke, head of A&R at EMI, and they wanted to sign me as a solo artist, *but* … I had to sign a new contract that day. Still in shock from the revelations, and feeling deserted, I signed. Can you believe it? Coletta even took me to EMI later that day to talk about my new and future plans.

I left 25 Newman Street a shattered thirty-year-old man, I don't mind saying it. The greatest band any guitarist could wish for had ended without a row or whimper, and a song-writing partnership that could have gone on to bigger and better things was terminated because of lousy management.

Am I being fair here? Is it too easy to blame management for everything? But equally, is it not reasonable to suggest that our manager should have been a creative force, looked after us, and pushed us higher? It's easy to blame John Coletta. I had no legal advice but I was the one who signed that contract. All I can say is that John Coletta was a very poor manager for me. They're my thoughts.

Another common question: was I fired or did Whitesnake just disband?

Well, you tell me. If I was indeed fired, then I am proud to say I was sacked at the same time as the best rock drummer in the entire world. Ian Paice just shrugged, and later joined the Gary Moore band.

Jon Lord continued to work with David Coverdale in Whitesnake, but everything else changed. Cozy Powell replaced Ian, Colin Hodgkinson replaced Neil, and Mel Galley replaced me. I did wonder if Gary Moore had ever been considered for my job, based on a mysterious encounter just before the band broke up. Gary turned up at Britannia Row, and looked a little bit ruffled when he saw me. It seems obvious now that he was there, and was put out to see me, because he was in the frame to join Whitesnake. I'm by no means certain, but I guess it did make real sense. Maybe I should ask David some time. Moody also returned to the fold, which surprised me, but this didn't last very long as John Sykes very soon replaced him.

I still stand by *Saints & Sinners*. Martin Birch returned to record David's vocals and mix the album. Mel Galley sang backing vocals, and I never got the chance to play the songs live, but I recorded them all and wrote the most important one. The line-up for that album is the classic: Coverdale, Marsden, Moody, Murray, Lord. and Paice.

I'm proud of all the albums I made with Whitesnake. It was a brilliant adventure. We started in a shitty little rehearsal room in central London that David called the 'cat piss cellar', but even without good management we still managed to claim Europe and Japan. Jon Lord often said that he had the best time of his musical life with Whitesnake, and I agreed with him. All credit should go to David Coverdale for taking it by the horns after 1984, and reforming an all-new line-up in the USA, which culminated in multi-million sales of the 1987 album, albeit with my input via what turned out to be the most important Whitesnake song, 'Here I Go Again'.

12.

BAKED ALASKA

I had been in one of the best rock'n'roll bands in the world from its start, and now – I was not. Big difference.

I thought a lot about the talk with David at Britannia Row. During those last *Saints & Sinners* sessions David must have been in considerable turmoil. His little girl, Jessica, still a baby, had contracted meningitis. I understood well enough that it was a bad thing but I didn't have children myself and I couldn't really appreciate the particular agonies of being a parent, how much he and Julia must have been going through on top of the band's internal problems. I have had two daughters since and the thought of meningitis now terrifies me. I wrote to David, saying that his family was the most important thing at that time and to contact me when Jessica was on the mend from her illness. Thankfully, as weeks passed, she made a full recovery.

I saw the new line-up of Whitesnake at Donington Park in 1983. It was the first time I had seen him in person since the split. It was emotional. He reiterated that we should still write together, which I was quite happy to do. I'm still waiting for that day, and I'm absolutely certain that our writing partnership would still be as good as it ever was, perhaps even better.

Whitesnake had an enormous audience that day. I could only watch and feel some sadness, especially as they pretty much played the old set list. I may be biased but I didn't think it was as great as it had been two years before. The bluesy feel that was so integral to the original band was almost non-existent. Mel Galley was playing my solo parts, and he told me himself a few years later about the pressure he was under to replicate my originals. One of my best mates was now on drums, but Cozy told me himself that he was never the right drummer for Whitesnake. They played many of my songs, but the only connection to them was David singing. Donington Park was bleak; not one of my best days.

Whitesnake underwent many more personnel changes. David had an encounter in a restaurant in Germany with John Sykes, then with Thin Lizzy, and pretty soon Moody was no longer in the band (for the second time). For a brief period both John and Mel Galley played guitars, until Mel had an accident. Bass player Colin Hodgkinson had also departed, and Neil Murray re-joined. Jon Lord left for financial reasons that I won't go into, and Whitesnake became a four-piece band for the first time. This was a pure rock incarnation that worked much better. I think 1987's *Whitesnake* shows that the bluesy days were history.

By this time Cozy had gone, and Aynsley Dunbar was playing drums instead, Neil was on bass, and even Don Airey was in the studio. Mike Stone produced an excellent rock album that sold many millions. 'Here I Go Again' was re-recorded for the album and released to quite devastating effect pretty much worldwide. A brilliant video was all over the newly formed MTV, featuring Tawny Kitaen slithering over a classic Jaguar car. It was quite a moment visually, and the song sounded fantastic. In October 1987, the song reached No. 1 in the USA and Canadian charts, and made it into the UK Top 10. It was nominated for the American Music award in rock and pop albums in 1988, that same year that David and I both received an American Society of Composers, Authors and Publishers award, and in 2016 I was given a BMI music award recognising four million radio plays of the song on US radio alone.

It's ironic that 'Here I Go Again' was the very last song I wrote for Whitesnake, and because of the incredible success of it I am able to write, of all things, a book! The song enables me to play as many gigs as I wish to do these days, and I always take great pleasure performing it in venues large or small. As David Coverdale wrote in his introduction to this book, ''tis a biggie for sure'.

My first post-Whitesnake band was SOS – a cry from the heart, in hindsight. I held auditions at the old Studio 51 club, where I had myself auditioned for UFO all those years before. At this point, I had already managed to hire Clive Edwards on drums. Early in the afternoon, a guy called Andy arrived for the bass gig. He was about my age, very thin, had long hair, and looked slightly dishevelled, but had a nice face. He was from Liverpool, and had a very strong accent.

He took his bass out of the case. He beamed at me, eyes wide, as I greeted him. He never said a word, but continued to beam.

I put it down to nerves.

I started a slow 12-bar shuffle, and told him to get into the groove when he felt right. Clive and I continued to jam without a a single contribution from the bass. Andy merely beamed a smile bigger than the room itself.

I stopped, and I asked if he might like to actually play the bass with us. Abruptly, he thrashed into life, hitting the bass so hard the strings bounced on the fretboard.

Clive Edwards looked at me in astonishment. We stopped again and I looked at Andy, who now resembled a rabbit caught in headlights.

'You can't play bass, can you, Andy?'

At last, he spoke for the first time. 'No, Bernie, I can't.'

'So, why are you here, mate?'

'So I can tell all me mates that I've played with Bernie Marsden!' he replied. He looked a little sheepish, but I cracked up. He put me in a good mood for the first time in days.

Andy was a huge Whitesnake fan, and I had been his favourite member. I asked him how he got to London and told me how he'd hitch-hiked all the way down from Liverpool, arrived in Euston in the cab of a lorry, borrowed a mate's bass guitar, and had no way of getting home.

'Can you make tea and coffee, Andy?'

'Yes, I can,' he said, his confidence soaring.

Steve Payne gave him some money in the vague hopes he might get some food for us. To Steve's surprise Andy returned with some sandwiches. We later took him to a café for some hot food with us; he was a very nice person. He stayed for two nights, sleeping in the studio on a bench, and insisted he would take care of all the equipment. After three days, he went back to Liverpool. I've never seen him again. I hope he reads this.

In the end, Steve Cherry joined SOS on bass, with Tommy Jackson on vocals. We played a short UK tour in July 1982, finishing up at a festival in Mildenhall. We played Nottingham too, and I couldn't help but think that the last time I had played in that area was at Donington Festival, with Whitesnake, with a hundred thousand people in the crowd singing my songs. Bernie Marsden's SOS was all over very fast. It wasn't the guys in the band's fault at all, they all tried very hard, but my heart just wasn't in it. What could I do?

I was also by now despising the act of signing the new contract with Coletta, with no legal advice for the second time: unbelievable stupidity! The promised big deal with EMI never materialised. I recorded some decent demos at Chappell and KPM studios, but nothing really happened with them. When SOS ended, so did my tenure with Coletta. I simply walked away and drove back to Chetwode in my Porsche 911,

On stage with
Whitesnake, 1979.

On stage with Whitesnake.

Donington Festival, 1980.

Our wedding day at Stowe,
26 July 1980. Fran with
two suited and booted boys!
Cozy was my best man.

Backstage before the
gig in Osaka, 1981.
We had a good time!

In my room after an hour in Tokyo holding the tour Marmite, 1981.

Alaska, 1984.

MGM, 1986. Mel Galley, myself and Neil Murray.

With Peter Green in Hell, Norway, 1996.

With David 'Honeyboy' Edwards and that sixty-thousand-dollar Jaguar.

With Ian Paice rehearsing for Tony's Benefit Gig, Abbey Road Studio One.

With Robert Plant, Paul Rodgers and Brian Johnson.

On stage with Gary Moore.

With the Allman
Brothers Band.

Playing with Robert Plant.

With Joe Bonamassa at the
Royal Albert Hall, 2019.

seriously considering packing it all in, for good. I couldn't stop thinking about the fact I was no longer in Whitesnake.

At length some good news came my way, when Yamaha invited me to Japan to do some guitar clinics towards the end of the year. Still deep in the trauma of the split, I didn't want to travel alone and asked my old friend Nick Griffiths to come with me as my technical support. Nick had been the engineer on *Look at Me Now*, and had previously worked with Pink Floyd, both on the road and in their Britannia Row studio. But even with him around I still had to deal with my memories of the old band. Stopping in Anchorage, Alaska on the way reminded me of the first time I had been there with Whitesnake. Feeling pretty alone and somewhat sorry for myself, I stepped outside the airport building into the sub-zero temperatures. I was also planning to start a new group and I wondered what I should call it.

I took in the fabulous sight of the frozen White Mountains and the stunning blue sky dotted with perfect fluffy white clouds. It looked spectacular, and I reminded myself that, despite all the recent shit, I was still in a very enviable position: I played guitar for a living and I was travelling to Japan with my work. I went back inside the terminal and saw a big poster on the wall, 'Welcome to Alaska'. It occurred to me that 'Alaska' was a good name for a band.

A sad thing happened as we arrived in Japan. Nick was contacted at our hotel by the British consulate to let him know that his mother had died suddenly in England while we were in the air. Nick, understandably distraught, flew back to London that evening. Now I was now very much alone in Japan. I felt so sad for Nick, missed my own family, and generally felt very sorry for myself. The end of Whitesnake was very much sinking in.

As it turned out, I was not entirely on my own so far from home. Over breakfast in my hotel I was astonished to see

Aston Villa's manager Tony Barton arrive one morning. The side was in Japan to play the Intercontinental Cup against Peñarol of Uruguay. Mr Barton was soon enough joined by other European faces: Dennis Mortimer, Tony Morley, and my old friend Peter Withe. Peter did a real double-take when I waved across the room. Peter is a great, straight-talking Liverpudlian, big in stature and big in heart. He was a real pro. He played for England eighteen times, made 182 appearances for Aston Villa and was man of the match and scorer of the winning goal for Villa in a European Cup Final. Not many men can say that.

I first met Peter when I was on the road with Whitesnake in 1978, when he played for Newcastle United, through a friend of the band who owned a nightclub in the city. We got along very well and he gave me his No. 9 United shirt. I still have it today, although it sadly no longer fits. In Tokyo he introduced me to all the great Villa players and invited me to the game. I'm sorry to say Villa lost 2–0, but it was a good, bruising match. Peter and I kept in touch, and he even helped to put a celebrity team together for a fundraiser in my village. Watching a European cup-winner at work on the Tingewick village football pitch was quite something.

The Yamaha crew in Tokyo were very good, and made me feel welcome. I travelled to Tokyo, Osaka, and Nagoya and was treated as quite the star. In Nagoya I stepped out to explore on my own, without the rep from the company. It was a dumb thing to do, as I spoke no Japanese, and I got lost pretty quickly in the outskirts of the city. I was beginning to panic when I spotted a cab. But I had no idea where I was, much less where I needed to go, and the driver didn't speak English. Then, I had a flash of genius. I had a packet of matches with the hotel logo in my jacket pocket. I pointed to the name on the matchbox. The driver looked very confused.

'Go here, please,' I said, but I didn't get much response.

I pointed to the tiny matchbox again and again until, suddenly, his face burst into a smile and he nodded vigorously. We started to drive. After some time, I began to be concerned as we seemed to be moving away from the city. About half an hour passed. In the middle of another small town he finally stopped the car and turned around at me, looking very pleased with himself. He pointed to the building he had taken me to – the small factory that made the matches! I can laugh now, but I wasn't laughing at the time. Between the two of us and a very helpful man from the match factory, I found my way back to my hotel to tell the tale. The Yamaha guys were horrified.

The trip to Japan was a real success, although I do realise now that I didn't exploit my popularity as much I should have done. The guitar clinics were all absolutely packed, and the fans were attentive, respectful, and thrilled that I was there. In Japanese guitar magazines I had been voted one of the world's top ten guitarists alongside my heroes, Eric Clapton, Jeff Beck, Gary Moore, and Brian May. The work was very good for me as it took me out of my brooding mood, and I think it really helped my state of mind. I'm sure I would have been a total pain if I had been at home with Fran. She was always there for me and always supported me, but she knew how much I loved the band and how I was now feeling. I just wasn't in the right frame of mind to see that I should have concentrated more of my energy on Japan, where I had been totally accepted and loved both by fans and musicians.

Back in the UK I felt much more positive. I found myself writing songs using a keyboard, and I was pretty much ignoring the guitar. I had a quiet 1983. I did a hell of a lot of writing, and hung out at EMI with Malcolm Hill, who took very good care of me. I spent a lot of time at the office of the Whitesnake merchandise company, Concert Publishing, in north London. I became friends with everyone there, especially owners John Collins and John Lyons (collectively known as 'The Johns').

Many of the staff had come on Whitesnake tours with the band. In the summer I purchased a bicycle from Harrods which I would ride from The Dungeon in Paddington to the Concert Publishing office nearly every day. Believe me, the thought of regularly riding a bicycle down the length of the traffic-packed Marylebone Road, past Euston and King's Cross stations, now makes me shudder. But one day my bike was stolen from outside the Concert Publishing office. That thief probably saved my life.

The Johns encouraged me to put a new band together. They even said that they felt somewhat guilty at how much money they had made from their Whitesnake deal. They were amazed to see how little the band saw of it. The Johns were the partners in a new management company called London Pride, and they offered to finance a new band for me. This was very good news, and a really nice gesture because I didn't really have anywhere to go. It was a tough time for me, not only mentally but also financially. The Johns offered a monthly salary and I thought this was all very good of them at the time. The money did indeed appear in the bank and I was soon financially level again, with my head above the water. If the band did well, more money would be generated, and this made me feel better.

Now I had the means to put together the band whose name I had thought of on my Japanese travels – Alaska. I contacted singer Robert Hawthorn, who had auditioned for SOS, and asked him to be part of the line-up. I had Richard Bailey from Magnum on keys, Brian Badhams on bass and John Marter on drums. London Pride contacted Robin Godfrey-Cass at Warner Brothers and I soon signed a deal for Alaska with Music For Nations, a record label run by a former employee of EMI. We recorded the first album in a great little studio in Lincolnshire called the Chapel, where we all had some real rock'n'roll times.

I found myself writing a lot of new stuff and this time took a different musical path. I had no desire at all to try to recreate a Whitesnake line-up. The songs were good; easy-going, American-flavoured tunes, but I wasn't sure what the Whitesnake fans would think. We recorded during the first few months of 1983 and the first album, *Heart of the Storm*, was quickly released. David Coverdale called me to say he thought I should hire a different drummer, and with hindsight he was right, as ever, but I didn't. I hated the audition process.

There was much to be happy about at first with Alaska. Finally being free of my association with my previous management lifted a lot of my gloom, and the Johns were good company. I felt that they really wanted to be creative in management. I never signed a contract with them: perhaps I'd learnt my lesson at last.

While rehearsing with Alaska, I had the pleasure one day of meeting Shirley Bassey. But as is the way with these things, it was not to be entirely straightforward. There had been a whisper the day before that she was coming to the studios, but nobody really took much notice. The next day, I was sat completely alone in the studio café when I heard steps ascending the old and steep wooden staircase. Clip-clop, clip-clop, clip-clop. Then I heard a familiar voice, one I had grown up with. It had a a still, soft Welsh accent.

'Excuse me,' she said.

There in front of me, in all her magnificence, was Shirley Bassey. I stood up immediately; she must have thought I had army training. I said nothing, just smiled. 'I'm looking for the toilet,' she said.

My heart sank. The toilet was at the very top of the staircase and covered in used stage passes and graffiti. It was clean enough, but was very much for the boys and certainly not for the likes of this legend. Put it this way, if you needed a sit-down you'd wait for a trip to the pub. Ms Bassey looked every inch the superstar that she was, sporting an off-white winter fur hat, fur coat, and heeled boots. The coat made her twice the size she actually was, and I had to be honest. I said she would need to remove her outer garments if she was really desperate to go. The fur hat alone looked too large to fit into the cubicle. I explained that it was very much the men's room. She laughed, took off her hat and coat, and asked me to hold them while she went. Ms Bassey returned in no time.

'My dear boy, thanks for your help,' she said, and as she left, she turned around and added, 'By the way, I've played in a lot worse toilets than that, my darling.'

Shirley Bassey, one of the boys, just like the rest of us.

A couple of years later I was at Nomis Studios in west London when Shirley Bassey was due in. The lobby was always busy with managers, roadies, artists, and some pretty big names often came in and out. The crowd parted like something out of a biblical scene as Ms Bassey walked in. I was on one side as she walked past. She saw me, smiled a little, and momentarily stopped.

'I remember you. The toilets are OK here, I hope?' She gave me a lovely smile as she walked on. The Black Crowes were there at the studio at the time, but I felt like the main man, and I was an instant celebrity. I acquired tickets for my folks to see her in concert at the Albert Hall. They both said she was marvellous. I had grown up with her music in my house, and my mum in particular was a huge fan. Dame Shirley Bassey, I salute you.

Alaska did initial gigs with Liverpool band Spider, followed by a decent UK tour with Mama's Boys from Ireland. *Heart of the Storm*, was well-received in the press but there were some reservations. Where was the blues? I was accused of pandering to an American sound, which was true, but I was just very conscious of not trying to make a Whitesnake album. That would have certainly been a disaster, these guys were good musicians, but don't get me wrong, there was no Jon Lord or Ian Paice, and there was certainly no David Coverdale in the mix.

Alaska toured Poland, playing in Warsaw and Katowice, then to Germany, when Richard Bailey suddenly left. Don Airey joined in his place, and took to the road with me once again.

We had quite a bizarre experience in Europe with the early heavy metal band Manowar. They had Ross 'the boss' on guitar, Eric Adams singing, Scott Columbus on drums and a totally over-the-top bassist with leader Joey DeMaio, who wore leather outfits that looked like Roman tunics and a four-foot sword strapped to his side for good measure. That's metal for you … They played songs with titles such as 'Warlord', 'March of Revenge (By the Soldiers of Death)' – the brackets are important – and 'Gates of Valhalla', which was certainly my favourite each and every night. Before Manowar took to the stage with their fearsome setlist, Alaska would present fairly soft rock'n'roll songs for their audience. We survived, but I think I have Whitesnake to thank for that. Strange tour, fierce guys on the stage, but quiet and nice as pie off it. I did constantly wonder what we were doing there with them, but it was enjoyable.

The second Alaska album proved to be more difficult to make. We started the backing tracks at Gerry Anderson's studio in Bray, which were the studios in which the iconic TV show *Thunderbirds* was made. We completed the tracks at a studio called The Clock, somewhere in east London. The people who worked there were nice, but the sound just wasn't working. I decided that I didn't want to do the mix at The Clock and was beginning to feel that the album would never be finished, when I moved the sessions to the Sol studio, Berkshire, then owned by Jimmy Page. It had formerly been known as the Mill and was the studio of Elton John's producer Gus Dudgeon. The house engineer was a man called Stuart Epps.

I was staying at the studio but my room wasn't ready when I arrived. The future Mrs Bill Wyman, Mandy Smith, was still checking out, following Bill's recording session a week earlier.

Mandy's mum made me a cup of tea. I had no idea I was almost a witness to the infamous Bill and Mandy affair – I must admit I thought Mandy and her mum were both studio staff.

After a few days' working there I saw the signs that Jimmy Page was in the house. Stuart had told me that I would know when he was about as Jimmy always left his cigarettes on the filter tip until they burned out. The man himself came into the control room while we were recording. He was very nice, quiet, but very much in charge. He had been recording with Paul Rodgers for an album called *The Firm*. We chatted about guitars, and I was more than a bit in awe of him. We were overdubbing the song 'SOS' for the album when he arrived and Jimmy asked me how many guitar tracks were on the song. I said there had been two.

'Two!' he screamed at Stuart, 'Two!'

He looked at the Gibson guitar and my Marshalls and asked if they were mine. I told him they were. He asked if I would mind listening to a mix of a track he'd recorded for *The Firm*. Stuart put the track through the studio system and I listened to the big guitar intro.

'How many guitars on that then, Bernie?' Jimmy asked me.

'Three?' I replied.

'About six,' he said. 'Your guitar sound is much thicker and clearer. It's a great sound.'

This was Led Zeppelin's guitar player. He had influenced a whole world of guitarists, including me. And he had just described my sound as 'great'. That put a smile on my face. I compared our Les Pauls and checked the serial numbers. Jimmy's number two was very close to The Beast, and I was interested to see that – they were probably made the same month in Kalamazoo all those years ago in 1959.

We finished the mix on the second Alaska album, and we called it *The Pack*. It was released on Music for Nations in the UK, and they in turn licensed it to small European labels. But, in a major change, I did sign this album to Bronze Records for the USA. I always liked label manager Gerry Bron and his son Richard, the A&R director. He wanted remixes of some tracks and so we went into the old Bronze studio in Camden – the same studio where I recorded the Babe Ruth albums.

Richard Bron was full of enthusiasm and he thought Alaska would be very successful in the USA. As far as he was concerned, he would make it happen. It didn't happen! We took *The Pack* out for a European tour, but Alaska had lost its novelty and was becoming a weight around my neck. So I decided to call an end to the band.

London Pride thought I should form a band with guitarist and vocalist Mel Galley. He had been jettisoned from Whitesnake under some strange circumstances. He told me himself what had happened. He had a bad accident while on the road with Whitesnake and broke his wrist badly. He and John Sykes had been car-jumping, and they both fell off the roof of a vehicle. John landed on Mel and Mel broke his wrist. Not great for a guitar player. Mel had the bones reset but they just would not mend and he was finding it incredibly difficult to move because of damage to his nerves. He found a genius doctor who designed a mechanical piece of equipment that Mel had to wear on his wrist. This enabled him to play the guitar, but soon afterwards he left Whitesnake. Now the guy who had taken my place in the old band was about to form a new band with me.

I soon called Neil Murray and the initials of our surnames together made MGM. I was concerned about having the same name as a certain little movie company and raised this at London Pride's offices. John Collins simply said that our MGM would be so big that we would be the ones to sue the Americans. I told you he was keen.

A key factor behind putting the band together was that both Mel and I were strong songwriters. Mel had contributed the song 'Gambler' to Whitesnake and it became a stage favourite very quickly. With us working together, how could MGM possibly fail? Well, read on and you'll find out. To begin with, I made a very big mistake retaining John Marter from Alaska as the drummer: I should have remembered David Coverdale's words. We hired Angel Studios, London, with engineer Tony Platt, a place much used for recording classical music and it had a magnificent live room.

We recorded four tracks, including a very good song called 'Welcome to the Real World', which was Mel's work, and a number of mine, called 'Abuser'. This was the next problem for MGM – Mel and I always wrote separately. It had always been easy to write songs with David Coverdale but with Mel it never happened. I don't know why, as we got along very well and he was a great singer. We chatted a lot about Trapeze, his first band that he would then re-join in the 1990s, but we never really talked much about Whitesnake. This may have been because Mel always felt as if he had taken my place in the band, which I suppose history shows he did. He was also suffering badly with stage nerves at the time, perhaps as a result of the accident, and maybe because of his rapid exit from Whitesnake, but as far as I could hear he was singing and playing great.

Out of the blue one day, the office received a phone call from Bobby Kimball, the former Toto vocalist. Somehow, he had heard the MGM demos, liked what he heard and knew that we needed a singer. I was a little sceptical as Toto were a huge band from the USA, and I wondered why Bobby would be in London. But I was a huge fan. Who doesn't like 'Africa' or 'Hold the Line'?

With Bobby on board, we relocated to a small studio called the Old Smithy, Worcester. Tony Platt engineered and we started reworking the backing tracks we'd recorded at Angel. Bobby had some song ideas of his own, and all appeared to be good. We wrote a track together in the studio called 'Where's My Little Girl'. He added his voice to the recordings that we already had, and Mel's song 'Welcome to the Real World' was a particular success. Then, it all started to go very wrong. Very quickly, over a couple of days, the sessions descended into acrimony, to the point that I packed my bag and drove home in the middle of the night.

That was the end of Kimball and, I thought, the end of MGM. But the band was still booked for festivals in Germany and Switzerland so I had to do something. I considered working as a four-piece again but then remembered that, when Alaska had ended, I had sent a plane ticket to a young singer from Ireland called Rob Cas. He was now in London and I put him into the MGM band as a guest vocalist for the European gigs. Because we were added late to the festival shows, the promoters had made credit-card-size promos for MGM:

Marsden – ex-Whitesnake

Galley – ex-Whitesnake

Murray – ex-Whitesnake

Some clever wag had added, 'Featuring Kimball – ex-Toto, and now ex-MGM', in time to pass them out to us. They were pretty hilarious, I still have one somewhere.

In July 1987, MGM played shows in Germany, Switzerland and Austria with, among others, Bad Company, Kansas with Steve Morse on guitar, and the great Status Quo. They were all memorable gigs, and being on the road with Quo was never boring. The night before the Reading Festival, we played a show where I was told shortly before we went on stage that Mel would not come out of the dressing room. I sat down and had a talk with him, we talked for quite a long time. I think it was a combination of his nerves, the accident in Whitesnake, not being in Whitesnake and suddenly playing big shows again (the Reading Festival was 30,000 people). But he was fine, he played and sang his heart out.

By the time we had got to Reading I had added a singer called John Saxon. He was very good and very easy to work with; he proved himself when he learnt the set in about ten days. John was local to Reading, and I think this affected his performance on the day. He was in his home town playing some huge Whitesnake songs with three previous members of Whitesnake by his side. I'd presumed he was fine to walk out to a crowd so big, but I'd put him in a position he'd never been in before. Despite his nerves, he actually did a very good job. I believe John is no longer with us today, but I remember him with warmth and respect, one of the good guys. But Reading was to be the end of MGM. I headed back to London Pride to give the Johns the news.

13.

SHOOTING THE BREEZE

I had never seen any royalties whatsoever from the songs I wrote during my entire tenure with Whitesnake. I only ever received my weekly payment. In the late Eighties I decided to take John Coletta to court.

The law firm of Kanaar and Holmes investigated and represented me. The lawyers did a fantastic amount of work – Nick Kanaar, stand up and take a bow. We sued for payment – or lack of – and the case rolled on, and on, and on. In all, more than two long years elapsed. The other side were continually stalling for more time, using their considerable financial heft to freeze me out of my own case. Nick knew this, and he resolutely believed in me and worked for relative peanuts to win justice. He said he would get his firm's fee from the settlement. I was very worried about what it would mean for me, but felt I had to fight for my songs.

After a final day in court, my barrister won. I was so relieved. The whole of the Seabreeze/Sunburst scenario was finally over. I was awarded all of my copyrights back for the total cost of, I think, one penny. Ian Gillan has always praised me for being the only one to go back to John Coletta and win. Years later the subject also came up in a car journey with Ian Paice. By then we were able to joke about how little money we had earned, although when Ian innocently mentioned the wages he negotiated, I let out a loud sigh: it was far more than the rest of us ever earned. But by then it was all long in the past and, to be honest, Ian was worth every penny he was given, and the same goes for Jon Lord – although I suspect he too never earned as much as Ian either.

David Coverdale had always said to take care of myself, and I suppose that I could have done it better. But although I might have been naive, as were most of the other guys, the fact is that Coletta was just a really bad manager – for me. He was greedy, had little morality, and wasn't creative in the slightest. I've discussed it with Iron Maiden's Adrian Smith, and we both believe that if Whitesnake had been managed as well as Maiden, we could have been as successful as Queen.

Nick Kanaar advised me to go to court again, this time to claim my earnings, the unpaid song-writing income over the Whitesnake years, but I had had enough. I was out of it at last, and I was now free to sign my whole Whitesnake catalogue to a new publisher, where I would at last receive my royalties. At last, I had some money and I believed I was free from financial problems. But I was wrong to feel so positive. There was another mess to come, and this one really upset me.

Concert Publishing, and by extension London's Pride, was in serious trouble, although I didn't know quite how badly it was going for them. John Lyons and John Collins received a cheque from Nick Kanaar's office for a very decent amount of money, and made out to me. I was ecstatic when they told me – this was the first real income I had ever seen from my work with Whitesnake. I was expecting smiling faces in the office, but the room was very sombre.

The Johns explained to me that things were very bad at Concert Publishing and that cash flow was zero. They needed money, and they needed it fast. Suddenly, and at a crucial time for them, they received Nick Kanaar's cheque or, to be ac-curate, my cheque. They asked me if I would loan them the money, and guaranteed they would pay me back with interest as soon as they were in credit. Well, what could I do? These were the very people that had picked me up, both mentally and financially, when I was at my lowest and they were asking for my help. I said 'Yes,' and they promised they would only need it about a month. A month went by, and then another, and I saw absolutely nothing. Oh dear, I had done it again.

London's Pride totally defaulted on my loan, and the result was I walked away from their operation. A very upset John Collins asked if I thought he was another John Coletta. 'At least Coletta didn't pretend to be my friend,' I said. I could see that this hurt him.

On many occasions these days at gigs, parents with musical kids who want to go into the industry ask me for advice. For me it goes back to signing a contract, with reading it properly, or reading it at all. That I didn't back in the day was my fault, nobody else's. I have a somewhat glib answer for mums and dads now, although it is true. I tell them if their kids wish to succeed in the music business, they should train as a lawyer.

During this very shaky time, I received a call from Duran Duran guitarist Andy Taylor. He asked to meet at a studio in north London, Swanyard Studios, not far from the Concert Publishing office. I arrived, guitar case in my hand, and was impressed from the start by smart glass doors opening into a very plush reception. The studio, a former dairy, was newly converted and very glam indeed. There were lots of busy people buzzing around, and superb equipment installed almost everywhere I looked. This was all looking good, except that there was no Andy Taylor. I waited in reception, was given a coffee, and treated very well. After a long while, an enigmatic, very good-looking blonde lady arrived. She had a very piercing voice that I can still hear to this day. She looked over, instantly dismissing me, and continued into her office. It was a memorable introduction to Margarita Penelope Hamilton, owner and CEO of Swanyard Inc. She was wearing about two thousand pounds' worth of clothes, and the same amount again in jewellery – and this was in 1988.

Andy finally arrived wearing a sharp suit and introduced himself. He was very much the pop star, but affable and friendly. We went into the studio, where he played me a couple of songs which I liked a lot. He wanted me to write and play on his forthcoming solo album. I was very taken with this little man (I can say that: he is shorter than me!). We talked as if we had known one another for years, which I suppose, reputation-wise, we had. Within fifteen minutes he had sold the plan to me, sealing the deal when he told me that we would be working with none other than Bernard Edwards. He was the bass player and producer on the very successful Power Station album that Andy had recorded with Robert Palmer. That was it for me. When could we start? I was very excited.

The top floor of the Swanyard building was a production suite decked out with computers, small recording systems, and a self-contained demo studio. Jazzie B was a regular visitor, putting Soul II Soul tracks together. Andy and I stayed for a few days, checking out each other, really, and we got on very well. He was a very amusing guy with lots of Duran Duran tales although, in truth, I had no sense of just how big Duran Duran were until I happened to be on a train to London a few days after our meeting. Opposite me sat a gang of girls, prob-ably in their early twenties. They saw my guitar case and asked me if I was famous – that hurt a little bit. Then I told them I was working and writing with Andy Taylor, and they almost passed out.

By the second week of the sessions, Andy and I were getting some decent stuff together, and putting the recordings on a cassette for Margarita. Several times during the day, her driver, Tim, would pop his head into the studio to listen. One after-noon he spoke to me. 'I seen you at Hammersmith, Bernie, ain't I?' Proper Londoner. He was a nice guy.

What I didn't know was that Andy Taylor was telling Margarita that all the new stuff was his, and that he was playing the guitar parts. He basically neglected to tell her that I was there at all. Driver Tim put her right about my identity.

'Why didn't you tell me who you were?' Margarita screamed when she saw me next.

'Well, you never asked,' I told her in a quiet voice.

'Bastard!' She roared with laughter, and motioned for me to follow her into her office. She then told me that the songs I was working on were for a film she was producing called *Runaway Dreams*. It was currently in production in Florida. Hmm … I thought, not an Andy Taylor album, after all. She was not happy with the situation: Andy was working on his own solo album in her studio while simultaneously writing tracks with me for the soundtrack.

I was very keen to work with Bernard Edwards, and I felt that this was as close as I was ever going to get to the man behind Chic. A compromise was reached: I would continue with the Duran Duran star on his solo album, but I was given the go-ahead to be the composer for Margarita's movie.

To record Andy's album, we relocated to studios in the middle of the Oxfordshire town Chipping Norton, with pubs and markets close by; it was very quaintly English. This was where Alaska had recorded demos. Swanyard engineer Spencer Henderson was sent to work with us, and I met keyboard player Simon Webb, who is now a good friend of mine. He was a fine musician who had been involved with Andy for a couple of months.

The legend that was Bernard Edwards was a joy to be with. He had so many tales, especially from his time with Nile Rodgers, and I told him that Whitesnake had carried tapes of Chic all over the world: he laughed at that a lot. He was a larger-than-life figure – and what a musician. I always called him Bernard, and he called me B. Once I got to know him I asked a question that had long been on my mind.

'Bernard, how do you make a Chic record?' I asked.

He grinned and said, 'B., you have been making records a long time: how do you make yours?'

So when I told him, he laughed out even louder.

'Well Mr M., that's how we made Chic records too!'

He paid me a great compliment when I was overdubbing some guitar fills. The engineer Spencer Henderson asked him at what point he should drop in during the track to begin recording. Bernard looked at him: 'Spencer, record every damn thing this man plays.' I felt good, very good. In all the time I worked with Bernard, both in London and in Oxfordshire, I always looked up to him. To me, he was a consummate player and producer, and it was only after we lost the great man that I found out he was younger than me – he always seemed like the grown-up.

Andy was somewhat absent from the sessions but always said that we should carry on, and that we didn't really need him. In fact, I don't think he ever played a guitar solo on anything we recorded. Drummers came and went at a great rate. Simple Minds' Mel Gaynor was there for a day or so, and David Palmer from ABC lasted an afternoon. They all played very well but Andy wanted a certain sound, and that was to arrive a few days later, when Bernard took me to one side and told me that Chic drummer Tony Thompson was coming into the studio. I was so excited. I was going to be playing with the Chic rhythm section – I was about to become Nile Rodgers! Tony was a very cool and dapper guy in a sharp suit, fedora and sunglasses. He was funny, too. Bernard introduced us.

We got stuck in, and recorded a song of mine. (That's another one I should rescue from the archive.) In all we spent about a year working but Andy's album never saw the light of day. The only tangible result was a track on the *Tequila Sunrise* movie soundtrack. I didn't mind because, thanks to Andy, I had worked with Bernard Edwards and Tony Thompson, and what an honour it was to be in their company.

Margarita Hamilton pretty much became my manager after those sessions. I continued to work on her soundtrack and returned to the Swanyard studios, where her movie *Runaway Dreams* soon became known as 'Runaway Budgets'! I wrote most of the music and hired a bunch of really talented players: Jimmy Copley, Jaz Lochrie, Simon Webb, and two really good singers, Kipper and Chris Thompson. We recorded with a very good engineer called John Lee. The resulting soundtrack and the songs sounded pretty good, and Margarita was very happy with the results.

The film was premiered at the prestigious Deauville Film Festival in France.

After some problems in Florida with the soundtrack we were booked into a suite at Pinewood Studios to redub the whole sound. It must have cost a fortune. It's a shame the film was so bad as the actors worked so hard. At least it sounded good ...

I was very unexpectedly recommended to Cliff Richard's live band in 1989. David Bryce of his management team called me at The Dungeon on the advice of Malcolm Hill, my mate at EMI, as ever looking out for me. Cliff's team had been talking about how they might revamp his sound, and they thought it would be a good idea to introduce a hard-rock feel. David Bryce's idea was for me to be the bandleader and songwriter in the vein of Richard Marx, a very popular singer of the time. I was seen as leftfield in terms of where Cliff Richard's image was, and that appealed to David Bryce.

Margarita Hamilton thought this suggestion was utterly crazy and advised me very strongly to have nothing to do with it at all. This, of course, made me call David Bryce immediately to say OK and confirm a meeting. EMI flew Malcolm and I out to a very wet Paris to see Cliff play a live show during his *Stronger* tour. The rain was pouring so hard that we first had to go out and buy new clothes, before heading to the Zenith arena to meet the tour manager for our 'access all areas' passes. We wandered backstage.

I could tell there was a certain amount of surprise at my appearance from those around Cliff Richard, and a lot of eyes were watching me. I could feel a bit of an uneasy vibe – why the hell is this ex-Whitesnake guitarist at a Cliff Richard gig? I watched the show with Malcolm and made mental notes of just how many changes there needed to be. I could see that a lot would need to be done if David Bryce's idea was to come to fruition. I met Cliff for dinner that same night. While I sat next to his sister, Cliff and I spoke about the music business, my time in Whitesnake, me as a songwriter, and it was actually a very pleasant evening. I told him I'd pass on my thoughts to David Bryce and that I'd see him back in England.

Back in the UK, David Bryce called to brief me on rehearsals at Bray Studios and sent me some cassettes with some new material and some old songs that were to be retained in the set. Among the songs was 'Carrie', which I rearranged into what can only be called a classic Whitesnake/Bad Company vibe. I arrived at Bray Studios in my Porsche 911, which didn't go down very well with the crew. It was immediately obvious that the previous line-up of band and crew had been close, which I could understand. You might already have guessed that David Bryce hadn't told the rest of the band that there were going to be additions to the line-up and there was an air of resentment that things were changing. Another new boy was former Kajagoogoo bass player Nick Beggs, who I already knew from EMI.

During the first few days of rehearsals Cliff wasn't there, and the keyboard player, who was clearly the bandleader, kicked off by giving me some sheet music. I looked at him and asked him what it was for. I told him exactly what we were going to do – we were going to play the new version of 'Carrie'. He was somewhat confused by my approach and there was quite an unpleasant atmosphere, bordering on a standoff. Damn, I could hear Margarita in my ear, screaming already.

Fortunately, David Bryce arrived later in the afternoon and did a pretty good job of smoothing things over. We did play 'Carrie' and a couple of other tunes I had worked on from the cassettes Bryce had given me. He told me later on in the afternoon that, as part of the new band, I would have to play some of the classics too. I could hear Margarita's voice again in my head, but by now I was in the band and I just had to get on with it.

The sound guys played a few tricks during the rehearsals by introducing an echo in the monitor system. It really messed with Nick Beggs, and I felt pretty strongly, telling them to stop playing around with Nick's career. That further distanced me from most of the crew. They perceived me as a rock star with a Porsche who shouldn't really be there. On reflection, this was probably true.

By the end of the third day, people were coming into the rehearsal room from other rooms to check us out. It must have sounded so different. Cliff at last joined us and I have to say, it was a great personal thrill for me to play guitar on 'The Young Ones', standing next to Cliff Richard.

We enjoyed a full day and, as far as I was concerned, it was sounding fine and it was plain to see that Cliff liked it. Over the next couple of days, his entire management team came to see what we had been up to. As we played 'Carrie', I could see the mouths dropping one by one, all except for David Bryce's. We would speed through anything outside of the classic numbers, and the faces of the management became increasingly dour. The gig I'd seen in Paris stayed on my mind. I realised that there were between three and four thousand people in the crowd at the Zenith, and at least three-quarters of them were British. This was obviously the management's dilemma – Cliff Richard is a household name with very loyal fans in the UK, and I knew he was very popular in Australia, but not in many other countries. By including me as part of the so-called new 'rock regime', they could see his audience disappearing. Their grim expressions made sense.

By the last day of the rehearsals, I knew that the writing was on the wall. Cliff asked me to join him for a cup of tea on the side of the River Thames at Bray, where he explained how much he was enjoying the music but – aha, here was the 'but' – his management felt he was making too many changes, too soon. Shit, I thought – Margarita would have a field day. Cliff and I shook hands and, although he was very gracious and wished me well for the future, I must admit that I lost a little bit of respect for him in that moment. If I had thought something was so good, I'd have told my management that I wanted to give it a go. But, business-wise, I respected his decision.

I made a much more successful foray into another unfamiliar area in June that year, when Zak Starkey asked if I would like to play a gig with him and some friends of his in London. I almost didn't agree. Fran was due to give birth to our first daughter, Charlotte, and I didn't want to be away. But Fran had always loved Zak and encouraged me to go – she said the baby would understand!

When I arrived at the venue I could hear music already pounding out. I found Zak and he took me to meet world-famous tennis players Pat Cash and Vitas Gerulaitis. I soon realised I was surrounded by all the top tennis pros in the world, in London for the upcoming Wimbledon tournament. Pat was a big rock fan, particularly of the classic Whitesnake years. He was very friendly and gracious, and told me that it had been him who had asked Zak to call me.

Speaking to many of the younger players, I soon found out the vast majority of them were really into music and a significant number played instruments themselves: mostly guitars and drums. Vitas Gerulaitis was a lovely guy, played decent guitar, and really liked the Eagles. While I was there he got together with a group of other tennis players – the lone musician was Zak Starkey on drums – to play 'Hotel California'. Some of it was pretty good, some of it excruciating, but the worst part was that they couldn't seem to end the song, which went on, and on, and on. It was a day of great fun, nonetheless, and the gig that night was great.

The following year, the director of the Association of Tennis Professionals (ATP), Bob Green, asked me if I would put together a house band for the 'ATP Bash' that was always held in London at a venue before the Wimbledon championships. I was more than happy to do this, and ended up running the band for about five years. We always rehearsed at the Nomis studio in Shepherd's Bush for a gig at the Hard Rock Café. Passes for these shows were like gold dust and I was a very popular man at the time. I was keen to draw the band members from the tennis-playing world but, inevitably, a lot of musicians would show up as well.

At the 1991 show, a big bonus on the night was the arrival of half of the Allman Brothers Band. They were gigging in London that week, and it was here that I met Gregg Allman, Warren Haynes, the late bassist Allen Woody, and one of the original drummers, Jaimoe. Warren took me to one side and asked if it would be OK for him to use my rig as he thought it sounded the best. This meant that he'd take my place on stage. Other guitarists, who I will not name, were so embarrassingly desperate to be photographed onstage with Gregg Allman that I freely sacrificed my spot to accommodate Warren. He told me after the gig that we would get along very well as that was the kind of thing he would have done too. I'm still very close to him, and see him any time he comes over to the UK.

I finally did get to play with the Allman Brothers Band with Warren in New York at the Beacon Theatre in 2014: it was an extremely special night. I got to play 'One Way Out' with Jaimoe and Butch Trucks drumming, with Warren Haynes on one side and Derek Trucks on the other side … how much better does it get than that? After each night at The Beacon I would walk back to the hotel with Derek Trucks. That's a story I like to drop into conversation when I'm with other guitar players.

Over the years I spent organising the ATP bashes, I got to know a lot of the tennis players. I was quite the novelty for them, especially to the Americans who had grown up with 'Here I Go Again'. I had the likes of Jim Courier, Pat Cash, John McEnroe, Peter Lundgren and the rock'n'roll tennis brothers Luke and Murphy Jensen as band members. It was fun, and unlike anything I'd been a part of before.

Being this close to the ATP team made me one of the gang, and I was invited to various events with them. I had dinner at the Dorchester on the night of the ATP awards: this was particularly special. I sat a table with Ken Rosewall and Rod Laver, who were both very chatty and most interested in the fact that I was coaching players in guitar-playing. I was also given full access to all of Wimbledon, with an all-access ATP pass. Walking around Wimbledon at that time with Pat Cash was like having my own automatic door-opener – he even gave me a pass that said I was his coach!

In 1991 I was having lunch with John McEnroe, Jimmy Connors and Pat in the players' restaurant when Cliff Richard came in. I could immediately see Cliff's awkwardness, even two years after our unsuccessful pairing. He knew that he knew me, but in this setting he was clearly struggling for the detail. He walked down the aisle, smiling, and as he approached, I stood up to shake his hand.

'Hi, Cliff, Bernie Marsden, we had tea on the river at Bray, do you remember?' I gave him one hundred per cent recognisable information, just in case.

'Of course ...' he said, but his attention was elsewhere. 'How are you?' he asked, looking at all the tennis stars: Cliff Richard was a huge tennis fan. Then he spotted my pass. 'Coach of Pat Cash?' Now he looked very confused.

In time, I became disillusioned with the ATP gigs which, as the years passed, became much more orientated towards rock stars, and I didn't think that was the point. I loved my time playing with the tennis guys, and hanging out with them, but my time doing the ATP gigs had to come to an end. Bob Green retired from his post as the director, and I resigned as MD for the Bash Band.

I didn't entirely break contact with the tennis world and met up with Pat Cash again when I was in New York in 2010. He invited me to Flushing Meadows for the US Open. It was raining very hard that day and I wondered whether there would be any play. With my splendid ATP 'guest of Pat Cash' pass around my neck, I waited in the players' lounge. My phone buzzed, and a text from Pat informed me that there was not going to be any more play that day. The official announcement would be made in half an hour, and he advised me to get away as soon as I could before the crowds left and we would meet at his hotel. I got into an elevator. One floor down the doors opened and in walked ... Cliff Richard – we meet again! Dressed in a white suit, he was with some friends and hoping to see some tennis.

'Bernie, how are you?' he beamed. I could see him looking at my pass. Cliff's face was transfixed by my big ATP New York Open laminate. 'How did you get that?' he said, almost longingly.

We exchanged pleasantries, and I told him that play was suspended and passed on Pat's advice to get out of Flushing Meadows as soon as he could. We ran into each other again at the cab rank, and no doubt I'll find him again sometime at another ATP event – I think we're probably due to meet again soon.

I do look back at those ATP days with great love and I made some terrific memories. Seeing world-class sportsmen having fun thrashing a drum kit, slapping bass guitar, or rocking out on an electric guitar was great fun. I remember John McEnroe's tongue half hanging out as he attacked a blues solo, and Pat Cash by his side always looked the complete rock star. Pat's playing is more than fine, by the way – much better than my first serve, I can assure you. I was happy just to be another ex-rock star at those gigs playing a few songs.

I returned to the music world when I started the Moody Marsden Band in 1990. Us reconnecting had been the most positive thing to come out of doing the *Runaway Dreams* sessions. We had both realised that we should put a band together. Without any doubt, Micky and I had a profound understanding of each other's playing. No less a person than Thin Lizzy main man Phil Lynott, backstage at Hammersmith Odeon after a Whitesnake show, said that he wished his guitarists would play together like we did – praise indeed (he did use much more colourful language).

Margarita was excited about the new project. I called Zak Starkey and he was immediately up for the gig, and bass player Jaz Lochrie also agreed to join. Gigs were soon in the book. We played mainly blues and covers, with some classic Whitesnake songs thrown in to please the crowd. The band was incredibly powerful. Zak Starkey – later with Oasis and still now with The Who – was an utterly brilliant drummer by that time. I loved to tease him about the Tittenhurst Park days when I saw him leaving for school when he was a teenager. By the time he joined my band he was married with a daughter of his own.

I had expected to go into the Swanyard Studios to record, but the truth was that we didn't have nearly enough material to justify recording. I suggested a live album and Margarita agreed. We had a gig coming up in Bristol, and made a plan to record it, and then stay at Margarita's home. She lived only half an hour away, at Walton Castle – yes, a real castle. We eventually recorded two gigs – one in Bristol and one in Dudley. The Bristol recording came out really well and Tony Platt took charge of the mixing. That album still sounds very good today. We had one new song in the set, 'Never Turn My Back on the Blues'. Was this a subliminal message, perhaps? The crowd were very loud, and we had a very good gig.

Zak Starkey and Jaz Lochrie were the first of many to pass through the band. We never did record a studio album for Swanyard, as by the time we were ready for it Margarita and I had drifted apart, although we didn't ever fall out. The truth was, I wasn't easy to manage. I know what I want, and I do my own thing. But Swanyard had been a great place to work and Margarita in particular was a superb help to me. She put me in a much better place than I had been when I first met her during the Andy Taylor sessions. I'm very thankful to her.

In 1991 we were due to play at the Cambridge Corn Exchange with Otis Grand and the Dance Kings. We were the opening act, added late to the bill, but we helped to shift a load of tickets. For reasons unknown Otis Grand pulled out of the gig and I walked into the backstage area to be met by a smiling Steve Marriot. Steve and his band Packet of Three were the replacement act. I was delighted. I had always been a very big fan of Steve, and we both knew bass player Jimmy Leverton – Micky had played with him in Juicy Lucy. There was a short discussion about stage times, Steve assumed we were headlining, but I assumed he was and I won that discussion.

We played our set to a pretty full room, and were very well received. A few songs in, people began to shout out for Whitesnake songs. Micky told them that we didn't play that stuff any more, that it was a past life and they were at the wrong gig. This was perhaps not the best way to word it. We ended our set and there was lots of applause, but I had heard more than a few more moans for Whitesnake songs.

Steve was ready to go on, I wished him good luck and he gave me a strange look. I dismissed it. He went onstage and performed brilliantly, playing his blond Gibson 335 through a small Marshall rig, creating a lovely guitar tone, and sang with that fantastic voice. I watched the show on the side of the stage, soaking up every note. Steve played the most exquisite blues I had heard in years on the Eddie Boyd song 'Five Long Years'. He chatted to the audience and made self-deprecating jokes about his age, the loss of his hair, that type of thing, but when he went into 'Thirty Days in the Hole' from Humble Pie I felt a shiver down my spine and as far as I was concerned, at that point in time he was better than ever, regardless of any hair loss. I was riveted by this performance. He continued with 'All or Nothing', the classic Small Faces song. Before I knew it, the tears were streaming down my face. I watched him perform, with incredible passion and commitment, a song he must have played a thousand times.

Steve ended the set and said, 'Thank you,' and looked at me, steely-eyed, ringing wet, before heading for the dressing room.

'Steve, that was fantastic, such soul, great delivery, you were fantastic, mate, the crowd loved every minute of it.' Expecting a thank-you, I waited for his response, and he tore into me something vicious.

'Where were the fuckin' Whitesnake songs in your set, Bernie boy?' I was silent. 'You owe those songs to your punters, you twat, they fuckin' made you!'

I felt about thirteen years old, being told off by my teacher. Steve had been watching us play covers and, in his opinion, being rude to the audience. The penny had dropped. It was then that he thanked me for my comments about his own gig.

'Come and have a drink,' he said laughing his head off. 'This bollocking is over, Bern.'

Steve Marriot was right, and he opened my eyes just at the right time.

We arranged a meeting in London, when he was due to play Dingwall's, and he told me to take my guitar with me so we could play some blues together. Then came the terrible news that Steve had been killed in a fire at his house. What a man, what a musician, what a loss.

The Moody Marsden Band went on to play throughout Europe, and we went down very well. I had a call from a friend of mine in Norway, where blues music is huge, who had been speaking to the Hell Blues Festival committee. This particular Hell is a small town about twenty miles from Trondheim, and they asked if I would put a band together for their inaugural event in September 1993. We played an acoustic session in the afternoon at the Rica Hotel, Hell, playing Whitesnake, some blues, and a new song Micky and I had written for the festival, called '2000 Miles Back to Hell'. The show was recorded, and I'm so glad it was, as it was very special. Mick and I were very well received, and we were both made official 'ambassadors of Hell' and were presented with official documents from the mayor of Hell himself.

I have been associated with the festival ever since, playing it many times as it has grown. Peter Green played there in 1997, arriving after Gary Moore had played the night before. I had asked Gary to stay an extra day in Hell and, to everyone's delight, he did. I already had a great band – dubbed the Hell Blues Band '97, made up of Colin Hodgkinson on bass, Henry Spinetti on drums, Mark Feltham on harmonica, the irrepressible Tony Ashton, and myself, with Mr Peter Green sitting in the audience. Most people had seen Peter and expected him to be the surprise guest. I knew that was never going to happen, but when I brought my old friend Mr Moore out the packed crowd in the Rica Hotel went mad. He was on stage with me for over an hour, smiling, very happy and, of course, played astonishingly well. Gary never let me down.

Another Hell Blues Band included Jon Lord, with Miller Anderson on guitar, Colin Hodgkinson again on bass and the great Chris Farlowe on vocals. The last song of the set was Chris Farlowe's big hit 'Out of Time', and the crowd loved it. We went backstage and could clearly hear the crowd cheering for more. Chris laughed their enthusiasm off, and suggested that nothing could top what we'd just done. Jon Lord looked at me, winked and in that unmistakeable voice said, 'Oh, I do believe we can, Chris.'

I knew what was coming. Jon strode out onto the stage to a great reaction – people really loved him – and played some devastating solo stuff on the Hammond organ. He then went into the 'Smoke on the Water' riff. Cue total pandemonium in the hall. The Lord was in control, again. The next day in the bus on the way to the airport he looked at me and said, 'Great ending last night, Bern.'

A remarkable man named John Jackson played a town bar show in that festival. Born in 1924, John was a player of Piedmont blues, a sweet, fingerpicking, troubadour style. He was an absolute master, a joy to listen to and watch. His very strong Virginian accent accented words with extra syllables – 'Bernie' would be 'Ber-n-i-e'. I was in the audience during his set and there were a couple of very rowdy tables close to mine. Norwegians do like their beer, and as he played, the noise increased. At last I had to go over and ask them to let John play his gig. The table – about eight men and a few women – looked at me like I was the crazy one, but at last they dropped the volume. I was later told that my esteem in Hell grew even more as I had chastised the festival's biggest sponsors.

I saw John later, and he thanked me very much, drawling that they had been getting on his neves ('ner-ve-es'). I played John's treasured 1950s' Gibson J50 that afternoon. He called the guitar 'Standby' because it was always with him. A couple of his friends had liberated it from a pawnshop for fifty dollars in the 1960s when John needed to go back out on the road.

I had the pleasure of him visiting my house when he was in the UK. He played a 1930s' Gibson guitar, singing songs to my daughter Charlotte, who was about eight years old at the time. He was amazing, and she was captivated. We stayed in touch, until I got the sad news that he passed away, in early 2002. Try to find his records on the Arhoolie label, or listen online. You won't be disappointed. I remember him with great affection: his smile, his stories and above all his infectious goodwill.

Paul Oscher sat next to me on an early morning flight after one of the Hell festivals when he played with remnants of the Muddy Waters Band. He had first played with Waters in 1967, was a first-class harmonica player and did a perfect imitation of Muddy Waters' slide guitar style. Paul and I got to talk about the legendary Muddy Waters. Paul was the first white musician ever to play in his band, which gives you an idea of just how good he must have been aged eighteen. As we talked he complained about their drummer, who had been so late that morning that the band had almost missed the flight.

We all had to get a connecting flight and my seat was next to the drummer who had so annoyed Paul Oscher, this was the amazing Willie 'Big Eyes' Smith. I had a ball listening to Willie's wonderful stories about Muddy and Howlin' Wolf. I told him I was a guitar player and he told me all about Hubert Sumlin, Pat Hare, Willie Johnson, and Buddy Guy. Each name was a piece of treasure – the man was a goldmine of blues tales and glorious anecdotes. It was easy to see how much he loved Muddy Waters. Willie Smith had recorded well over fifty sides with the man. He gave me his business card, and told me that should I ever need a drummer in Chicago to call him up. He said he was pleased to see a fresh face and get away from the bands, adding, 'Sometimes I get frustrated, man. I hate waitin' on people: today I almost missed the plane because of Paul Oscher being so fuckin' late!'

There are two sides to every story.

Speaking of Hubert Sumlin, in 2017 I was in Anaheim, Los Angeles for the NAMM music show, a yearly gathering of musical instrument dealers, makers, players. It is trade only. I was there as a PRS guitars endorser. I was walking around the vast building when I literally nearly ran into none other than Hubert Sumlin. He was in good form, he was part of the Fender entourage, and was wearing a blue and red suit that had 'That's Right' on the lapels, and the back of the jacket was the emblazoned 'I Ain't Done Yet'. He was very friendly, and very easy to talk too.

Then something happened that you couldn't even rehearse. Paul Reed Smith called me at that moment on the mobile phone, and my ringtone at the time was 'Smokestack Lightning' by Howlin' Wolf, with Hubert Sumlin playing guitar! Hubert looked totally shocked.

'Where's that comin' from?' he said.

I explained to Hubert that it was the ringtone, and he wanted to hear it again. I asked Paul to ring me again so the great Hubert Sumlin could hear himself as a mobile ring tone. He was delighted. 'I wonder what Wolf would make o' that!'

I spent a few minutes with Hubert Sumlin, thanked him for 'Going Down Slow', to which he replied that I was not the first one to say thank you for that. 'Eric Clapton an' Keith Richards like that one a lot, too,' he said with a smile.

I had another interesting Norwegian airborne encounter one cold morning in 1990, when I arrived fairly late for a flight from Gatwick to Oslo. I used to fly a lot with a family company called Braathens Airways because they tended to let passengers sit where they liked. I rushed my way onto the plane as quickly as I could. Seeing as I was so late, I was surprised to see that the first row had a vacant seat. I happily sat down next to a very attractive lady who had some packages on the seat next to her. She said, 'Good morning,' and we chatted politely. I pointed to the packages on the seat, and asked if she had been shopping for Christmas presents in London. She said that she had. I asked her where she had been staying, to which she replied with family and friends. I asked if she lived in Oslo to which she replied, 'Most of the time.'

Just then, a very tall and robust man appeared in the aisle next to me. 'I'm sorry sir, but Her Highness's lady-in-waiting has to sit there.' He pointed at my seat.

'Pardon?' I said.

'Would you mind sitting a couple of rows further down?' he said very politely. I had been chatting to Sonja Haraldsen, better known as the Crown Princess of Norway, who would later become Queen Sonja of Norway. She was very nice.

Between Hell and Moody Marsden, I had other projects to keep me busy. In 1994, I recorded and self-produced the album *Green and Blues*, a tribute to the guitarists John Mayall hired and the musicians who had given me so much as a young player: Clapton, Green and Taylor. I went to Battery Studios, London, where John Lee Hooker was recording at the time, with Tony Platt at the desk. Horns came from the guys in Gary Moore's Midnight Blues Band. They enjoyed the session so much that when they next rehearsed with Gary he was inspired to respond with his very successful *Blues for Greeny* album. This came out in 1995 and as a result (as he was a big star) I held my record back so it didn't look like I was jumping on Gary's bandwagon. So we held the album back for a few months. I played it to Peter Green to see what he thought of it, and he said quite nonchalantly, 'sounds like Fleetwood Mac'. Well that was praise enough for me – although I don't think he intended it that way!

I made my own personal pilgrimage to the home of the blues in 1995. For many years I had been reading about 'blues field trips'. This was when people, whether in a group or alone, go in search of the blues – stories, guitars, records, and even players themselves. These journeys were usually pretty academic, and so I decided to have me a field trip. I flew to Nashville and stayed with my old mate Graham Nolder, part of the old Deep Purple management team, and one of the good guys. I hired a white Ford, and was soon on my way to Memphis on my own, with the radio blasting out on the blues station. I found my way through Memphis onto Elvis Presley Boulevard and passed Graceland, by this time a hugely popular tourist attraction.

I drove onwards to Mississippi and thought about all the books on the real Mississippi blues I had been reading night after night back home. I was excited to go to the places I had been reading about for years. I was soon on the fabled Highway 61 and had Bob Dylan's great song in my mind. It was a special experience for a lifelong blues guitarist, and all the places featured in all the songs were now on the road signs ahead of me. It was magic.

Driving down Route 61 out of Memphis I saw the sign for Helena, Arkansas, where the *King Biscuit Hour* radio show with Sonny Boy Williamson was broadcast. Soon after that I saw a sign for Robinsonville, now in Mississippi, the birthplace of Robert Johnson. I had Johnson cassettes with me and could not resist putting the great man on the car stereo. But, as I pulled the Ford into Robinsonville I was a little disappointed. I was probably the only person in the town that day trying to find the house of Ike Zimmerman, the man who taught Robert Johnson to play. I never did find it or the street Johnson was born in: Robert Johnson's Robinsonville was long gone. I cranked up some Memphis Minnie in the car as I approached her home town, Walls.

Blues man 'Honeyboy' Edwards had known Memphis Minnie and later told me that she was as good as any man playing the guitar and could sing incredibly well. He was a huge fan of hers. The English blues singer and guitarist Jo Ann Kelly had been a big fan of Memphis Minnie's work, and in the 1960s played benefit gigs in the UK for the ailing blues singer who was living on a meagre income in very old age.

I was very excited as I drove the very dusty Ford into Clarksdale – the real home of the blues. Muddy Waters, John Lee Hooker, and Ike Turner were all local blues men, and Robert Johnson and Howling Wolf had played the street corners in the 1930s. It was starting to get dark as I drove into the town, and I needed to find a hotel. I stopped to fill the car with fuel, and waited for a few moments as the fast-approaching night came in. This was my first-ever trip to Mississippi, and I would go back many times afterwards, recording, and even making a film, but this first time in '95 I was more than a little nervous.

I made for the Uptown Inn to stay overnight. A storm was brewing, and I could see lightning flashes. On the TV in my room all the local TV news stations were warning about the weather. It hit town at 1.30 in the morning and was truly torrential. Rain cascaded down the roof of the motel, the traffic lights outside my window were swinging wildly, and trees were bending thirty per cent of their height in the middle of crashing thunder and violent lightning. Clarksdale was at the centre of a very big storm.

By about 3.15 the storm had subsided but I was awakened again, this time by loud shouting. I pushed a chair against the door of my room, and looked out of a crack in the curtain to see three police cars not fifty feet away from my room, their lights flashing, and officers with their guns drawn and seemingly pointed in my direction. I dropped to the floor between the bed and the wall and I wondered in that moment what the hell I was doing there. I was picturing the headline, 'Ex-Whitesnake guitarist shot dead in Mississippi'. I was a dedicated blues fan, I know, or I was a nutter …

The man they were actually after was a few rooms down from me and eventually gave himself up. He was bundled into the cop car. I checked the chair against my door handle and got back into bed. I turned the TV on for a little while and after a couple of minutes *Are You Being Served?* came on. Can you believe it? I'm in the heart of the delta with a tornado and a potential gun battle and Mrs Slocombe is on the telly arguing with Captain Peacock. It was surreal.

I met one of the policemen the following morning in town and he told me what had happened. A 'lady of the night' had been using a room at the hotel for her work, and there had been an altercation with her client. Supposedly shots had been fired, but I must have slept through that. He told me to be careful in Clarksdale, he was eyeing my new Nikon camera. 'That is a lot of crack money around here,' he said. 'Be careful round here.'

I planned to take my camera into the old part of town, under the railroad and into the old quarter of Issaquena Avenue. This was the site of barrelhouses in the 1930s, where black people would gather to drink, play music, dance, and gamble. The policeman was very concerned about me visiting what was by 1995 being called Crack Alley. I could drive but taking photos would be too risky.

Visiting the street was like being transported back in time. It seemed as if nothing had changed since the Twenties and Thirties. The Roxy Theatre still stood, empty and roofless, but with a presence. It was fascinating, but I didn't stop or get out of the car. I drove around the street a couple of times, trying to film shaky video and trying to take photos on the move with the Nikon.

I had been given an idea of what relations were like between the communities. At breakfast in a café had been three men, all over seventy, all white, complaining in very racist tones about their black employees and how slow they were getting

214

their farms cleaned up after the storm. I was quite shocked but had the sense to hold my tongue. This was Mississippi. It could have been a scene from *In the Heat of the Night*.

I headed to Tutweiler, the birthplace of Sonny Boy Williamson. Once more I overheard incredibly racist comments, this time from a gas station owner. And yet, when I asked where the memorial was, the man went on about how famous Sonny Boy was. He was very proud of the bluesman, which didn't make sense to me given his previous racist comments. I went on to Itta Bena, the hometown of BB King. I arrived with 'Lucille' playing on the radio and the little town looked like a scene from a blues LP cover I'd bought when I was a kid. I left it feeling better than I had after my visit to the other towns.

I have some good friends in Mississippi these days. I once played a Saturday night show at Clarksdale's Ground Zero blues club, owned by Morgan Freeman – he was dancing in the aisles. I had lunch there the next day with Morgan and town mayor Bill Luckett. I also made a documentary in the state, *A Day in the Delta*, a labour of love that is still unreleased. I was last in Mississippi in 2016, and Clarksdale has changed a lot since my first visit in 1995. It's part of the established blues trail now, and I met fans who knew me from England, Norway, France, and Germany; they were all delighted to see me in the home of the blues.

The Delta came to England – to Buckingham in fact – in emphatic style the year after my own trip to Mississippi in 1995. I was backstage one day, leafing through a copy of *Blues in Britain*, and was astonished to read an ad for blues player David 'Honeyboy' Edwards playing at my old town hall. I knew he had been part of the Fleetwood Mac *Blues Jam at Chess* double album, but had thought he probably wasn't still with us by that point and certainly not in my local area. I swiftly offered to introduce him at the gig, much to the relief of promoter Graham Sharp, who told me that ticket sales so far had not been as good as they hoped.

My first sight of the eighty-one-year-old bluesman was as he strode up the stairs of the town hall on the day of the show. I had taken a bottle of whiskey as a gift and was standing two feet away from the man who had played throughout Mississippi and Tennessee with the likes of Charley Patton, Tommy Johnson, 'Big Joe' Williams, and Johnny Shines, and was close friends with the one and only Robert Johnson.

Honeyboy was a small man. He wore a baseball cap, coloured socks, pressed trousers, and brown leather brogue shoes. He was quite dapper. 'How ya doin', Danny?' he said to me, flashing a smile and revealing some gold teeth work. Someone said my name was Bernie. He was a little hard of hearing.

In the evening I was pleased to see that, in the end, the room was full, and I could tell that there were some serious blues lovers in the audience. My job was to say a few words about this old man for those who had been born long after he was in his prime. Did they know that Alan Lomax, the historical field-recordist, had captured Honeyboy in Clarksdale in 1940? Lomax had then asked Honeyboy if he could suggest anyone else. Honeyboy pointed him south to Rolling Fork, and a young blues singer called McKinley Morganfield – better known as Muddy Waters.

After my introduction Honeyboy came out to play a semi-acoustic Gibson through a Fender amp. His hands moved over the fretboard a little slower and he was not as smooth as his old recordings, but it was still Mississippi blues. I was quite emotional, watching this grand old man playing and singing his heart and soul out. The crowd soon realised they were witnessing something real, the real deal. The lighting was poor, but it strangely added to the performance. In any case, the sound was very good, his voice was haunting, it was real folk blues, delta blues in Buckingham. Afterwards he signed my 1926 acoustic Martin guitar. He looked back at his signature and smiled. 'That's my name,' he said with pride in his eyes. There were a few tears in mine. He enjoyed playing my guitar – and the fact that it was nine years younger than him.

Graham Sharp said I should play something myself. Honeyboy had no idea who I was or even that I was a guitarist at all. I sat next to the veteran bluesman and started tearing out some finger-style blues licks. His face lit up, his white and gold teeth gleaming. 'Danny, you son of a bitch, hell, you can play that thing!' He was very funny and extremely animated. He shouted to Dave Peabody, his guitar player, 'Lookee here – Danny playin' the blues!'

Dave smiled, and told Honeyboy all about me, which I can honestly say meant very little to him. But he did like my guitar playing and that was more than enough for me. 'Damn sure you got the blues,' said the man who played with Robert Johnson.

The next day I took him for a drive in my aging racing-green Jaguar XJ6. He was convinced it was worth sixty thousand dollars and nothing could convince him otherwise. I was surprised when he asked to see churchyards, but that was his thing – he loved old churches, the smaller the better. We finished our tour in the old churchyard in Hunter Street, Buckingham, in the centre of town, where I watched him happily hunting for really old gravestones. It had been a very memorable thirty-six hours, and watching him play his blues was astonishing. I get chills, still, just thinking about it. I took photos of him in his hotel room, and in the car park with the much-admired Jaguar and promised to take him copies when I was next in the USA.

The following year I did visit him in Chicago, and he really took me to places I could not have ever gone without him. Along the way he told me some outrageous stories about

Robert Johnson, Memphis Minnie, Big Joe Williams, and so much about Chicago when that city was the electric blues centre of the universe. We kept in touch, and I always saw him in England at his gigs. I was at Newbury once where I found a pile of posters in a gig office, got him to sign them, and sold them for fifteen pounds each that night. He was amazed when I gave him the cash. Even at the age of ninety-two he was still full of energy, flashing those gold teeth, shaking my hand, and eagerly accepting another bottle of whiskey to take home. He retired not long after and in 2011 he died at the age of ninety-seven. He always did call me Danny – he must have wondered who the Bernie Marsden was on the CD that I left for him in Chicago, but he was the man that walked and played the streets with Robert Johnson, and he could call me anything he wanted. Danny misses you!

Alongside my other projects, the Moody Marsden Band continued to gig across Europe in the 1990s. Don Airey played some gigs with us, as did bass player Peter Stroud, drummer John Trotter, great pianist Geraint Watkins, Tony Ashton, and ace drummer Terry Williams from Dire Straits. On a 1995 tour, we even had the old Whitesnake player Dave Dowle join us to play, which was an absolute delight. We played an open-air street festival in Berne, Switzerland, to about ten thousand people. We had a great line-up: Zak Starkey on drums, Steve Price from the reformed Bad Company on bass, his wife, Monica Reed, singing. Such a fantastic array of musicians played with the MM Band over the years, and it's only writing this down now that I see how high the quality of playing really was.

The headliner in Berne was an American band called Great White. I didn't know a thing about them, except that they were fairly obnoxious backstage. We played at about seven in the evening, and by now we included a lot of Whitesnake in the set. Those songs were always huge crowd-pleasers. We ended with 'Fool For Your Loving' and 'Slow and Easy,' and the crowd always made a hell of a noise as they sang along. We finished the set, waved our goodbyes and went off-stage. We didn't know that the Great White camp had been trying to get us off for about fifteen minutes. Oops. There were huge rows going on backstage.

'Why are they playing fuckin' Whitesnake?' they screamed at our German tour manager.

The manager was a very cool guy. 'Well, that would be because they wrote the songs.' Great White were quite shocked, by all accounts. Meanwhile, the crowd was still screaming for an encore and the promoter was very clear that we hadn't run over time. We returned to the stage and played 'Here I Go Again'. The crowd erupted. Great White and all concerned were fuming backstage. Our driver told us all later that he took great pleasure in seeing their fury. Thousands of people were still chanting 'Whitesnake' – and definitely not 'Great White' – as they went on stage to little excitement. 'Great' White? Well not that day.

We then located to Stuttgart to record at the On Air studio. I enticed Tony Platt to join us as I wanted his authority and had enjoyed working with him on the aborted MGM sessions in '86. Tony had good ears, and was an old-school producer and engineer – the type I liked. We took the tracks back to England to Great Linford Manor, courtesy of Pete Winkleman, who had formerly been my label manager during the Alaska years, who owned Grand Linford Manor and is now the owner of Milton Keynes Dons football team. We overdubbed some horn players from Gary Moore's Band, and we'd already spent far too much money on the album, *Real Faith*, considering that it was only ever released in the Stuttgart area. The guys at the label were lovely people but totally localised. The album hardly made it to the UK, let alone anywhere else. It's very rare these days. It's a shame, because we had written some very good songs, and everybody worked hard. We persevered with promotion but it was plain to see that it was quite a waste of money and time.

We had put it all together between March 1995 and May 1996 and then released it before going on the road in Germany. I did a radio tour with the wife of one of the main label guys, Raphaela. I will never forget the day we were in Baden-Baden, a famous spa town in Germany. Raphaela suggested we head to the spa to relax a little after our hectic schedule. I hadn't got any swimming trunks, and she had told me my cut-off jeans would be fine. Imagine my surprise when she joined me by the sauna utterly naked. She asked me nonchalantly if I wanted to swim before the sauna. This was Germany, folks, where nudity is normal, but I was very conscious of the fact I was wearing very dodgy cut-offs. I was also aware that I was the only person in the area wearing clothes of any kind. She walked away towards the pool. What could I do? Well, being the Brit abroad I was, I followed her into the pool still wearing my dodgy jeans, swam for a few minutes and then removed the jeans in the sauna, which, by the way, contained several more naked stunners. Life on the road can be so difficult.

A man named Horst Zwipp had a management company in Stuttgart and tried, in vain, to become my manager. But one of the first things he did was fix a sponsorship with a lawn mower company – yes, lawn mowers. The firm sponsored a local handball team and Micky and I were invited to make a personal appearance at a game. It was all a little surreal – we were not the most informed people about handball at all.

Towards the end of 1994, Zwipp held talks with ZDF in Munich, one of the biggest German TV companies. ZDF said they wanted to meet me, and I flew out to see Christian, the director of a new show. His face lit up when we walked in, and I thought he might be bit of a fan. This was not the case. The reason for his delight was that a character from his newly written script had just walked into his very plush ZDF office

– me! 'Big Ed' was the character's name, and now he'd just walked into the office in person. Zwipp had tricked me, knowing full well that if he'd asked me to act in a TV show, especially in Germany, I'd have never agreed.

So I told Christian I was reluctant to be an actor, but he somehow talked me into it. A deal was struck, and we shook hands. He wanted an authentic person who could be natural on screen. Big Ed was the aging, former rock star guitarist who becomes the mentor for a new upstart rock star. He had sideburns and grey hair, and was about the same age I am today – and thanks to the top-notch makeup girls I have been aware of what to expect in my looks for over twenty years.

A few days later I was at the nearby studio of the musical director, Harold Faltermeyer – the man behind the *Beverly Hills Cop* movie music. We got along very well; he was a big fan of rock and knew all about Whitesnake and 'Here I Go Again'. We quickly put together four songs and we were both very pleased with the results.

The TV series was shot in several cities in Germany, and it turned out very well. I did speak some German dialogue but they dubbed most of the long sequences. The show was called *Frankie*, and went out in six parts that have been repeated many times. I turned on the TV in my room in Germany one morning during a tour years later to see myself playing a Gold Top Les Paul and speaking German! Some people in Germany still believe I am fluent in their language but I can assure them that I'm not. It was a pleasure to do, even if I still can't quite believe it happened. The actors and musicians were lovely people and I even arranged for my old friends The Scorpions to have a cameo appearance in the show.

Eventually, the MM Band drifted to an end. There were no problems between us, but the spark was gone and there was a feeling that we were going around in a bit of a circle. It had simply run its course.

14.

IN THE COMPANY OF SNAKES

As the Moody Marsden Band came to an end, I spent a lot of time in Norway with my friends Willy Bendiksen and Sid Ringsby. We had played many shows together after I produced an album for their band Perfect Crime. Willy, Sid and I went out on the road – the very icy road – in the very north of Norway – a beautiful environment. After one of the shows, Willy played me a cassette of what I thought was a Whitesnake bootleg. But it wasn't Whitesnake, it was actually his own band, with a vocalist called Jørn Lande, who then had a day job with the Norwegian tax office. His voice was spectacularly close to the classic David Coverdale: it was quite astonishing.

Willy suggested that Jørn join us on the road. We toured Norway as 'An Evening of Whitesnake Music' and were very well received throughout the country. After the tour, we recorded an album called *Once Bitten* and called ourselves The Snakes.

I then bowed to the Norwegian musicians' requests to fix up some shows in the UK. But this was a big mistake. My seemingly perennial problem with lead singers seemed to strike again with Jørn Lande. I could handle him singing like David, but when he started to show a Coverdale-inspired attitude, the end was nigh.

The Norwegian expedition had at least shown me that playing Whitesnake stuff was the best way to go forward and so I contacted singer Robert Hart, who had been with Bad Company, and asked him to join the band. In what I thought to be a stroke of genius, I christened the band the Company of Snakes. I called Neil Murray to join, my old mate John Lingwood came in to play drums, and Don Airey joined on keys at a later stage.

My former UFO agent Rainer Hansel had a record label in Germany and he called me out of the blue to offer a deal for the Company of Snakes. The trouble was that by the time we went into the studio to record, Robert Hart had disappeared to America with Barbara Orbison to write for her publishing company. The widow of the legendary Roy Orbison called me herself one Sunday afternoon to explain that she needed Robert in her writing studio, and that he was contractually bound. She was very polite, but was very definite that Robert would have no time to record with me.

By this time, the Company of Snakes was already booked for the Wacken Open Air Festival in Germany, a huge affair with a lot of heavy metal music. We recorded the show with former Michael Schenker vocalist Gary Barden, who I knew from the Alaska days when he was in a band called Statetrooper. The fifty-thousand-plus crowd in Germany that day received the Company of Snakes very well and the Whitesnake songs went down as well as they ever had. I thought it all sounded great, but I was proven wrong when we heard the tapes back in a Hamburg studio. Gary hadn't learnt the songs well enough, rendering his vocals unusable. We had tracks with excellent playing but no vocals. The studio engineer suggested overdubbing the songs with a vocalist named Stefan Berggren, who lived in Stockholm. He was in a band called, spookily enough, Snakes in Paradise. He flew to Hamburg and a week later we had a live album, kind of, that I mixed with Rainer Hansel.

The album was released – rather predictably – as *Here They Go Again*. We had to photoshop out Gary Barden, as he had been in the photo session at Wacken – oh, the joys of modern life. The album was well-received, especially in Europe, although the distribution in the UK was not that good. Overall, Rainer was very happy with sales and wanted me to commit to a studio album as soon as possible.

Stefan had become the permanent singer and we went to Hamburg to record *Burst the Bubble*. It turned out very well and Rainer's label, SPV, put the album out, although it hardly got heard outside Germany – maybe that's another one I should dig out and re-release. We toured the set in Germany, France, Spain, Portugal, and the UK.

We were at Cologne airport on the way home one time when we boarded the same plane as Slade. My old mate Len Tuckey, Suzy Quatro's first husband, was managing a later line-up of the band with Dave Hill, Don Powell and three new guys. We were late boarding, and the Slade boys were already on the plane. Len saw me get on and stood up to salute as we walked along the plane: 'Stand up, you lot, real bloody musicians are on the plane now!' he shouted to the rest of the Slade boys. It was very funny.

As seemed to be a pattern for me, I became somewhat disinterested in the Company of Snakes and so for a while, I took a break. I was interested in keeping up a variety in my work, even if the blues was never far from the heart of what I did. One of these projects involved recording with Alabama-born blues musician Larry Johnson when he played in the UK.

He was appearing at a weekend of folk and country blues at the Stamford Arts Centre, Lincolnshire, in June 1999, organised by my friend Michael Roach. I had first heard Larry back in the Sixties, on a Blue Horizon LP called *Presenting the Country Blues*. Michael's festival featured the cream of UK folk guitar players: John Renbourn, Bert Jansch, Martin Carthy, and Davey Graham. This was basically the chance to see the acoustic equivalent of Clapton, Beck, Page, and Green together at one small event.

I saw Bert Jansch arrive first, guitar case in his hand, and then they all began to appear. I have to say that I was pretty gobsmacked when these legends began to come together on the same bill for the first time for a number of years. To see Bert Jansch and Davy Graham hugging one another was very moving.

I caught most of Davey Graham's set and there was still a lot of magic in his hands, although he was not the man he once was. After part of the Bert Jansch set, which I would have liked to have seen more of, I had to prepare for Larry's show. He was a great guitarist, and an unusual player, having spent a great deal of time with the Reverend Gary Davis in 1960s. Hearing Larry's interpretation of the Davis material was uncanny.

That night Larry played a superb set and the recording and filming turned out very well. I wanted to take the opportunity to record Larry in a regular studio and he agreed. I booked the Audiolab Studios, Buckingham, where he was welcomed by studio owner and engineer Nigel Kneale. Larry was dressed in a sharp suit, crisp shirt, and shiny shoes. Nigel, Michael and I stayed in the control room and Larry Johnson set up in the studio with his Washburn guitar. He was wonderful, a human jukebox of the blues and American folk music that I had not even heard before. We recorded hours of material and even did an interview that was a revelation.

Larry was very happy with the performances that became the album *Blues from Harlem*, and it was an honour to be so close to one of the last remaining authentic bluesmen. He showed that the real blues could be recorded anywhere – even in Buckingham, in England – which I like to think of as the south-east delta. I hope that the two recordings we made with Larry helped to re-establish him as one of the most original and best blues artists still performing. I believe that Larry is a great favourite of Bill Wyman, and if that's true then Bill Wyman has very good taste.

Moving right out of my comfort zone with the blues, I was offered a theatrical job by Simon Webb in March 2001. I first worked with him on the Andy Taylor project; Simon was a great musician and composer, but also had a lot of rock'n'roll in him. At the time he called, he was the musical director of the National Theatre's modern adaptation of Shakespeare's *A Winter's Tale*, and asked if I would be interested in being in the house band. Nicholas Hytner was the play's director, a real force to be reckoned with. I was well up for it, and the agreement was that I'd play a twelve-string guitar, a mandolin and acoustic and electric guitars (although not all at the same time). For the first time since I turned pro I was on a wage that involved a pay packet!

I needed to be in London for the start of rehearsals at 2.30 in the afternoon every day, and arrived on time for my first day's work at the National Theatre with my guitars and amplifier. I had already decided that this was a completely new venture for me, and so I would abide by the theatre rules.

The Winter's Tale rehearsal room was No. 5, and I was strangely nervous as I approached. I had met Simon's friend and artist liaison manager Kevin Leeman a couple of times, and he came to the rehearsal to welcome me. I was given my NT card and was firmly informed that no card meant no entrance, no garage parking, and no canteen. Yes, sir! Simon and I were allotted our dressing room on the second floor. Backstage at the National is a warren of corridors and doors, and there are two theatres in the main building. Ours was the Olivier, but almost identical to it was the Lyttelton.

I was delighted to run into Dennis Waterman, then appearing in *My Fair Lady* in the Lyttelton. I knew him from my EMI days, and he was really great. He made me feel very much at home in the theatre, taking me backstage to meet a lot of the carpenters, electricians, and set-builders – the bones of the building. To my delight, I was signing autographs for them over the following weeks – they were Whitesnake fans. He introduced me to some of the cast of *My Fair Lady*, including Nicholas Le Provost.

The canteen was the hub of the National, and I saw some famous actors in there from day one. You soon got to know the people around you, and I was really enjoying myself. I met Bill Paterson the first day. He was in *A Marriage Play* with Sheila Gish, a striking blonde lady I had seen on TV many times. I was so keen to be part of this new world, but things didn't start too well with Ms Gish. I got in a lift with her, and I was probably smiling far too much considering nobody had ever introduced us. I told her that I was part of the Olivier production. I thought she might be impressed, but she had every right to be wary of this complete stranger. I rather think she wanted to get out of that lift as soon as possible. Never mind – Bill Paterson, he was the cool guy.

Simon had composed some music for the show, but a lot of my input was made on the night. I had to 'feel' the mood of the scene, and often played David Gilmour-style guitar using a Fender Strat. I wanted to feel a different attitude, and this always seems to happen when a Stratocaster is in my hands. A few members of the cast asked how I made the sounds – I was quite the novelty it seemed. Even when the run began, I was still wrapped up in being a part of a Shakespeare play at the Olivier Theatre. This is something Dennis Waterman never did stop ribbing me about. 'What the fuck are you doing here mate?' he would say, 'you're a fuckin' rock star!'

I agreed with him though when it came to doing the technical rehearsals. They turned out to be long, and very boring and I came to dread them very quickly. Dennis had warned me what to expect, and he was right. Sometimes we worked fourteen-hour days.

Nick Hytner's version of the original marketplace scene in the play was like a sort of Glastonbury Festival, something rather bohemian. He at length decided I would be a part of this scene on stage. I was carefully measured for my costume, and trod the boards every night. What odds would I have gotten from a bookie in 1990 that I, Bernie Marsden – guitarist/songwriter/Whitesnake – would be in a Shakespeare production on the Olivier stage at the National Theatre? I would have made a fortune.

I had to follow a complicated sequence each night to get to my part on stage. I would leave the area where Simon and I played, high above the stage, and hurry down a flight of stairs to the dressing room to get my costume. The crew helped me dress, and I then had to go down one more floor in the lift – or run down the stairs. Already sweating in the woollen costume, I would wait at the rear of the stage for my cue. I was on stage with the hot lights beaming down for about ten minutes. After an extended dance sequence, which I must reassure you I was not part of, I would grab the lift, disrobe and get back up to Simon. At least four shows out of the eight shows a week I had to groan up the stairs, as the elevator would be unavailable. Some nights I barely made the return for my guitar cue. As Hermione came back to life and Leontes wept, the auditorium would be totally silent as I played haunting volume swells on the guitar to create the perfect mood. This emotional, haunting scene was enacted every night, while I could meanwhile feel the sweat dribbling down my back.

Some very fine British actors were in the cast, including a whole bunch of young actors, most of them at the National for the first time, just like me. Phil Daniels was also in the show, and his character, Autolycus, played an old Fender Telecaster … I could see why a few Shakespeare zealots were confused.

One night, towards the end of the run, all of this modernity in the play got too much for one of the audience and, just after that dance scene, he stood up in the aisle, screwed up his programme and threw it at the stage. 'This is not Shakespeare!' he exploded, before leaving the auditorium.

For me, on the other hand, it was a fabulous experience, if not something I ever imagined I would do. *A Winter's Tale* was a top show in London over the summer of 2001. Simon and I took our bow in the balcony, with the likes of Helen Mirren and Kenneth Branagh applauding us from below. It was special.

I hadn't entirely stopped gigging with the Company of Snakes, but I did turn down shows because I was having such a good time in the play. As the run came to an end I couldn't help but feel a little sad, as it had been so wonderful to do. We all got together to have a send-off on the terrace of The National after the final performance. Many tears were shed by all, but many memories remained.

On 16 March 2002, I flew to Monte Carlo for a weekend of music that I would not have dared to dream of when I first picked up the guitar as a young boy. I was on my way to the world-famous Monte Carlo Sporting Club where I would be rehearsing with none other than Ringo Starr.

Zak Starkey had called me about three weeks earlier to ask on behalf of his dad if I would do the gig. I obviously needed no time to think of an answer. I spent a day at Zak's house rehearsing with Ian McNabb, Gary Nuttall and Peter Gordeno. I'd known Gary since he was a lad. He was a talented player, lovely guy and had played with Robbie Williams since the 1990s. Gary insisted he would play rhythm.

'You are the lead guitarist round here, mate,' he said to me. Nice man.

As soon as I agreed to the gig, which probably took milliseconds, to be quite honest, I booked into Nigel Neale's studio in Buckingham to get my parts of Ringo's music just right. This was a gig with one of The Beatles, and I was determined that there would be no mistakes. I pretended to be cool but I was very nervous.

Despite that, we were very much looking forward to the gig. No matter how old or young you were, or where you were from musically, playing with Ringo was special. Zak was happy with the rehearsals and told us that his dad would be pleased. That meant a lot to me, and I hoped everything was in place. On the plane to Monaco I remembered watching *A Hard Day's Night* in 1964 in a small cinema in Bletchley. I queued up straight away for the second showing. I was utterly transfixed.

My time in Monte Carlo would complete an astonishing circle. In 1962 when 'Love Me Do' was released I was eleven years old. I had Beatles pictures on my wall in my bedroom, along with the millions of others who wanted to be John, Paul, George, or Ringo. I have been fortunate enough to meet three of The Beatles. On that Saturday night I played guitar and sang harmonies with one of the two surviving members of the group, this gig coming just a few months after George Harrison had passed away. After a while, I would even be asked to address Ringo as 'Ritchie' – and only those who knew him well did that. According to Zak, by now one of my closest friends, when Ringo asked me to call him Richie I became part of the team.

The show was part of the Red Cross Ball at Monte Carlo Sporting Club. The guest of honour was Prince Rainier, his son Albert, and daughters Caroline and Stephanie. His guests were the king and queen of Spain, and the king and queen of Holland, alongside a long list of other dignitaries. Marianne Faithful opened the show – boy, this was a long way from Buckingham town hall.

I admit to feeling very spaced out that night in Monaco, and not from booze or drugs. It was a natural high, the best feeling;

I was *on* stage with a Beatle. During rehearsals and the sound check I was excited but it didn't hit me until Ringo himself walked out in front of the audience. The moment he sang a line from 'With A Little Help From My Friends' and I sang the response, it all came home to me. We opened with 'Photograph' and then 'Boys', a song I had played a thousand times after school in 1963. The showstopper song was, of course, 'Yellow Submarine', which was a very complicated piece of work, instrumentally and vocally. I watched the audience as they looked at Ringo Starr in the flesh: I was doing it myself. It was a magical experience, he was very encouraging, and I could see he really enjoyed the band's playing.

We were all invited to a very grand lunch at the Café De Paris brasserie the next day. I went with with Zak, Ian McNabb, Gary and Peter. The doorman tried to turn us away, until he saw Ringo, at which point we were immediately swept into the magnificent dining room within seconds. It was like the scene in *A Hard Day's Night*. I made sure I was sitting close to Ringo.

My great friend Steve Lukather, from Toto, plays with him, and we have talked about what it's like being on stage with a Beatle, and he could appreciate how I felt this first time. It really is unlike anything else. Enough said, I think. The week-end was over all too soon and we flew back, leaving Mr and Mrs Starkey at home in Monte Carlo. Sitting on the plane I could see that all of us, with the exception of Zak who, after all, was only playing with his dad, had experienced something special.

I got to play again with Ringo in June that year at Cowdray Park, Sussex. We rehearsed again at Zak's for the gig and had got to 'I Wanna Be Your Man' when Ringo arrived, all smiles, and listened to the band finish the song, which I was singing. He said the band sounded great, and then Zak asked him if the drum part was good. I wondered why he'd asked.

Ringo said that it sounded fine, 'if that's how you want to do it'. This seemed like a kind of stand-off, but not a musician thing: this was father and son. Gary Nuttall and I exchanged slightly concerned glances.

Zak instantly passed the sticks to his father. We went again with Ringo on the drums.

By this point we had played the song a few times, and it really was sounding great, but the moment Ringo Starr played drums it just sounded like … well, The Beatles. All of us in the room knew something special had happened. Zak had a huge smile on his face, 'Good, ain't he,' he said as Ringo returned the sticks. He only needed to play it once, and we all knew what we had to do. Ringo was taking none of the credit, saying only that he based his original part on Ray Charles's classic 'What I Say'.

The Cowdray bill comprised Donovan, David Gilmour, Lulu, Mike Rutherford, Paul Carrack, Robbie McIntosh, and Gary Brooker. This time I insisted that my two daughters were at the gig. Charlotte was twelve, and Olivia just eight. I'd insisted they were there because I wanted them to be able to say when they were older, 'I saw my dad play with a Beatle', and these days they do. Ringo made a big fuss of my girls, even giving Olivia his drumsticks and signing her bandanna. She still prizes both those objects very highly, and it was again a brilliant evening. Not long after that, I was invited to the Albert Hall with Ringo and Zak for the George Harrison memorial concert on the first anniversary of his death, another wonderful night, featuring Eric Clapton, Ringo, and Paul McCartney. I always dreamt of playing with The Beatles – well, didn't we all? Let me be the one to assure you that dreams really do come true.

The following year I was pleasantly surprised to receive a phone call from Simon Webb to ask about the possibility of my working at the National Theatre again. Nick Hytner had called Simon to put the old team together, this time for *Henry V*. Birmingham boy Adrian Lester became the first black actor to be in the title role at the National. We became friends, and I even gave him some guitar tuition.

It was a radical production that was staged at the time of the second Iraq war, which had begun in March 2003. There were jingoistic overtones in an obvious reference to the conflict started by Bush and Blair. I always looked at the stage with amazement, fully decked out with working, camouflaged Land Rovers, realistic weaponry and the actors in modern army fatigues. Theatrical luminaries were in the audience each night – it was the hottest ticket in town.

In July the National Theatre canteen became very excited – Kenneth Branagh was in the building. He was making his debut at the National in the David Mamet play, *Edmond*. He could have asked me for advice if he wanted; I was an old hand by now. A highlight of my run was being in the maze of back-stage corridors when the Tannoy crackled into life with a very important announcement: 'Mr Marsden and Mr Branagh, this is your thirty-minute call.' I wish I had recorded that. Simon Webb had heard it in another part of the building and he cracked up, knowing that I would be absolutely delighted. I frequently saw Branagh passing by, and he always said, 'Hello.' He seemed a very down-to-earth kind of guy, but with an extraordinary talent.

Watching actors on a daily basis was so different to seeing and working with musicians. Observing Adrian Lester in the lead role of Henry was tremendous. Each night he gave a slightly different twist to his performance, and I was always stunned by the ability he had to subtly alter his voice with such ease from a bloodcurdling rage to a gentle whisper. I mentioned my intrigue about this aspect of acting to Adrian in the dressing-room area. He told me that he thought acting was like playing a guitar solo, and asked if I ever played exactly the same solo in a song. He made a very good point. Perhaps there is not such a difference between the two professions after all.

My two gigs at the National were really great, and although I haven't been back there since, I do still have my NT card. The card is printed proof that I am a National Theatre player, and not many lead guitarists have that.

In 2004 the three Ms got back together – Marsden, Moody, and Murray, and that was exactly what we called ourselves: M3. As with the Company of Snakes, we continued to work with a Whitesnake theme, and Stefan Berggren came along from the earlier group to sing with us. It was good to get back with Neil Murray – we've been working together since 1974. He has always been a very gifted musician, and is a really exceptional bass player. Just listen to some of his work on the Whitesnake albums. He and I still have an understanding, both in the studio and on stage. We don't talk about it but I think we both know it's there. I joke on stage that I don't have the time to list all of the fine people he has played with, but there is a great deal of truth in that.

Former Magnum keyboard player Mark Stanway also joined the group, and he christened us 'Them 3' during an interview in Russia. Mark was an excellent musician, and I had worked with him when Magnum opened for Whitesnake. He was a very funny guy to have on the road. I had also immediately asked my old mate Jimmy Copley to take the drumsticks: I'd always wanted to work live with Jimmy. After spending time on stage and in the studio with the likes of Cozy Powell and Ian Paice, I had always been very hard on drummers, but Jimmy Copley combined all of the best aspects of Powell and Paice. He had a superb technique and an even better feel for the music. On top of that though, he was a bloody brilliant person to be around. As well as having a love for music, we also both loved football. On an M3 tour, Jimmy and I shared a train cabin travel in Russia and I couldn't have wished for a better companion. He was full of stories of London's east end in the 1960s: some light, some very dark. Jimmy was always a pleasure to be around, and having him in M3 was the best musical decision I made in the 2000s.

Even without a record company or manager, M3 managed to put together a very good live album and DVD, with a lot of help from my good friend Mark Smith. We recorded a show in the Burnley Mechanics theatre and the whole project still sounds and looks very good to this day. We toured in the UK, Europe, and in Russia, doing well on stage, although we constantly faced promoters who insisted on billing us as Whitesnake, and posters would feature Whitesnake's logo used larger than our own. It wasn't as if people would really believe that Whitesnake would be playing a five-hundred-capacity club in Hamburg, but it was an annoyance. M3 was a great live band, yet I wondered about its future.

In 2005, M3 were flying to Switzerland after ten days of shows in Germany. We were routed to Berne. The band and crew were on a small jet-propeller aircraft, and I carried a very useful, many-pocketed Fender gig bag with me at the time. After ten shows in Germany it was pretty heavy with cash, my passport, air tickets for all the people and my personal gear for the road – headphones, CD player, DVDs, etc. We crammed our luggage and guitars into the small hold but I kept the Fender bag with me at all times for obvious reasons. I still wince at my decision to ask our roadie, Ian Bintliff, to take charge of the Fender bag – why I did this I still don't know. The repercussions were huge.

Ian B. was a heavy smoker, but no smoking was allowed on the flight, and he was getting a little desperate for his nicotine fix. We landed and Ian couldn't wait to get off the plane for a cigarette.

We gathered the bags from the carousel; I took the guitars from outsize baggage, while Jimmy Copley and Mark Stanway gathered other bits and pieces, and Ian picked up the rest of our stuff.

We cleared customs and went outside. Ian was by now desperate for his smoke. We loaded the bags into the minibus waiting for us from the gig; Ian had disappeared to have his smoke, returned, and we boarded the minibus.

It was about twenty minutes to our hotel. Unloading the bus at the hotel I started and very quickly felt a panic. 'Where is my Fender bag. Ian?'

The look on his face was unmistakeable. 'Oh, fuck,' he said, looking absolutely terrible. 'I know where I left it, boss.'

Moody, as per usual, along with Mark Stanway, found it very amusing. I said, 'I don't know why you're laughing – all the gig money is in that bag.'

So, not so funny after all.

The driver immediately drove us back to the airport. I was distraught, Ian was almost in a state of collapse, but I didn't shout or complain: after all it was my error, my bag, my passport, and I was only asking myself why I had changed the set routine.

We arrived back at the airport to an ominous vibe: the promoter pointed to the sky where there were a lot of aeroplanes circling in a holding pattern. Nothing was landing, and nothing was taking off – the airport was in lockdown.

We went inside the terminal.

I was rather frightened: this was going to be very difficult.

I found the security people, and I was frantic, but trying to appear collected. They were all very calm.

I apologised for leaving my bag unattended, as you're never supposed to do, and then it dawned on me. A large black bag had been left randomly at the airport. Not a great thing to do. Airport security was a major deal in 2005.

'Ah! So *you* are responsible for leaving the bag, sir. We have destroyed the bag, sir.'

My heart sank. 'I am so sorry, it's my fault.' What else could I have said?

'The bag was brought to our attention, and dealt with.' It had had been picked up by a machine and taken to a steel container and destroyed with a controlled explosion. They could all see my face. I'm sure I must have looked terrible.

'There was a lot of money in the bag, sir' said one of the officers.

It took a moment for me to process what he had said. But hadn't it been blown up? 'How do you know that?' I asked, explaining the reasons for the large amount of cash: they didn't seem bothered.

'We have your money, all of it, your passport is good, but some of your things are ruined.'

What a huge moment. I couldn't stop saying 'Thank you' – I thought Ian was going to self-combust with relief.

I had been incredibly lucky – the controlled explosion had detonated on the side of the bag where my personal stuff was. I had put all the cash in small cloth bank bags, and then wrapped those bags inside towels, and it was this that had saved the money.

Then it occurred to me I might be about to be fined a million pounds for the airport situation, but the officials couldn't have been nicer. I tried to leave a little bit of cash for them to have a beer or two, but they politely refused. I didn't even get a rollicking. I lost a few CDs, a couple of shirts, and walked out of the terminal as a free man.

There was a committee waiting at the hotel: Jimmy Copley was genuinely concerned for my state of mind, 'Fuck the money, Bern, are you all right?' That was J. C.!

No grinning from the others this time, either, just huge sighs of relief when I filled them in. I still see Ian these days, and never once have I attributed any blame to him, but he still feels bad about leaving the bag to have a smoke. And I lost that great Fender gig bag.

M3 came to an end around 2008, and I decided that if I was going to carry on gigging it would be as a solo artist. This has more or less been how I've been doing things ever since. Jon Lord had suggested that I make the move years earlier. 'You put it all together, so why not put your name on the top of the poster?' Jon's advice was always solid, and his words came back to me as I considered my next move.

By this time, I had been working with an agent for some time – Alec Leslie, who had a very illustrious career going back to the Sixties. He had booked out Steve Winwood with the Spencer Davis Group at a time when Steve was too young to be in licensed premises. Alec had to sign the young musician in on local police station logs to get him in and on stage. He was one of the original Island artists' bookers, tour-managed Free at the height of their fame, and had his office at the legendary Basing Street address. He booked many shows for Bob Marley, and managed Elkie Brooks at her peak. Tiring of the London rat race, Alec eventually relocated to Cheshire and with his company, Consolidated, now handles four artists: Manfred Mann, Ritchie Blackmore, Steve Lukather, and yours truly.

I have gone on to become very close with Alec over the years. He remains old-school and very straight in his dealings, and I'm sure you'll know by now that I haven't come across that quality many times in my career. If I had known Alec when I finished in Whitesnake I do believe I would have had a very different career over the last thirty years or more. His expertise in promotion and management would have been exactly what I needed.

When I made the decision to go it alone I had been running the whole show in both the Company of Snakes and M3, but not doing well in financial terms. Alec knew this and when I told him of my plans he was delighted.

The road does go on and, under my own name, I have since found myself being busier than ever. There are always more gigs to play, more recordings to make, and more dreams to fulfil.

15.

GOING AGAIN ON MY OWN

In 2011, I was invited by David Coverdale to appear with Whitesnake for the first time in thirty years. The backdrop for this momentous occasion was the Sweden Rock Festival. I flew out to meet the guys in Copenhagen, and got to see Adrian Vandenberg as well. I really enjoyed meeting Doug Aldrich, Reb Beach, and Michael Devin, who were all very keen to hear stories of the original band. They had great respect for all things Whitesnake, which was very nice.

Sweden Rock was quite the return for me. I pointed out to David just before the show that we hadn't played 'Here I Go Again' together since the day we recorded it in Clearwell Castle. Indeed, the gig tonight would be the first time we ever played it live on stage. He was quite moved at this observation and made a great fuss of me when I walked out on the stage in front of 35,000 people. That moment was incredibly special. Since then I have played several times with the band, including a very emotional return to Hammersmith Odeon in June that year. Jimmy Page was also at the gig, and I asked him if he was going to play.

'Tonight is about you and David, Bernie,' he graciously replied. What a gesture.

In other areas of my musical life, I am lucky enough to have continued doing a great variety of work. For one thing, I always enjoy doing acoustic sessions with Jim Kirkpatrick. I've been working with him for the last ten years, and he's a very fine guitarist. As I've said many times on stage, I've got guitar strings that are older than he is! He's a particularly talented slide player and he's an absolute pleasure to be out on the road with.

I recorded my double album *Big Boy Blue* in 2002, and it was very well received in the USA by blues stations. I was lucky enough to have harmonica player Phil Wiggins playing beautifully on that album, and my old friend Michael Roach helped me out too. I had the great Henry Spinetti on drums, Andy Pyle on bass, and Geraint Watkins on piano. It was a really fun album to make. I recorded a session at the now demolished Pebble Mill studios in Birmingham for Paul Jones's BBC radio show. This session led to an album I am very proud of, called *Stacks*, featuring Jimmy Copley on drums. We tried to keep a live feel, and that worked well. I still play some of the tracks live today. It was only ever officially released in Japan in 2006, I'm still not really sure why. I do know that copies sell for large amounts on the internet, so I might rectify that soon and release it properly.

I always enjoy being involved in charity gigs, and in September 2006 I was the guitarist at the first Sunflower Jam. This was a charity founded by Jacky Paice – Ian's wife – that raised money for cancer patients by organising high-profile, classic rock events. I was excited to play this gig as it meant I got to perform with Robert Plant. I had a bit of a shock when we discussed the setlist and he nominated Zeppelin's 'Ramble On', 'What Is and What Should Never Be', and 'Good Times Bad Times'. I thought he was winding me up. We were really going to play all of these great Led Zeppelin songs, alongside numbers by Buffalo Springfield and Elvis. Jon Lord and Ian Paice were in the band as well, and that made an already special night even better. I've spent quality time with Robert over the years, and I'm still humbled to be friends with people I first admired when I saw them from the audience.

I had my own charity show, Party in the Paddock, that was held in my village in Buckinghamshire in the early 2000s. I organised the events with Fran and some friends in the village, Jeannie and Duncan, who owned the paddock in question. The final edition was in 2008 and featured The Who's Roger Daltrey topping a considerable bill. We divided the money between various cancer and kidney research charities, and raised more than eighty thousand pounds. I'd like to do another one.

In 2010 I made a Rory Gallagher tribute CD, *Bernie Plays Rory*. Anyone who knew me in the Seventies will tell you that I did my best to emulate his look. We already had a strong physical and facial resemblance, but I enhanced it as much as I could with check shirts, Levi's and tank tops – you can see just how close I got in the sleeve image of *Bernie Plays Rory*. I must have been asked a thousand times in all sorts of places if I was Rory Gallagher. When I saw him for the last time, at a German festival in 1994, just a year before his death, he told me with great delight that only a few weeks earlier somebody had asked him in an airport if he was Bernie Marsden from Whitesnake. I didn't let on to Rory himself, but I was absolutely thrilled. I was just as excited when Rory's brother, Donal, gave me his blessing for the record.

I contacted bass player David Levy and drummer Richard Newman, who had both played with Rory for the last five years of his life, and guitarist Jim Kirkpatrick completed the line-up. I'm very proud of that album, and one thing I know for sure is that, as long as I play, there will always be a little of Rory Gallagher's spirit in my heart. That same year, I was asked by Donal to headline a hometown gig for Rory in Ballyshannon, in Ireland, and again in 2014. People from all over the world make the trip to be in the great man's hometown. It was a real honour for me to be there, and those shows are highlights of my solo career.

Far too many of the central players of rock and blues are no longer with us, and I guess that will always be the one major downside of having such a long career. But – and it is an enormous but – I have been incredibly privileged to have been able to work and play with some of the greatest rock and blues musicians in history.

In May 2009, I spent a great afternoon and gig with one of my heroes, Johnny Winter. He was playing at the Stables in Milton Keynes, a fantastic local gig for me, and I sat with him in his trailer outside the gig. We talked about BB King, Muddy Waters, and the blues. He was very amiable and upbeat, but at this point was quite frail and wore an eye-patch. He only entered the Stables itself to play his show. I can understand that. Johnny had been on the road all of his life and being in his vehicle is a little like being at home. I have done the same thing myself. He was not in the best of health, but he played very well and very loud that night, and I had the thrill of playing his beloved Gibson Firebird in that trailer.

I had the pleasure of spending a couple of days with Glen Campbell in 2011. I went to see him in Northampton at the Derngate Theatre when he was in the UK as part of what was, due to declining health, his final world tour. There had been some talk that Glen had been diagnosed with Alzheimer's disease, but I was looking forward to meeting him. His tour manager introduced me to Glen's son Cal who took me to the dressing room. I met a smiling and, I thought, very healthy-looking man in his seventies. We talked about life on the road; he answered many of my questions and knew that I played the guitar. I told him about Whitesnake – I think Cal knew more about them than his dad – and the meeting was terrific. I was pleased to see how well he seemed. His show was fabulous and very emotional in places. He did struggle a little with some lyrics, but then so do I. His guitar playing was first-rate and I had a lump in my throat when he sang 'Wichita Lineman'. I saw him briefly after the show, shook his hand, and said how much I enjoyed it.

'Come see us again,' he said. A couple of weeks later I took him at his word and drove to the Symphony Hall in Birmingham, this time with my autograph book and little Martin guitar. I ran into Cal again, who was pleased to see me and I was once again taken to see Glen. Smiling, he had no idea we had met before, asked the same questions and told me almost the same stories as he had in Northampton, just twelve days earlier. I realised that he was indeed in the cruel grip of Alzheimer's. He still looked great, signed my book and guitar, gave me his plectrum, and we had our photograph taken together. The gig turned out to be even better, and I admit to being in floods of tears when he sang 'Lineman' again. What a singer, what a musician.

A great personal loss for me was Jon Lord, who died in July 2012. I was proud to be at his memorial gig in 2014 at the Royal Albert Hall, playing guitar on two Paice Ashton Lord songs with Paicey on drums. It was a fantastic gig, but I have to say that I was sad that no Whitesnake music was performed that night. Jon was an integral part of the band and added so much and it was a shame that this was ignored. Politics were involved but I'm sure Jon would have wanted to hear some of that music. Jon's number is still in my phone, as is Cozy Powell's. These men will never leave my thoughts or my heart.

Music and friends were very far from my thoughts in November 2013. Indeed, after a very late finish in the recording studio I was not planning anything of note the next day. All that changed when my dad appeared in my bedroom at around 11.30 in the morning. It was not his habit to suddenly turn up at my house without warning, and certainly not my bedroom. But he had the best opening line ever.

'You'll need to get up, son, the prime minister wants to see you at 4 o'clock.'

All that time I was involved at the time with a cross-party project, Rock the House, and was a patron alongside Brian May, Alice Cooper, and Ian Gillan. MP David Morris, a friend of mine, had discussed a possible meeting with David Cameron a few weeks before, but I had forgotten about it, but it was suddenly happening.

I got myself together, and a smiling father drove me to Milton Keynes railway station. In the car, he said, 'You have always surprised me with your many achievements, but today takes the biscuit,' he said.

I arrived at Westminster and got through security to find that David Morris seemed a little more nervous than me. There was yet more tight security to reach 10 Downing Street, including armed guards in the street, and then one of them simply waved me through before David: 'Carry on, Bernie, I know who you are. I seen you at Hammersmith Odeon, mate.' I was inside No. 10 Downing Street.

The prime minister's PA met us and we walked up the famous stairs, past the many portraits and photographs of former occupants. I was shown into the cabinet room, and waited, thinking of Churchill, Eden, Macmillan, Wilson, Thatcher, Blair, and the decisions made where I was sitting – before David Cameron entered. He was a decent man in a job nobody should want: I'm not really political, but he seemed genuinely interested in our project. In any case, he was pretty well-informed about my career and very fond of Thin Lizzy, so that made him all right in my book. It was a most surreal day.

I had just that one brush with politics and otherwise continued with my guitar day job, although I never thought I'd sign another record deal. That was until the Dutch label Mascot Provogue approached me and the result was another solo album, *Shine*, in 2014. I recorded at Abbey Road Studios with Ian Paice, Don Airey, Joe B., Jimmy Copley, Simon Webb, and

I also had harmonica maestro Mark Feltham. The producer was Rob Cass, my old singer from Alaska days, and I also called David Coverdale in the hopes that he might sing something. There were no music-business shenanigans to get in the way, and he agreed to it immediately. He sang one of the first songs we ever wrote together, 'Trouble', and made a magnificent job of it as well.

Next up in the guest spot was Joe Bonamassa. I had first seen him play in May 2009 at the Royal Albert Hall. Backstage at the post-gig party I was on my way introduce myself but, before I could say anything, he got there first: 'Bernie Marsden, great to see you.' We have been close friends ever since, and Joe was instrumental in me signing with Mascot. I went on to play with him on many stage shows over the next few years. He is truly a phenomenal talent and watching him play The Beast was something special. While I was making *Shine*, Joe had a day off from touring and when I asked if he'd be up for coming to the studio he was there in no time at all. That's the kind of guy Joe is, ladies and gentlemen. He played some stunning guitar on the title track. Having him was a double win, as anyone hearing the track for the first time might just assume it was me playing! Joe an I have worked together a lot since those early days, especially on the Keeping the Blues Alive Cruises and now we are a songwriting partnership which I hope goes on for many years.

Shine was very well received in Europe, and reached No. 1 on the iTunes blues chart within a week of release. I promoted the album towards the end of 2014 on a tour with the talented guitarist and performer Joanne Shaw Taylor. That was a real pleasure and I loved to talk to people after those gigs. I was truly humbled by the praise I received.

By contrast, more than six months of emails regarding song choices, arrangements, of rehearsals planned and cancelled, rebooked and cancelled again went past before I finally got to do the gig with Ginger Baker. It was April 2019 and we were in Brighton for a sound check rehearsal. I had a nightmare drive but fortunately the former Cream drummer was even later than I was.

My old friend Andy Chard, Ginger's long-serving (and suffering) tech, met me at the Dome, where Herman Rarebell, formerly of the Scorpions, and his band were to be found, German guys, and big Whitesnake fans. Pete York was also there, the original drummer with the Spencer Davis Group, affable as ever. He played on all their hits in the Sixties and was a close friend of Jon Lord and Tony Ashton. And then, finally, Ginger was in the building. Definitely in a bad mood, he greeted each of us with barely a touch of a handshake. Abbas, his supremely cool long-time associate and a very gifted percussionist, and Andy took care of him.

I had suggested 'White Room' for the rehearsal, and Ginger duly messed around with the arrangement and blamed me. 'This is going to be a disaster,' he enthused, after less than twenty seconds of the rehearsal. How nice, I thought. I had dropped my fees for this gig considerably, as I had been involved with the Cream Revisited project for some time and thought I should do it. Bass player Mike Mondesir and I had to follow Ginger somehow, but he just went on complaining and criticising. At last he almost smiled and, during the guitar solo, I asked if we were all OK. Ginger was delighted – no more playing for him and he could go back to his hotel. The rehearsal and sound-check came in at under six minutes. It had taken me longer to unload my gear from the car. Abbas and Andy had seen it all before but Ina – Ginger's nervous agent and gig promoter – was amazed.

'That's it, and that was a long one,' said Andy and Abbas in unison.

Mike and I stayed at the same hotel as Ginger. Most guitar players I know would have been on their way home by this point in the day: maybe I should have left as well. But I was here, and I knew the songs (if not the way the drummer seemed to want to play them). I thought of Jack Bruce, Gary Moore and, of course, Eric Clapton. If they could get through working with Mr Baker, I'll give it a damn good go, as well.

On the day of the gig, I walked over to the venue with Abbas and, to my surprise, Ginger showed up for a run-through after lunch. He seemed to be in a better mood. False confidence. By the time of the show that evening the arrangements were all changed again. The audience, though, were very respectful, applauded, and we were soon into 'Toad', although played much slower than we did in the afternoon. We were on stage for about nine minutes before it was time for intermission, I kid you not.

During the break I met a young member of Ginger's immediate family, who was most interested in my guitar. She asked me if it was easy to learn. Ginger wandered into the room, acknowledging nobody except Andy, even though he was now in my dressing room. As I played something for the little girl Ginger shouted, 'Stop that noise!' Suddenly, I understood a lot about this near-eighty-year-old man. He needed and wanted to be the centre of attention, always.

There can be no disputing that Ginger Baker is a legend. Yet, regardless of what happened in his long life, his main failing was that he has no love or compassion left for his music. I am sure that people – including myself and his band members – will always respect his past legacy but I decided that the second half would be on my terms. I let him and Abbas start 'Sunshine of Your Love' before I began the classic guitar riff. I had seen Cream play live in 1967, and I believed I was in heaven that night, and in my wildest dreams I could never have imagined I would be playing Cream music on stage with Ginger Baker fifty years later. But would I do it again? No, I don't think so. To me it seems as though he genuinely has no interest in people in general. After the show, Ginger, left without saying a word to anybody.

Inevitably, the narrative of this book returns one more time at its conclusion to the biggest band of my career. Hooking up with David Coverdale again in 2011 resulted in a renewed friendship, and I think having each other back in our lives has been a very fine thing. Sure, there were times when I thought we would never speak again. I had taken leaving the best band in the world very hard. In the late 1980s, Whitesnake became the enormous success in the USA that the original line-up had craved so much. I like to think I had something to do with it with 'Here I Go Again', which has turned out to be the biggest song the band has ever produced, and is still used over and over again in TV shows, ad campaigns, and movies. No less than Mary J. Blige and Tom Cruise sang the song in a movie called *Rock of Ages*.

Being part of Whitesnake has enabled me to choose the work I want to do, and for this I will always be grateful, no matter who is in the band. That will never change. When I play with Whitesnake these days it is a real pleasure, and my full respect goes out to my friends Adrian Vandenberg, Doug Aldrich and the current line-up of Reb Beach, Joel Hoekstra, Michael Devin, Michele Luppi, and Tommy Aldridge. When I'm on stage with David Coverdale, I smile at how different we are since the days of Central Studios, Clearwell Castle, the splendid Tittenhurst Park, and my stable in Ridge Farm – writing all those fabulous songs late into the night, and playing all those shows with Dowle, Paice, Lord, Moody, and Murray. I have nothing but respect for the man who still steers the good ship Whitesnake.

I have to mention the boys on the road in those days: John Ward, Steve Payne, Barry Evans, Dave 'Dustin' Paterson, Jack 'ZZ' McGill, Ashley Williams, Willy Fyffe, Youth, Nick Sholem, Stuart Wickes, Tapper, Joe Brown, Tasco, Adrian

Hopkins, Louis Ball, Gary Marks, Rod McSween, Jimmy and the Johns, Barry Newman, Ossy Hoppe, Tina Beans, Robbie Dennis, and Malcolm Hill – all of them and many more, those who helped to make Whitesnake the band it was.

I have played with so many musicians over the years and met a host of utterly superb people out on the road. Yet, despite the number of famous people I've met and worked with, this book is for the people who go out to work in the morning, go home in the evening, have some dinner, change their clothes, and then they go out to see the gigs. They're the people for me.

See you out there, folks.

GUITARS AND THE SICKNESS THEY INDUCE

Guitar collecting is a disease, and there is no cure as far as I am aware. Most guitar players of note are collectors, some public, some secretive, but all on the lookout for guitars, all the time.

Guitarists are strange. They are very open when it comes to giving others advice but when push comes to shove they are singularly selfish individuals – especially if there is a rare guitar in the midst! Way before I turned pro I contracted the collecting condition, albeit in a mild way. I would always try and hang on to the guitars I had and wouldn't trade one in for the next one unless I really had to.

While I was working at the much-loathed hairdresser in Bletchley there was a Jim Marshall shop in the high street. Hanging on the wall was a brand-new Les Paul replica by British company Grimshaw and my hero at the time was Les Paul-playing Peter Green – although he obviously played the real deal. I had to have the replica. Hanging next to it was a 1960s' Gibson 335 in red. The guitar police reading this will understand the haunting text that follows. The brand-new Grimshaw was £135, while the second-hand and very used Gibson 335 was just £115. But Peter Green didn't play a 335 at the time, and I wouldn't look at anything else. This is probably the worst guitar decision I have ever made, but I was a Peter Green acolyte and it made total sense to me.

Skinny Cat first opened for the Keef Hartley Band at Banbury art college in 1969. I got a great sound from that Grimshaw, as I always did, through a Marshall 50 head with a Marshall 2x12 cabinet. Keith Hartley's singer and guitar player, Miller Anderson, was very impressed and called guitarist Spit James over. After the gig, Spit made an astonishing proposal, he offered me a straight swap – the Grimshaw for his gleaming, cherry-red Gibson SG Special. I thought he was having a laugh. But Miller was in the room and I could see this was for real. A genuine Gibson guitar was way out of my price range, and I was still paying for the Grimshaw. This was a deal people could only dream of: a cherry Gibson SG Special was going to Buckingham that night.

I took that guitar up to my room when I got home and woke up early just to stare at it and touch it, making sure that it was real. The following week a truly desperate Spit James phoned to say he simply could not get a decent sound out of the Grimshaw. He had plugged it into Impact amps, other amps, and still more amps, and still no good sound came. He needed his guitar returned. Now I was the desperate one! But it had to go. My beloved new Gibson guitar, only three days in my keeping, was soon in the back of a Ford Anglia driven by my mate Trevor Fenables to Spit James in Watford. With great sighs – relief and sadness – we exchanged guitars. The weight of the world clearly fell from his shoulders. He asked how I managed to get such a great sound from the Grimshaw. I just shrugged.

Miller Anderson never forgot that exchange, and we've now been friends for over thirty-five years. Miller later told me the other side of the story: Spit's anguish had been real. Miller told him that the sound came from me, not the guitar, and that he had me marked down for a positive future. I have always remembered that.

When I turned pro in 1972, and I was at the house with Mick Ralphs he showed me what guitar collecting was all about. Mick was the first chronic guitar collector I really knew. He was in the first vanguard of British musicians to realise the greater availability of affordable Gibson, Gretsch, and Fender guitars in the USA. On tour, Mott the Hoople would raid pawn shops, buying up Les Paul Juniors for fifty dollars, Strats for a hundred dollars, and top-of-the-line, original Les Paul Standards for $250.

One guitar in particular haunted both me and Mick: and this one was in the UK, an original 1958 Gibson Flying V with the original brown case. It hung on the wall of Top Gear in Denmark Street. The guitar was £599, a lot of money for such an item in 1974, and was advertised as the guitar of the year. I used to go into Top Gear and get it off the wall to play. It had a good sound, but the V-shape always annoyed me. If they didn't have a strap for it in the shop, and with its odd shape, it always slipped off my leg: after a short while I'd always put it back on the wall.

Mick also thought it a bit pricey – after all, he might find two for that kind of money in the US. A month went by, the guitar stayed on the wall, and the price was reduced to £450. I joked to the staff that it would be there for ever, but they laughed and said that sooner or later either me or Mick would buy it. Not long after, I had a call to say that Mick was indeed on his way to buy the guitar. If I really wanted it, I needed to get down to the store with the cash, ASAP. I was in Wild Turkey at the time, doing OK, but I had no savings. Still, I thought a brand-new guitar would look good on stage and Chrysalis agreed to front me the money. I flashed the cash at the shop.

'What's that for?

'I'll have the V!' I said in triumph.

'No, you won't,' they giggled. 'Mick Ralphs has just bought it.'

I found out that the guys at Top Gear had phoned us both but, nevertheless, I was devastated. Mick kept the guitar for a while and played it on stage with Bad Company before selling it for a lot more than he paid. Worse was to come. I later found out that it was the very first Gibson Flying V ever made, and it was shipped from the Gibson factory in April 1958. Today that V is worth at least a million dollars. And to think I was devastated when it was just £450! Ah, well: the important thing to remember in guitar collecting is to never look back.

I was in Guitar Village when Gary Moore sold his Gibson SG to buy Peter Green's Les Paul. Manager Nigel Tannahill did the deal, and I think Gary received £140 for his guitar, and then bought the Les Paul for that amount. Gary took a lot of flak over the years for that – people said that he ripped Peter off but this wasn't the case. They had a deal and they both stuck to it.

In 1974 I purchased a beautiful 1959 sunburst Les Paul from a guitar player called Cosmo Verrico, who played with a band called Heavy Metal Kids. This Les Paul was one of the first of its kind in the UK and had belonged to none other than Keith Richards. I liked the guitar, although it wasn't even remotely close in sound to The Beast – it still had a Bigsby tremolo unit, and wouldn't stay in tune. I used it for a couple of Wild Turkey shows, but the tuning became a real problem. I removed the tremolo, obtaining a second-hand tailpiece from Top Gear for about seven pounds. It now stayed in tune better, I already had The Beast, so I decided to sell it. I called my friend, Mike Jopp, who was the guitarist in the rock-jazz band Affinity.

We struck a deal and I wrote a receipt: 'From Bernie Marsden, sold to Mike Jopp, one original Gibson Les Paul (ex-Keith Richards).' That tiny piece of paper would feature in a lawsuit and those brackets became very important, because a few years later when another guitar was sold as being the Keith Richard Les Paul. There was a court case but Mike Jopp won because of those brackets. The good part of that deal is that I doubled my investment. I paid around £300 for that guitar and I sold it for £600. I know now that I should have kept it – just have a look at how much that guitar costs now.

Hindsight is a dangerous thing, you see, I suppose I should also have kept my Hiwatt 100-watt stack that belonged to Pete Townsend, and the Bob Marley Fender amp I had for about a week. Another piece of memorabilia I should have maintained in good condition was Peter Green's Norwegian army coat that featured in the early Fleetwood Mac photos. It was hanging up at Glen Cornick's house in the winter of '73 and he told me that Peter had left it behind many years before. I wore it until it disintegrated the following winter. But I'm not the only collector to have let things go, and I won't be the last.

When I was recording with Cozy Powell, ex-Humble Pie guitarist Clem Clempson and I swapped guitars. He took a real shine to my cherry red Gibson 335, circa 1963, and so I swapped it for his 1956 maple-neck, sunburst Fender Stratocaster. He'd bought it from Steve Marriot, and the guitar can be seen on a clip from *The Old Grey Whistle Test* with Humble Pie. I kept that guitar a long time: it looked just like the Strat on the back cover of Clapton's 'Layla'. But I never really warmed to the sound and I soon understood why both Steve and Clem had moved it on.

I took it to Doug Chandler's shop in Richmond, always a pleasure to visit. I asked for three thousand pounds and he nearly fell over. He said the resale would be about £1,750. He would not budge but I spotted a very nice 1960s' Gibson Firebird III hanging on the wall which was £700 and sensed a move.

'I'll buy that if you up the Strat deal.'

'Sorry B., it can't be done,' said the boss.

That was it then. No deal. Just as I was leaving another customer stopped me to say he would pay cash for my Strat and at my asking price. I was somewhat sceptical. He asked me to wait a few moments, as he had to go to the bank to withdraw the cash. I thought that would be the last I saw of him, but I went back into the shop to tell Doug what had just happened.

About fifteen minutes later the guy returned with the money. Out of courtesy to Doug I went into the street to complete the deal. I counted off three wads – it was all there. No names, no pack drill, I passed him the guitar. And then to my amazement, he took it out of its tweed case, put on a guitar strap that he pulled tight around his body, jumped on his bike, and cycled away, looking just like a 1960s Fender guitar advertisement.

Back in the store, there was a bit of a vibe. Doug thought he deserved some commission. I pointed out, 'If you had offered me two thousand pounds I would have taken it, and you would have just made a grand.' Doug reluctantly agreed and immediately put up the prices of his entire vintage Fender stock. Strat prices went up everywhere after that deal. I also offered him five hundred pounds for the Firebird, and he rightly told me to fuck off. We did strike a deal though, and I still have that Firebird III today. I hung onto the tweed Strat case and later swapped it for a Gretsch Country Gent guitar – another hell of a deal that was.

In 1978, in the early days of Whitesnake I was looking through the guitar ads in *Melody Maker* and I saw: 'For sale: original 1964 Gibson Firebird, very good condition.' The single pickup Firebird was already a rare guitar, and this one was more so because it had a straight line of six tuners, just like a Stratocaster, rather than the unusual banjo tuners. I was gutted to phone and hear the guitar had just been sold.

Imagine my surprise, then, when Micky Moody swanned into rehearsals with a brand new Gibson Firebird. The seller had told him that 'a Bernie' had called about it, and that led to him purchasing it immediately, and laughing his arse off at my obvious annoyance. I couldn't believe it. Moody was never much bothered with vintage guitars but he was grinning from ear to ear with his purchase.

I soon noticed that he switched from the new Firebird back to his Les Paul, picking up the Firebird for another song, but switching back again and again. Micky was easy to read in a situation like that. Sure enough, towards the end of the day he asked me if I wanted to buy a guitar.

'What guitar?' I asked, innocently.

'This Firebird,' he said, looking pretty sick.

'No, thanks,' I replied. He had paid about four hundred pounds and just wanted his money back. I could tell that he really didn't like the guitar at all and I offered him £250.

'Fuck off,' he said.

I had already owned three Firebirds by this time, and I can tell you that they are tricky to play. They're not well-balanced, they use heavy banjo tuners, the headstock drops down, and Firebird pickups are notoriously trebly. There is a knack to playing them, it takes time, and Mick just didn't have the patience. We settled at just over £350 – a real bargain. I kept that guitar until 2012 when sold in America for a lot more than I'd paid for it. Some you win, some you lose.

I did return the favour a little though. I had learned from Mick Ralphs that he was going to sell one of his vintage original Les Paul guitars and I told Micky. He snapped up a cracking 1958 sunburst. At that point both of us were then using original Gibson Les Paul guitars live with Whitesnake – pretty cool.

I bought The Beast in 1974, when I was still playing with Wild Turkey. I had met Martin Henderson, a guitar collector who came to our gigs in London on a regular basis. He owned a really fine Les Paul Standard from 1959 and he thought it would suit me. I could never afford the six hundred pounds he wanted but nonetheless he showed up a couple of weeks later at the Marquee, with the guitar in question, and said I should try it out on stage. Through my Marshall rig it was about 20 per cent louder than any guitar I had ever played – pure tone, phenomenal.

I appreciated the brilliant sales pitch, but I just didn't have the money. He said I could part-exchange my black Les Paul and a Fender Stratocaster and I could pay the balance when I could. That Les Paul has been such an important part of my story to this day. Thank you, Martin. He had bought the guitar from Free's Andy Fraser, who had bought it from Paul Kossoff, who had either traded it or bought it from Eric Clapton. It is also possible, if that's the guitar, that he got from Andy Summers. (I was told that recently, but I haven't been able to confirm it – there are many guitar-origin rumours out there.)

I used The Beast when I played with Ringo Starr at Cowdray Park. David Gilmour said afterwards, 'It's been a long time since I heard that guitar. What a great tone.' I thanked him, and he asked me how much I would sell it for. Maybe he's checking me out? I thought.

'Not sure, David, £150,000, maybe more.'

'Very cheap,' he said, with a wry smile. Guitarists know about these things.

In 2012 Gibson Guitar Company asked me if they could make a limited edition of three hundred replicas of The Beast. I have the very first one. The rest sold out before leaving the Gibson plant in Tennessee. This was really a proud moment for me, as I can still remember all those Gibson catalogues I used to send away for as a teenager.

Joe Bonamassa and Warren Haynes have played The Beast on stage more than I have over the last few years and, when I hear it in action, I know what all the fuss is about. It has become a legendary instrument. Younger players like Jared Nichols, Chris Buck, Ariel Posen and Joey Landreth have all played the guitar, all just holding it (and sometimes smelling it!) for a few seconds. This always makes me smile, but I understand why. People long to hear it live, dream of holding it, touching it and even being in the same room as it. When I play a gig, people always hope and pray that I'm bringing it with me, and if I do they want photographs of it, look upon it with awe in their eyes, as if it's an ancient artefact. Well, I suppose it sort of is. It's certainly been on the cover of more magazines than I ever have, and rightly so, it really is a truly remarkable guitar.

SEMINAL MOMENTS IN MY MUSICAL EDUCATION

The Woburn Music Festival, July 1968

I didn't have a ticket for the shows on the Saturday afternoon: Pentangle, Roy Harper, Al Stewart, Alexis Korner, and Shirley and Dolly Collins. It was all a little folksy so I wasn't too bothered. The Saturday night line-up, however, was mega: Jimi Hendrix, Geno Washington and the Ram Jam Band with Pete Gage on guitar, Tyrannosaurus Rex, Family with Roger Chapman, Little Women and New Formula (I'm afraid I don't remember anything about them).

Geno Washington and the Ram Jam Band were very poorly received. They were very good, but a soul band and so really weren't suited to a night with Hendrix. To general astonishment, he opened with 'Sgt. Pepper's Lonely Hearts Club Band'. The Beatles had only released the landmark LP of the same name a month before and so nobody in their wildest dreams expected Hendrix to open with such a new track. He also managed to blow up about three Marshall amplifiers in the first few songs. Good job the Marshall factory in Bletchley was close!

I had read and seen so much about Hendrix in a short period just before that gig. His outrageous appearance and guitar playing meant he had been a godsend for magazines, TV, and radio but he had only been in England for less than two years.

He was quite the phenomenon. He played with his teeth, and rattled the guitar against his microphone stand – all outrageous stuff. Mitch Mitchell and Noel Redding was the perfect pair behind him. Watching him that day was a really important moment in my life. That night's ticket cost me all of £1 – the Sunday night was cheaper at 15/- (75p) but, believe me, Hendrix was worth the extra five shillings.

First up on a very wet Sunday was Duster Bennett, the one-man band. He was a superb writer and performer. Next, fresh from Ireland, came a band called the Taste and this was the first time I laid eyes and ears on Rory Gallagher. They didn't play very long, probably about half an hour, but the reception they received was thunderous. I queued to shake his hand after their short set – this was the start of my lifelong admiration for Rory Gallagher.

The superb blues piano player Champion Jack Dupree played a solo set at the piano: he was absolutely fantastic. I remember him telling the story of how Ray Charles stole 'What I Say' from him in the 1940s. He added a few choice expletives, telling the story with a toothy smile as he tore into the song.

Fleetwood Mac were due to headline but for some reason never turned up, and so the headliner that night was John Mayall and the Bluesbreakers: Mick Taylor on guitar, Jon Hiseman playing drums, Tony Reeves on bass, Henry Lowther on trumpet, and Chris Mercer and Dick Heckstall-Smith on sax. Although disappointed that the Mac were not going to perform, I have to say that the Bluesbreakers were magnificent.

I should thank my friend John Ridley for making sure I was at Woburn. I didn't really have the money to go but John insisted and made sure I was there. I'm eternally grateful that he did. Thanks John, you made it happen, you're responsible for getting me to see Jimi Hendrix for the first time.

Fleetwood Mac, Bluesville, 1968

Bluesville '68 took place at the Manor House pub in Seven Sisters Road, north London. I got there early and I offered to help the crew. Peter Green and Mick Fleetwood arrived together, and I stayed way in the background as they sound-checked. I was captivated by what was really a rehearsal.

I couldn't believe my eyes when I saw Peter Green walking over to me holding a bottle of beer. The small crew had told him that I had helped hump the equipment in and this was a thank-you. He was very quiet and polite, asked me where I had come from and whether I played the guitar. I didn't say very much! Peter let the bluesman know that I was with him, and I was allowed to stay without a ticket.

There was no stage and that meant the crowd and band was on one level. With a capacity of around 150 people it was quite intimate, but the atmosphere was electric. By this time they had released both their debut album, *Fleetwood Mac*, and *Mr Wonderful*. Just to hear 'Merry Go Round' live was incredible for me. Fantastic memories – and I have a bootleg recording of it somewhere.

Fleetwood Mac, The California Ballroom, Dunstable, 1968

On 7 September 1968, about a week after I first saw them, I gathered up all my gang to see the band who now had a new guitar player, eighteen year-old Danny Kirwan. God, I was jealous. In my mind I wanted to hate him because he was about my age and actually playing with Peter Green. But it was impossible to hate him – he was a sensation. I was able to get on the upper floor to look down at the stage. It was packed out.

Peter had his Les Paul high up on his body and wore his standard rugby shirt. John McVie stood motionless and was so solid on bass, and Jeremy Spencer was all over the stage, swearing, shouting, and abusing the crowd as Greeny just stood back and laughed at his antics. Danny Kirwan was playing his Watkins Rapier guitar and looked about thirteen years old. He looked so nervous and I felt for him – all my jealousy was instantly gone and all I wanted to do was cheer him on. He really was fabulous that night and superb things would come from that collaboration. In fact, Danny wrote one of my favourite Mac songs, and I re-recorded it in 2014 for my solo album *Shine*. The song was 'Dragonfly' and it still is a beautiful piece of music. I left the gig that night not only worshipping the Green God but the new kid as well.

Fleetwood Mac was probably the biggest draw in the country. Peter Green's writing only became more and more eclectic and I loved it. You can notice a very big difference between 'Merry Go Round' in 1967 and 'Oh Well' in 1969. As it was Green, of course, I liked anything. I got pretty close to him with the Splinter Group in later years, hanging out with him and Gary Moore in Norway. I filmed a whole gig at the Oxford Playhouse, and later played with him at his manager Mich Reynolds' wedding. I became a hero that night as I persuaded him to sing 'Need Your Love So Bad' for the first time in years. As you can imagine, that went down a treat. He sang, we both played guitar, and my old mate Neil Murray was on bass.

Rory Gallagher, The California Ballroom, Dunstable, 1968

I went to see The Taste one Friday in Dunstable, arrived early – no change there – and went inside the hall to find Rory with a drink sitting on a chair at the side of the stage. I chatted to him whilst he waited for the support group to set up their gear. He was quiet, charming and thoughtful. I liked him instantly. We talked about the Woburn gig, and when I mentioned I'd queued to quickly shake his hand, he thanked me. We talked about guitars and he explained how he had acquired the famous Strat, which even then had very little finish on it. What a sound the man made with it later that evening. Rory was a real gem of a person, the kind of guy to never forget your name. I got to know him pretty well in the years to come. He was a great guy.

Fleetwood Mac, the Bath Festival, 1969

Peter Green's last show with Fleetwood Mac was on 28 June 1969. I was on the pitch in the centre of Bath football ground for the one-day festival. It had been publicised that Peter was leaving the group and so the gig was very emotional. I shed a few tears as I watched and listened to him.

The rest of the bill was so strong that I need to list the artists for you: John Mayall, Led Zeppelin, 10 Years After, The Nice, Chicken Shack, Jon Hiseman's Colosseum, Mick Abraham's Blodwyn Pig, the Keef Hartley Band, The Taste, Clouds, Liverpool Scene, Savoy Brown, Group Therapy, Champion Jack Dupree, Babylon, Deep Blues Band, Just Before Dawn, and Principal Edwards. They were introduced by John Peel on two stages. It was truly a remarkable line-up. Promoter Freddie Bannister was a clever guy. Just check out the guitarists I saw and heard play live – Mick Taylor, Peter Green, Alvin Lee, Rory Gallagher, Stan Webb, and Jimmy Page. It really was an incredible time to be a developing guitar player. At such a young age I was exposed to some of the greatest guitar players to ever live, and I hope you can see why I was so determined to try and be just like them.

Blind Faith, Hyde Park, 1969

An away day of note was Saturday 7 June 1969. I travelled alone to London – no way was I going to miss Eric Clapton, Steve Winwood, Ginger Baker, and Rick Grech. It hadn't occurred to me that roughly 39,999 other people would feel exactly the same way. I was alone with many others.

The atmosphere was electric as I walked in the summer sunshine to find the stage. It was a very hot day but I got as close to the front as I could, hoping to be as near Eric's amp as possible. First act on was the Third Ear Band, and then the Edgar Broughton Band. I had seen the Edgar Broughton Band a few times before, and Skinny Cat had even played with them. They were very popular in 1969: their theme song, 'Out Demons Out', was always played at gigs. Richie Havens was on next; it was the first and only time I ever saw him on stage. He was amazing, thrashing his guitar, and his extra percussionists were a great addition. We had a surprise that afternoon as well. Unbilled, Donovan appeared and played quite a few songs. It was a really nice surprise and it went down really well.

As the sunshine softened, Blind Faith came on stage. I was fairly close to the stage and Eric Clapton was in my eyeline – his hybrid Fender had a Telecaster body and a Stratocaster neck. I couldn't help but think he looked very miserable. They opened with Buddy Holly's song 'Well … All Right', and Steve Winwood sang the beautiful 'Can't Find My Way Home' and then they sang 'Sea of Joy'. It sounded brilliant, but something wasn't right up on that stage. I could feel unease in the crowd – the band was not going down very well. I was having a lovely time, watching a hero play onstage in the middle of the largest group of humanity I had ever seen, but there were shouts from the crowd for Cream songs. The huge crowd grew restless, especially the throngs nearest the stage. People wanted to hear

'Crossroads', 'White Room', and 'Sunshine For Your Love', but the guys absolutely refused to play them. This was Blind Faith, not Cream or Traffic. Eric Clapton and Winwood were making a point about their new band. Clapton maintained a stern look on his face and offered no smiles or made any visual connection with the rest of the band. I think it was all over very soon. Blind Faith only played this one show in Europe. They later did an abortive USA tour but it was soon all over.

Freddie King, The California Ballroom, Dunstable, 1969

I feel honoured to be able to say I saw Mr Freddie King play live, along with Chicken Shack. Freddie had everything: feel, heart, soul, style, great tone, and terrific showmanship. We arrived early, and as usual Ray Knott was chauffeur, and parked around the rear of the building quite close to the stage door. The hood of a Ford Transit van was up and a man was bending over the engine. To my total surprise it was the great Freddie King himself. He was fixing the van as he knew about engines. Who'd have thought that same man would two hours later plug in a red Gibson 345 and send many, including me, into wonderland?

I managed to see Freddie King on most of his trips to the UK. One of my only regrets is that I never got to speak to him after a gig – I was far too polite to interrupt him while he was fixing the van. Chicken Shack guitar player Stan Webb became a friend of mine over the years and confirms that not just vehicle maintenance but other mundane matters, too, were all taken on by the great bluesman. Stan told me he loved to play cards; I think we would have got along fine.

Freddie always had a pickup UK band, and he recorded in England, too, including three albums at Mike and Richard Vernon's great studio in Chipping Norton. I still get frustrated at the thought of the great King walking around the market only thirty miles from Buckingham and me not going to find him. The Vernons told me that Freddie would go into the market when he was in town, then into a pub for a pint. What a brilliant image.

In the early 2000s I got to play with Freddie King's keyboardist Deacon Jones, a fabulous Hammond organ player, a couple of times in Oxford and in Bournemouth. When we played 'Hideaway' he had a glaze over his eyes. 'Freddie would have loved you,' he said. I was moved.

Derek and the Dominos, The California Ballroom, Dunstable, 1970

A year and a half after Blind Faith at Hyde Park, I saw a completely different Eric Clapton gig. On 8 August I was in Dunstable to see the new band everybody was talking about. During the brief Blind Faith USA tour, Clapton had become very closely associated with Delaney & Bonnie and Friends, who opened for them. Eric, obviously disillusioned by the Blind Faith setup, started to play with Delaney and Bonnie instead. They arrived in Europe to play in December 1969, and George Harrison sometimes played with them too.

The first Derek and the Dominos show had been at The Lyceum in London on 14 June, when they were simply billed as 'Eric Clapton and Friends'. Tony Ashton told me that he had suggested 'Derek and the Dominos' before the gig. He always used to call Eric either Del or Derek – and it stuck that night, after he introduced them under that name.

At the California they played songs from Clapton's debut solo album, and some from the not-recorded *Layla and Other Assorted Love Songs*. It went on to be released in December that year, was not critically well-received, and didn't sell well at all. Polydor issued a second run with a sticker on the front to let people know that 'Derek is Eric'! The music press might not have liked the album, but take it from me – on stage it was marvellous. They really were a wonderful live band, Bobby Witlock on keys, Carl Reade on bass, Jim Gordon on drums, and Eric Clapton playing the Stratocaster or a Gibson Les Paul special. It was very very good. The California Ballroom was a perfect venue for them. The atmosphere was brilliant, and it was jam-packed. Of the twenty-seven shows they played in the UK in their short existence, I still feel privileged to have been at the California Ballroom that night.

The California Ballroom, the Cali, has since been demolished and a housing estate now stands where some of the greatest artists of all time played live. It should have had a preservation order on it. I wonder if the people that live there today have any idea of the musical memories their homes are built on.

I could make an extensive list of wonderful venues that have disappeared, from small theatres in Manchester to old cinemas in Liverpool – all to make way for new housing estates, office blocks, garages, and dual carriageways. It's a real shame. I am proud to have played those places that helped me make the grade, so to speak. The Victorian theatres built by Frank Matcham had the greatest acoustics in the country. I have been fortunate to play in many of them, some still standing, from The Gaiety in the Isle of Man, to the Shepherd's Bush Empire, the Victoria Palace, the Blackpool Royal theatre, and the famous Buxton opera house. One gig designed by Frank Matcham has eluded me – the London Palladium in Argyll Street. I hope one of these days I'll play a gig at the Palladium … perhaps.

I got to headline the California Ballroom myself in 1974. It was wonderful to think that I was headlining the same stage as these fantastic musicians I had seen before. It was as packed in the audience as a gig by Fleetwood Mac or Derek and the

Dominos but all I could think of was the people – Freddie, Eric, Rory – who had all trodden the very boards that my feet were on. I still get that feeling today.

Opening for Fleetwood Mac, Oxford, 1970

A real watershed moment for me came in 1970. Skinny Cat was booked to open for Fleetwood Mac, thanks to a booker we had known at the Oxford polytechnic – I'm sure this is a fact very few people know. We played Headington in Oxford. Peter Green wasn't there but I did talk with Danny Kirwan and John McVie. Danny Kirwan was no longer the lost-looking boy I had seen in 1968 in Dunstable but was confident, calm and collected onstage. He played brilliantly with his black, three-pickup Les Paul Custom – the very guitar he would smash to pieces before leaving Fleetwood Mac about a year later.

I had some old photos from an early Fleetwood Mac gig in Windsor. John McVie looked at them with great fondness, especially two single shots of Peter Green. I remember his face and exactly what he said: 'It'll never be like that again.' I didn't really take his words in at the time, but now it's clear that he was reflecting upon the loss of Peter Green to the band. How could John imagine they'd ever be the mammoth success that they still are today. I will always remember John's face as he looked at those old photographs. Looking back now Skinny Cat opening for Fleetwood Mac was probably the highest thing I ever did as a semi-pro. It's nice to know that all these years later I can still talk about it, remember it and write it down. So that's it, that's my story. Now, where's my guitar?

ACKNOWLEDGEMENTS

I need to firstly thank my terrific and solid team at HarperCollins UK. My intrepid editor Michelle Kane, media muse Naomi Mantin and the rest of the gang at 4th Estate: Jack Smyth for the fantastic cover art, Fran Fabriczki for project-editing and Jack Chalmers for his work on the audiobook. My thanks also to Lucian Randall and Julia Koppitz for the rigorous editorial work. Thank you all for making this book what it is. I am honoured to work with such a fine team.

Special thanks must go to my fabulously talented daughter, Olivia, for all her hard work – both on the original manuscript and this latest publication.

I must also thank the original *Where's My Guitar?* pledgers from 2016. You supported this book from the very beginning, and I am so grateful for that. With that, I thank Mark Smith and Dave Smith for their excellent work on the first edition.

Thank you to my darling wife Fran, daughter Charlotte, and to my parents, Joe and Kath, who have always shown me the utmost support. Thanks also to my brother Steve Lukather for the front cover quote, and to Anders Körling for the cover photo. Thanks to Robert Ellis, Alan Parry, Neil Murray, Andrew King, Andrew Thompson, Allan Messer and Peter Nobles for the photos.

Last, but not least, I thank you – the readers, the fans – who continue to support me indefinitely. It truly means so much. I'll see you out there …

BM